Char-Broil® GREAT BOOK OF GRILLING

300 Tasty Recipes for Every Meal

CREATIVE
HOMEOWNER®

CRE🏠TIVE
HOMEOWNER®

Char-Broil® Great Book of Grilling
Vice President–Content: Christopher Reggio; Editor: Laura Taylor; Design: Wendy Reynolds; Index: Elizabeth Walker

ISBN 978-1-58011-801-9

Library of Congress Cataloging-in-Publication Data

Names: Taylor, Laura, editor.
Title: Char-broil great book of grilling / editor, Laura Taylor.
Description: Mount Joy, Pa : Creative Homeowner, [2018] | Includes bibliographical references and index.
Identifiers: LCCN 2018000006 | ISBN 9781580118019 (pbk.)
Subjects: LCSH: Outdoor cooking. | LCGFT: Cookbooks.
Classification: LCC TX823 .C47 2018 | DDC 641.5/78—dc23
LC record available at https://lccn.loc.gov/2018000006

We are always looking for talented authors. To submit an idea, please send a brief inquiry to acquisitions@foxchapelpublishing.com

Printed in Canada

Current Printing (last digit)
10 9 8 7 6 5 4 3 2 1

Creative Homeowner®, *www.creativehomeowner.com*, is an imprint of New Design Originals Corporation and distributed exclusively in North America by Fox Chapel Publishing Company, Inc., 800-457-9112, 903 Square Street, Mount Joy, PA 17552, and in the United Kingdom by Grantham Book Service, Trent Road, Grantham, Lincolnshire, NG31 7XQ.

Photo Credits

Photos courtesy of Char-Broil except as noted below.

Glenn Moores: 9; 20–22; 23 (top left and top right); 61; 67; 70; 74–76; 93–95; 98–99; 110–111; 115–121; 126–128; 130; 132–136; 138–142; 145–148; 154–157; 182; 187; 194; 196–197; 199; 215; 224–230; 235–236; 243; 247; 254; 260; 263–265; 284–285; 288–291; 295 (bottom); 297; 298 (bottom); 302; 305–306; 311–313; 321; 325 (top)

Freeze Frame Studio: 31–52; 66; 68–69; 71–73; 82–92; 100–109; 149–151; 158; 181; 183–186; 188–193; 195; 198; 216; 222–223; 231–234; 237–242; 244–246; 248–253; 258–259; 261–262; 266–283; 286–287; 292; 295 (top); 296; 298 (top); 299–301; 303–304; 307–310; 314; 316 (bottom); 318–319; 325 (bottom); 326 (top); 326 (bottom)

iStock: dutchicon (15 bottom food icon); dutchicon (16); dutchicon (17);

Shutterstock: Victoria Sergeeva (inside cover illustrations); Syda Productions (4); from my point of view (8 bottom right); Masterchief_Productions (13); RedKoala (15 top food icon); Brent Hofacker (29); Brent Hofacker (62); Joshua Resnick (65); Darryl Brooks (77); Bochkarev Photography (78); Hannamariah (79); Lisovskaya Natalia (80); julie deshaies (81); Susan Stevenson (96); Wiktory (123); David P. Smith (124–125); Joshua Resnick (129); BGSmith (143); nioloxs (144); gkrphoto (152); a katz (153); jdwfoto (159); zi3000 (160); a katz (161); farbled (174); Charles Brutlag (175); Duplass (176); MaraZe (177); Brent Hofacker (178); Razmarinka (179); Rabbitti (180); Africa Studio (200); msheldrake (209); Bochkarev Photography (210); Africa Studio (211); Bochkarev Photography (213); Tatyana Malova (214); Ryzhkov Photography (220); Africa Studio (221); Ruslan Mitin (257); jmattisson (316 top); picturepartners (317); Olga Miltsova (320); Maks Narodenko (322); divinecusine (323 top); Michelle Lee Photography (323 bottom); Hans Geel (324 top); Kozlenko (324 middle); Anna81 (324 bottom); martin garnham (326 middle); Africa Studio (328 top); Jade Y (328 bottom); FeellFree (329 top); Acter (329 bottom)

Acknowledgments

This book is dedicated to everyone who loves to cook outdoors. Whether you favor using a traditional gas or charcoal grill, the modern digital electric smoker, or the oil-less Big Easy®, you'll enjoy discovering the delicious recipes and expert techniques in this book. Take your grill game to the next level!

Contents

1

People get a little bolder and more wild in summer. You've got things going on kebabs, things cooking on the bone. There's something about standing over a grill or outside with the family that inspires us.

–Guy Fieri

Cooking Outside

The material in this chapter and several recipes throughout the book were contributed by Barry "CB" Martin, host of the Guys in Aprons website (www.guysinaprons.com).

GRILLING, BARBECUING & SMOKING:
WHAT'S THE DIFFERENCE?

Many people mistakenly refer to any type of cooking on their grill as "barbecuing," but that's not entirely correct. Let's compare the outdoor cooking techniques needed for the recipes in this book.

GRILLING

Grilling involves quickly cooking individual portions of food at relatively high temperatures over a direct heat source. The first step in many grilling recipes is to sear the meat over high heat—between 350°F and 550°F. The higher heat browns the outside of smaller cuts of meat, sealing in juices that would be lost if the meat were cooked more slowly. My mother did this before placing a roast in the oven, and I do it every time I grill a steak. Cast-iron grates on a grill are also highly conductive, which significantly aids the searing process.

Once food is seared, you'll often finish cooking over indirect heat on another part of the grill. The reason food can continue to cook this way is that there's still plenty of heat generated by one or more of these sources: (1) convective heat from air heated by the fire; (2) conductive heat from the grill grates; and (3) radiant heat produced by either a charcoal or an infrared gas grill.

BARBECUING

Barbecuing is a slower way of cooking large portions of meat or poultry using an indirect source of heat at a lower temperature (usually between 225°F and 350°F). It takes time, but your end result is tender and juicy.

Here's the science behind barbecuing: when meat is placed away from the heat source, it cooks by "bathing" in the hot air—or convective heat—generated by the fire. Another way you might describe barbecuing is slow roasting at low temperatures. Cuts of meat that benefit from this type of cooking, such as pork shoulder and beef brisket, have a high ratio of collagen in the meat. (Translation: They're tough.) Slow cooking with indirect heat works magic on these cuts, breaking down the dense collagen and adding tenderness and flavor.

GRILLING is a quick way to both sear and add a smoky flavor to vegetables, steaks, and chicken.

BARBECUING "low and slow" works best for large, less-tender cuts of meat, such as pork shoulder.

IT'S ALL ABOUT
THE HEAT

The roots of modern grilling go back to prehistoric times when our ancestors placed a chunk of meat on a stick and held it in the fire. Judging by the number of people who love outdoor cooking today, there's something in the way the intense heat crisps the meat's surface that still appeals to our deeply rooted DNA.

While we've refined the caveman's cooking tools and techniques a bit over the ensuing eons, there are certain things that haven't changed. The most important of these is the management of heat. This is probably the most basic skill required of any good cook, whether they're preparing a meal in the kitchen or the backyard. But because this book is about outdoor cooking, let's start with some basic facts about the heat we use to grill, barbecue, and smoke food.

In outdoor cooking, the heat source we use most often is fire. Whether its source is the propane in a gas grill, the charcoal in a smoker, or the logs on a campfire, fire produces heat; and we can harness that heat to cook foods to our delight.

Fire requires three things to burn: combustible material, a supply of oxygen, and a source of ignition. There are many materials that can burn; yet only a few—such as wood, charcoal, and propane or natural gas—are suitable for cooking food.

Outdoor cooking enthusiasts often refer to heat as either direct or indirect. The most popular form of direct-heat cooking is grilling, which means cooking food directly over the heat source, usually at high temperatures. We typically grill steaks, chops, burgers, and fish. We can also use a grill's indirect heat to cook food more slowly and at lower temperatures further away from the heat source. Whole chickens, briskets, roasts, and other large cuts of meat are usually cooked by this method, which we generally call barbecuing.

SMOKING with wood or charcoal on a charcoal grill such as Char-Broil's CB940X uses indirect heat.

ROTISSERIE COOKING

Rotisserie cooking involves skewering a large piece of meat or poultry on a rotating spit set over your grill's heat source. The spit, usually driven by an electric or battery-powered motor, turns at a constant speed to allow for even cooking over the entire surface of the food. Rotisserie cooking is best for large roasts, whole poultry, and pork.

To check for doneness with rotisserie-grilled food, stop the rotisserie motor and insert an instant-read meat thermometer into the deepest part of the food. To avoid overcooking the food, check the temperature about 15 to 20 minutes before the final estimated cooking time. Always use heat-resistant gloves when removing the rotisserie spit rod from the grill because it can get very hot.

Talk to any long-time outdoor cooking enthusiast and sooner or later you're going to hear the phrase "low and slow." In fact, it's pretty much the official motto of all barbecuing. "Low" refers to temperature—generally between 225°F and 350°F. "Slow" means the time it takes to cook the food. Simply stated, "Good eating comes to those who cook low and slow."

SMOKING

Smoking is the process of cooking food on or near an open fire made from materials such as wood or charcoal. The fire releases particles of these materials into the smoker that impart a unique flavor to the meat. The more these materials smolder and generate smoke, the greater the number of particles to flavor the food. Cooking at temperatures between 140°F and 225°F is called hot smoking.

If the smoke passes through a cooling chamber and comes into contact with the food at a temperature of around 45°F, you are cold smoking the food. (Note: Cold-smoked food isn't actually cooked, it's simply being slow-cured and flavored.)

When moisture is added to the smoker to increase its humidity level, it is called wet smoking. A simple pan of water is placed away from direct heat inside the grill or smoker. If desired, you can use fruit juice or wine instead of water, or add these liquids to the water for an additional flavor boost.

ROTISSERIE cooking is ideal for evenly cooking large roasts, whole poultry, lamb, and pork.

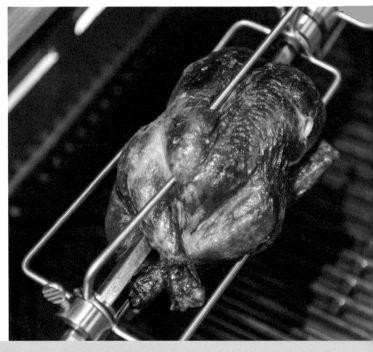

INFRARED COOKING: WHAT IS IT & HOW DOES IT WORK?

Infrared is a natural form of radiant heat we've all experienced in our daily lives. The warm rays of the sun are transferred to your skin by infrared heat waves. And if you've ever made "sun tea," you've brewed it using the sun's infrared heat.

Charcoal has been used to cook food for centuries and is still prized by some folks today for the flavor it imparts to food. But I bet that many don't realize that it's the infrared heat produced by a charcoal fire that helps food retain its juiciness and flavor. However, charcoal fires require a little more time and effort to adequately prepare them for grilling.

With the introduction of an affordable line of gas grills equipped with infrared, Char-Broil has made the technology used for decades by professional chefs available to backyard grillers. You'll find this exciting technology in Char-Broil's Quantum and RED grills, as well as The Big Easy, Char-Broil's new infrared turkey fryer that cooks without using a drop of oil.

HOW IT WORKS

Infrared heat is a great way to cook because it can generate high temperatures for quicker cooking and searing—up to two times greater than traditional grills. The infrared waves start to cook the food the instant they reach its surface, quickly creating a sear on the meat that locks in moisture and creates exceptional browning. Char-Broil's infrared cooking systems offer a wide temperature range, from high-heat searing to "slow and low" barbecuing and rotisserie grilling. Because most flare-ups are eliminated, you can simply drop unsoaked wood chips between the grill grates to create a slow-cooked smokehouse flavor in a fraction of the time, using one-third less fuel than standard convection gas grills.

INFRARED COOKING TIPS

Experience with your new infrared grill will help you determine what temperatures and cooking times deliver the best results. At first, you may want to adjust your regular cooking times. If you have cooked on a charcoal fire, this should be fairly easy to do. If you are more familiar with cooking on a regular convection gas grill, reduce the heat settings you normally use by at least 30 percent, and the cooking time by about 50 percent. Here are some other ideas that will help you master infrared cooking:

- Coat each piece of meat, fish, or poultry with a light spray of high-heat oil, such as canola.
- Plan your cooking according to technique, required times, and the best use of the grill surface. For example, steaks can be seared over high heat then finished over medium or low heat. Begin with steaks you intend to cook to medium doneness, and end with those you want rare.

NO-OIL "DEEP FRYING"

Deep-fried turkey is the juiciest, tastiest, most crisp-skinned bird you'll ever eat. The Big Easy is an oil-less way to "fry" a turkey using infrared technology. Turkeys cooked in The Big Easy are prepped the same way as for traditional fryers. One of the many bonuses of The Big Easy, however, is that you can use dry rubs and seasonings on the outside of the bird.

THE BIG EASY is a safe, easy, and delicious way to cook fried turkey, rotisserie-style chicken, BBQ pork, roast beef–even vegetables.

CARING FOR **YOUR GRILL**

Let's face it—it's easier to clean up after you finish cooking when the weather's nice. But when it's cold and dark outside, it's tempting to just run back into the house—balancing a plate of hot food while dodging the raindrops—rather than clean the grill.

Excuses. Excuses. We're all just lazy sometimes. Here are a few tips and tricks that will come in handy. Of course, be sure to check the manufacturer's directions for your grill before trying any of these.

Char-Broil Cool Clean Brush

WHY CLEAN?

If it's been a while since you last cleaned your cooking grates, here's a tip that could save you time and actually get your grates a lot cleaner. Place either a half-sheet aluminum pan or double layers of heavy-duty aluminum foil on the grates; close the lid; and turn the heat to the highest setting. (This method traps heat, causing the grill temperature to rise to between 500°F and 600°F). Let the grates "cook" for about 25–30 minutes. The crud should mostly burn off and, with a light scrape from your grill brush, it all goes into the trash. Beautiful!

GRILL RACKS AND GRATES

Before and after each use, you should burn off any excess grease and food that has accumulated on your grates. Turn the grill to high, and close the lid. Leave it on for around 15 minutes; this should turn most debris to ash. When grates have cooled, scrub with a cleaning brush or pad, and they should be as good as new.

Stainless-Steel Grates. Stainless-steel grates should be cleaned regularly with a heavy-duty grill brush. You can occasionally soak the grates in a mixture of water and vinegar. Periodically, remove the grates, and brush them off or lightly bang them together to remove burnt-on debris. Apply vegetable oil after cleaning to help prevent rusting.

Cast-Iron Grates. Treat your cast-iron grates the way you would a favorite cast-iron pan. To prevent rusting, cast iron should be seasoned frequently, particularly when your equipment is new. If rust occurs, clean with a heavy brush. Apply vegetable oil or shortening, and heat to season the grates. Note: Certain grills have cast-iron grates coated with porcelain. The porcelain helps prevent rust and eliminates the need for seasoning.

Porcelain Wire Grates. There are special brushes on the market, such as Char-Broil's Brush Hawg, that can clean porcelain grates without scratching. After you finish cooking, turn heat to high for approximately 5 minutes; then use the brush to clean the grates after the grill has cooled.

EXTERIOR SURFACES

For painted surfaces, warm soap and water work best. Some manufacturers offer an assortment of products for cleaning stainless-steel grills, from daily maintenance sprays and wipes to solutions that completely restore your grill's finish. Stainless-steel grills will develop rust if they are not protected from the outdoors. Check your owner's manual for detailed cleaning instructions.

KEEP COLD FOODS COLD AND HOT FOODS HOT

Uh, oh! Did you forget to defrost that package of chicken thighs you were going to grill for dinner? Should you run hot water over it to thaw it quickly? What if you remembered to take the chicken out of the freezer but left the package on the counter all day while you were at work?

Both of these scenarios are bad news. As soon as food begins to defrost and become warmer than 40°F, any bacteria that may have been present before freezing can begin to multiply. So, even though the center of those chicken thighs may still be frozen as they thaw on the counter, the outer layer of the food is in the danger zone. Maintain the temperature of frozen foods at under 0°F, and raw, unfrozen foods at under 40°F.

For hot foods, the minimum safe-holding temperature is above 140°F. Food can certainly pass through this temperature zone during cooking, but if it does not rise above 140°F, you are flirting with bacteria growth that will make you sick. Use an accurate meat thermometer.

As a rule of thumb, veal, beef, pork, and most seafood should be cooked to at least 145°F; ground beef, pork, lamb, and veal should be cooked to at least 160°F; chicken and turkey breasts, as well as ground poultry, should be cooked to at least 165°F.

THE BIG THAW

There are three safe ways to defrost food: in the refrigerator, in cold water, and in the microwave.

Refrigerator Thawing
Planning ahead is the key. A large frozen turkey requires at least a day (24 hours) for every 5 pounds of weight. Even a pound of ground meat or boneless chicken breasts needs a full day to thaw. Remember, there may be different temperature zones in your refrigerator, and food left in the coldest one will take longer to defrost.

After thawing in the refrigerator, ground meat and poultry can be chilled for an additional day or two before cooking; you can store defrosted red meat in the refrigerator for 3 to 5 days. You can also refreeze uncooked foods that have been defrosted in the refrigerator, but there may be some loss of flavor and texture.

Cold-Water Thawing
This method is faster than refrigerator thawing but requires more attention. Place the food in a leak-proof plastic bag, and submerge it in cold tap water. Change the water every 30 minutes until the food is defrosted. Small packages of meat or poultry—about 1 pound—may defrost in an hour or less. A 3- to 4-pound roast may take 2 to 3 hours. For whole turkeys, estimate about 30 minutes per pound. Cook the food immediately after it defrosts. You can refreeze the cooked food.

Microwave Thawing
This is the speediest method, but it can be uneven, leaving some areas of the food still frozen and others partially cooked. The latter can reach unsafe temperatures if you do not completely cook the food immediately. Foods thawed in the microwave should be cooked before refreezing.

GRILL **SAFETY**

Have you ever noticed grills on apartment terraces and backyard decks, and shook your head in disbelief? Many of these devices are way too close to wooden railings, siding, and fences. Regardless of the type of cooker you own, keep it at least 3 feet from any wall or surface, and 10 feet from other flammable objects. Here are some other tips for safe outdoor cooking from the Hearth, Patio & Barbecue Association (*www.hpba.org*).

■ Read the owner's manual. Follow its specific recommendations for assembly, usage, and safety procedures. Contact the manufacturer if you have questions. For quick reference, write down the model number and customer service phone number on the cover of your manual.

■ Keep outdoor grills outdoors. Never use them to cook in your trailer, tent, house, garage, or any enclosed area because toxic carbon monoxide may accumulate.

■ Grill in a well-ventilated area. Set up your grill in a well-ventilated, open area that is away from buildings, overhead combustible surfaces, dry leaves, or brush. Avoid high-traffic areas, and be aware of wind-blown sparks.

■ Keep it stable. Always check to be sure that all parts of the unit are firmly in place and that the grill can't tip.

■ Follow electrical codes. Electric accessories, such as some rotisseries, must be properly grounded in accordance with local codes. Keep electric cords away from walkways or anywhere people can trip over them.

■ Use long-handled utensils. Long-handled forks, tongs, spatulas, and such are designed to help you avoid burns and splatters when you're grilling food.

■ Wear safe clothing. That means no hanging shirttails, frills, or apron strings that can catch fire, and use heat-resistant mitts when adjusting hot vents.

■ Keep fire under control. To put out flare-ups, lower the burners to a cooler temperature (or either raise the grid that is supporting the food or spread coals out evenly, or both, for charcoal). If you must douse flames, do it with a light spritz of water after removing the food from the grill. Keep a fire extinguisher handy in case there is a grease fire. If you don't have one, keep a bucket of sand nearby.

■ Install a grill pad or splatter mat under your grill. These naturally heat-resistant pads are usually made of lightweight fiber cement or plastic and will protect your deck or patio from any grease that misses the drip pan.

■ Never leave a lit grill unattended. Furthermore, don't attempt to move a hot grill, and always keep kids and pets away when the grill is in use and for up to an hour afterward.

BEEF AND LAMB COOKING-TEMPERATURE TABLE

CUT OF MEAT	INTERNAL TEMPERATURE	VISUAL DESCRIPTION
Roasts, steaks, and chops: beef, lamb, veal	USDA guidelines	Depending upon how the meat is being prepared and which cut, different temperatures may be used.
medium rare	145°F	Center is very pink, slightly brown or gray toward the exterior portion
medium	155°F	Center is light pink, outer portion is brown or gray
medium well	Above 155°F	No pink
well done	Above 165°F	Steak is uniformly brown or gray throughout
Ground meat: beef, pork, lamb, veal	160°F to 165°F	No longer pink but uniformly brown or gray throughout

POULTRY COOKING-TEMPERATURE TABLE

MEAT	TEMPERATURE	VISUAL DESCRIPTION
	USDA guidelines	
General poultry	165°F	Cook until juices run clear.
Whole chicken, duck, turkey, goose	165°F	Cook until juices run clear and leg moves easily.
Parts of chicken, duck, turkey, goose	165°F	Cook until juices run clear.

NOTE: Always cook meat, poultry, and fish to at least the temperatures recommended by the United States Department of Agriculture to prevent food-borne illness. However, some parts of poultry, such as legs and thighs, cooked to 165°F, while safe, would be considered undercooked by many people. Consult individual recipes for finish cooking temperatures. ALSO NOTE: A 12-pound turkey can easily require up to 60 minutes of resting. During that time, the internal temperature can rise 30 degrees if not exposed to drafts.

PORK COOKING-TEMPERATURE TABLE

CUT OF MEAT	INTERNAL TEMPERATURE	VISUAL DESCRIPTION
Roasts, steaks, chops	**USDA guidelines**	
	145°F	Medium-rare, pale pink center
	160°F	Medium, no pink
	160°F and above	Well done, meat is uniform color throughout
Pork ribs, pork shoulders, beef brisket	160°F and above	Depending upon how the meat is being prepared and which cut, different temperatures may be used. A pork shoulder may be prepared as a roast and would be done at 160°F, whereas the same cut when barbecued "low and slow" for pulled pork may be cooked to an internal temperature of 195°F to 200°F.
Sausage, raw	160°F	No longer pink
Ham, raw	160°F	Dark pink color throughout
Ham, precooked	Follow printed instructions	Dark pink color throughout

STANDARD TERMINOLOGY AND TEMPERATURE GUIDELINES

HEAT SETTING	GRATE TEMPERATURE RANGE	PULL YOUR HAND AWAY (5 IN. ABOVE GRATE)
High	Approx. 450°F to 550°F	Approximately 2 to 4 seconds
Medium	Approx. 350°F to 450°F	Approximately 5 to 7 seconds
Low	Approx. 250°F to 350°F	Approximately 8 to 10 seconds

GRILLING TEMPERATURE GUIDELINES

METHOD OF HEAT	GRATE TEMPERATURE RANGE	DESCRIPTIVE LANGUAGE MOST OFTEN USED
Direct	Approx. 450°F to 650°F and higher	Sear, searing, or grilling on high
Direct	Approx. 350°F to 450°F	Grilling on medium
Direct	Approx. 250°F to 350°F	Grilling on low

ROTISSERIE TEMPERATURE GUIDELINES

METHOD OF HEAT	BURNER TEMPERATURE RANGE	DESCRIPTIVE LANGUAGE MOST OFTEN USED
Direct	Approx. 350°F to 450°F	Rotisserie or "spit" roasting

FISH AND SEAFOOD COOKING TEMPERATURES AND TIMES

FRESH OR THAWED FISH	INTERNAL TEMPERATURE	VISUAL DESCRIPTION
Salmon, halibut, cod, snapper (steaks, filleted, or whole)	145°F	Fish is opaque, flakes easily
Tuna, swordfish, marlin	145°F	Cook until medium-rare. (Do not overcook, or the meat will become dry and lose flavor.)
Shrimp	**Time Cooked**	
medium-size, boiling	3 to 4 min.	Meat is opaque in center.
large-size, boiling	5 to 7 min.	Meat is opaque in center.
jumbo-size, boiling	7 to 8 min.	Meat is opaque in center.
Lobster		
boiled, whole in shell, 1 pound	12 to 15 min.	Shell turns red, meat is opaque in center.
grilled, whole in shell, 1½ pounds	3 to 4 min.	Shell turns red, meat is opaque in center.
steamed, whole in shell, 1½ pounds	15 to 20 min.	Shell turns red, meat is opaque in center.
baked, tails in shell	15 min.	Shell turns red, meat is opaque in center.
grilled, tails in shell	9 to 10 min.	Shell turns red, meat is opaque in center.
Scallops		
baked	12 to 15 min.	Milky white or opaque, and firm
seared	varies	Brown crust on surface, milky white or opaque, and firm
Clams, mussels, oysters	varies	Point at which the shell opens, throw out any that do not open

ROASTING TEMPERATURE GUIDELINES

METHOD OF HEAT	COOKING CHAMBER TEMPERATURE RANGE	DESCRIPTIVE LANGUAGE MOST OFTEN USED
Indirect	Approx. 350°F to 450°F	Indirect grilling or indirect cooking
Indirect	Approx. 250°F to 350°F	Indirect grilling or indirect cooking, "low and slow"

SMOKING TEMPERATURE GUIDELINES

METHOD OF HEAT	COOKING CHAMBER TEMPERATURE RANGE	DESCRIPTIVE LANGUAGE MOST OFTEN USED
Indirect, with wood smoke	Approx. 250°F to 350°F	Hot smoking "low and slow" wood smoke
Indirect, with wood smoke	Approx. 150°F to 250°F	Smoking "low and slow" wood smoke

GRILLING & BBQ **ESSENTIALS**

MUST-HAVE PANTRY

- **Pure Vegetable Oil/Cooking Oil Spray.** This is an essential tool for lubricating meat and grill grates.
- **Kosher or Sea Salt.** The larger crystals of kosher or sea salt are wonderful because you can actually see where you have salted.
- **Garlic (granulated and fresh).** This is a basic flavor for most grilling sauces and rubs.
- **Cumin.** This spice is the secret of all great barbecue cooks.
- **Onions (powdered, granulated, or fresh).** You'll find that onions enhance most every barbecue recipe.
- **Apple Cider Vinegar.** This provides the flavor of apple cider without the sugar and is the choice of most master grillers. Use by itself as a spray or as a liquid component of wet rubs, mops, and sauces.
- **Ketchup.** This versatile ingredient can be combined with many others to form a quick sauce.
- **Brown Sugar.** Used for dry rubs. When combined with ketchup, it creates a sweet glaze for pork or chicken. Try sprinkling a touch on steaks.

**Char-Broil
Instant-Read
Digital Thermometer**

ESSENTIAL GRILLING TOOLS

- **Knives.** A good knife is essential to prepping and carving meat. Choose knives that feel good in your hand, work for different tasks, can be used outdoors, don't cost a fortune, and are easy to clean and sharpen.
- **Spatula.** Those with a wooden handle seem to be the best, along with a sturdy blade that supports a good-sized steak, and easily slides between the grate and the food. Try using two spatulas to remove the skin from a side of salmon during grilling.
- **Tongs.** Buy tongs in a variety of colors to indicate their purpose. You can use red ones for raw meat and black ones for meat that's cooked.
- **Fork.** Use the fork with the tongs and spatula when you need a little extra help.
- **Basting Brush.** Silicone cooking utensils are wonderful. The angle is great for getting to places without twisting your wrist, and the brush holds sauce and clarified butter quite well.
- **Thermometers.** The most important thermometer you'll own is a pocket instant-read thermometer. They are very useful for quickly testing meat in various areas to see if it's cooking evenly.

    Char-Broil offers a remote digital thermometer that has both a food probe and a dangling device that reads the temperature right near the grates. It will alert you if the temperature inside the smoker starts to drop, and it will inform you of the internal temperature of the meat.
- **Heat-Resistant Leather Gloves.** These bad boys are intended for heavy industrial use and can take sparks, heat, and hot metal. They aren't intended for playing in the fire but are very useful when you need to move hot grates and cast-iron pans, and when working around your grill, smoker, or barbecue.

**Char-Broil
Spice Stick**

BACKYARD COOKING **TIPS**

GREAT BURGERS

The criteria for acclaiming a burger as "great" is regional in both flavor and style. However, the best burger in the world is the one you'll enjoy making and eating on any given weekend. Try using coarse-ground chuck—coarse because it holds together better, and chuck because it has great flavor.

A good fat-to-meat ratio is no more than 15 percent fat. More than that and your burger will drip fat, shrink, and cause flare-ups—unless, of course, you are using one of the new infrared gas grills, where you will notice fewer flare-ups and less meat shrinkage. Note: You can always buy a leaner ground beef and add a bit of olive oil.

Prepping the Patty. Using a wine bottle, gently press the ground chuck to about ¼ inch thick. Seasoning is a twist or two of freshly ground black pepper, a couple of pinches of sea or kosher salt, and our "secret" ingredients: ground cumin and finely minced fresh garlic. Yeah, baby—now yer talkin'!

After seasoning, fold the meat over, and gently press it down so it's about ½ inch thick. The seasoning is now in the middle of the patty, which evenly distributes the flavors. Use a pizza cutter to form patties out of the seasoned ground meat, making them just a bit larger than the size of the buns you plan to use. Store the patties in the refrigerator, chilling them to about 45°F until the grill is ready.

Grilling Rule #1—Make it HOT. Spritz the patties with a little canola oil as you take them out of the refrigerator, and put them directly on the grill to sear. A searing temperature of approximately 450°F is ideal. An infrared grill can deliver the heat to create great, restaurant-quality sear marks.

After the patties sear and are no longer sticking to the grates, use a metal spatula to turn and place them on a fresh part of the grill. After grill marks are established on both sides, remove patties to an aluminum pan or tray, cover with foil, and allow them to finish cooking from their residual heat. Many folks like the meat seared on the outside and pink on the inside. (The USDA recommends an internal temperature of 160°F for ground beef, pork, lamb, and veal.) When using a conventional gas grill, brush patties with melted butter instead of canola oil before placing them on the grill.

Cheese Please! While the patties are finishing, add thin slices of cheese or brush with BBQ sauce.

SUCCULENT STEAKS

Beef cuts with marbled fat throughout the meat will cook better over direct high heat. If you prefer to grill without removing the external fat, and your steak is less than 1 inch thick, cut or notch the fat about every 3 inches to help prevent the meat from curling. If you can afford them, prime and choice grades will give you a better value for flavor and quality.

Marinades and Rubs. If you pay for a good cut of beef, you want to taste the meat, not the marinade or rub. However, some grill recipes call for seasoned or well-marinated beef. If you must marinate, remember that the acids in citrus fruit and vinegars will break down and tenderize the meat. Marinades containing sugar will quickly burn when exposed to high temperatures. The same holds true for rubs containing sugar.

Seasoning. Lightly sprinkle freshly ground black pepper and kosher or sea salt. Some folks insist that salting a steak prior to cooking will dry it out. This is only partially true. Salt draws moisture from the steak, but that moisture is composed of naturally occurring sugars and proteins. When these are exposed to searing temperatures, they brown and form the crust so many of us enjoy at a fine restaurant.

Searing. Searing the outside of a steak at a temperature in the range of 450°F to 550°F is the way professionals do it. Make sure you don't cook the steak at this temperature for the entire time, unless you enjoy meat that is crispy on the outside and raw on the inside. (See the cooking chart on page 15 to get a sense of correct time and temperatures.)

Steak on a Standard Gas Grill. Most folks cook their steaks at approximately 375°F to 400°F using a traditional convection gas grill. Charcoal grills can achieve temperatures of 400°F to 450°F. It requires temperatures of at least 450°F or more—similar to the heat used in a professional restaurant kitchen—to see grill marks form on a rare steak. If your grill doesn't get quite this hot, lightly coat the outside of a seasoned steak with clarified butter or a touch of brown sugar.

Always turn steak with tongs or a spatula, not a fork. Check for doneness using an instant-read thermometer inserted in the side of the steak, preferably through any fat on the edge. (The USDA recommends 145°F for rare; 160°F for medium; and 170°F for well.)

Steak on an Infrared Gas Grill. Set the temperature on your infrared grill to high, and place the steaks on the grill, lined up in the same direction. Cook steaks on each side for 1 to 3 minutes to sear. Remove steaks; place them in an aluminum pan or tray; cover with foil or top with another pan; and place on a cooler section of the grill to finish cooking. Check for desired doneness with an instant-read thermometer.

Roasting. Another trick you'll see in a restaurant kitchen is to pull a steak from the grill, and place it in a pan in a 400°F oven. If you try this at home, watch the internal temperature of the steak to avoid overcooking.

Resting. After cooking, it's important to allow a steak to rest for about 10 minutes before slicing into it. This holding period keeps every bite juicy.

JUICY CHICKEN

Preparing and eating chicken can be an enjoyable treat. Here are a few tricks that help ensure the most lip-smacking results.

Buy Fresh Chicken. Buy the best quality you can afford, and fresh is best. Organic chickens may taste more like the chickens you remember eating as a kid.

To Brine or Not to Brine. Your mom may have liked to tenderize chicken by soaking it overnight in buttermilk. Brine will produce the same results, and help retain juiciness.

Seasoning. Apply sauces and glazes during the final minutes of cooking. If you like the taste of a dry rub, check the ingredient list before using. Many spices will burn when exposed to high temperatures, which can ruin the flavor. Use only a light seasoning of ground pepper, as well as kosher salt if the chicken hasn't been brined. You can also lightly spray chicken with canola oil to prevent sticking.

Temperature and Time. First, make sure to remove your chicken from the refrigerator and let it warm up for just a few minutes before cooking. Be careful never to let raw poultry reach room temperature, but try to avoid putting ice-cold chicken on the grill because that interferes with proper cooking.

The second most important rule for grilling chicken is to cook it from the inside out. The USDA recommends an internal temperature of 165°F for both chicken parts and whole chickens. Use an

instant-read thermometer to gauge the internal temperature of the meat, making sure to keep the probe away from bones. If you cook chicken using the four-stage method suggested here, you can test the temperature at each stage.

Some things to remember: dark meat takes longer to cook than white meat; and larger pieces take longer to cook than smaller ones. The legs and thighs are dark meat. The wings, drumettes, and breast are white meat. Start cooking dark-meat chicken parts first. If you are cooking chicken halves, start them bone side down to speed up cooking.

Stage 1: Searing (450°F–550°F). This temperature range is perfect for searing steaks, and it's also a great place to start grilling chicken. A quick sear on both sides will help to lock in natural juices and flavor.

Stage 2: Grilling (350°F–450°F). On one-half of the grill, set the heat to medium-high (about 500°F). Set the heat to medium-low (about 375°F) on the other half. Start by placing fresh pieces of chicken on the hotter side. After searing for just a short time (2 to 3 minutes on an infrared grill, longer on a standard grill), the chicken will begin to get grill marks.

Although flare-ups on Char-Broil's infrared gas grills are rare, you may need to watch for them on other grills. Using your instant-read thermometer, check the chicken's internal temperature. Look for a temperature of approximately 145°F to 155°F to move from grilling to glazing.

Stage 3: Glazing (200°F). During the final ten minutes of cooking, reduce the heat under the chicken to low, and glaze the chicken with sauce. An apricot or peach marmalade is great depending upon what else is on the menu. Whatever your taste dictates, the chicken should be almost fully cooked and removed from any direct heat before glazing. For perfect glazing, simmer the sauce before brushing it on the meat.

Stage 4: Rest, Rest, Rest. When you're finished grilling, place all of the chicken in trays or foil pans, cover, and let it rest for at least 10 minutes. This will help redistribute the juices inside each piece and allow the internal temperature to rise an additional 5 to 10 degrees. If you like, you may also add more sauce.

TENDER, MOIST PORK

Depending on the thickness, cut, and amount of fat, muscle, and bone, the cooking times for pork can vary considerably. Generally, 160°F is considered a safe internal temperature for pork and yields a much juicier piece of meat.

Brining. Brining is similar to marinating because both methods involve soaking meat in a solution for several hours or overnight prior to cooking. Brining makes cooked meat more moist by hydrating the cells of the muscle tissue before cooking. You can brine pork shoulders, racks, roasts, and even chops.

Injecting Flavors. Flavors and moisture can be added by injecting meat with marinade solutions before cooking. Needle injectors incorporate marinades directly into the thicker muscle of the meat. Here are additional tips to help you prepare pork.

- Use an instant-read thermometer to check the internal temperature of the meat away from the bone and nearest to the thickest part.
- As you reach the end of the estimated cooking time, cut into the meat near the bone to determine doneness before pulling the meat off the grill. A pork chop is cooked when the meat is no longer pink near the bone.
- Brush on glazes or sauces that contain sugar or honey during the last few minutes of grilling.

Smoked Pork Chops with Polenta & Cranberry Chutney, page 154

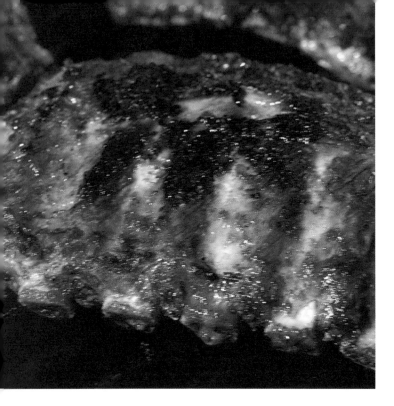

LIP-SMACKING PORK RIBS

There are several varieties of ribs, and each requires a slightly different technique to bring out its best flavor and texture. Here are some general rules for ribs.

- Apply a dry rub of herbs and spices before cooking.
- Cook ribs for ½ to 1 hour depending on the amount of meat, bone, and fat they contain.
- Baste the ribs with a light coating of apple cider vinegar during the last 10 minutes of cooking, or replace the vinegar with a glaze of marmalade or barbecue sauce.
- On Char-Broil's infrared gas grills, you may drop wood chunks directly between the cooking grates. They will flavor the ribs but not actually smoke them.
- Color is not necessarily an indication of when the rib is done. Smoke from burning wood chunks can turn the interior of the meat pink. Ribs are done when you can easily move the bones back and forth. To be certain, insert an instant-read thermometer into the thickest part of the meat away from the bone, measuring for an internal temperature of 160°F.

DELICIOUS VEGETABLES

Grilling vegetables requires little preparation and imparts a delicious, lightly smoked flavor.

- Set a standard gas grill to high; an infrared grill to medium-high.

- Lightly brush or spray vegetables with olive oil before grilling to add flavor, promote sear marks, and keep them from sticking to the grill.
- Some vegetables, such as corn on the cob, mushrooms, and baby eggplants, can be grilled whole. Others, such as zucchini, bell peppers, and onions, should be sliced or cut into wedges.
- Start vegetables over medium-high heat to sear their skins, turning every 1 to 2 minutes. Then move to low heat to finish cooking, turning occasionally.
- The easiest way to tell if vegetables are cooked is to pierce them with a fork or skewer. If it goes in easily, the vegetables are done.

Q: "HOW LONG DO I COOK IT?" A: "UNTIL IT'S DONE."

The only honest answer is that you need to learn from experience. Outdoor temperature, humidity, wind conditions, the thickness and type of meat, and the equipment you're using all factor into the finished product. Use the cooking times given in this book as a guide, and apply the USDA guidelines for safe internal food temperatures. (See charts on pages 15–17.) Remember, however, that most cuts of meat will continue to cook after they are removed from the heat, rising an additional 5°F to 10°F.

SAVORY SEAFOOD

Grilling adds a smoky flavor to seafood and also gives it a crisp, savory crust. Whole fish, firm-flesh fish steaks and fillets, shrimp, and scallops are great on the grill. Hard-shelled mollusks, such as oysters, clams, and mussels, are often grilled in the shell, which causes the shell to open but does little to enhance the flavor.

- Set a standard gas grill to high; an infrared grill to medium.
- Before you begin, make sure the grill surface is clean and very hot to prevent sticking. Rub the grill quickly with a paper towel dipped in some oil before you add the seafood. (You can also use a grill basket or topper to grill seafood above the grill surface.)
- Whole fish, such as snapper, pompano, and sea bass must be handled carefully to avoid sticking and falling apart. Firm fish steaks, such as tuna, swordfish, and shark, are particularly good on the grill because they hold together well and don't stick.
- Grilled shrimp are tastiest when the shell is left on. Lightly sprinkle the shrimp with salt, and grill for about 5 minutes until the shells turn pink.

GRILLED FRUIT FOR DESSERT

Lightly grilling fruit—especially stone fruits, such as peaches, nectarines, apricots, and plums—caramelizes their natural sugars, enhances their flavor, and provides appetizing grill marks.

- Set a standard gas grill to high; an infrared grill to medium.
- Generously oil grill grate to avoid sticking.
- Slice fruit in half and remove pits. Grill with pulp side down, turning once, until tender, about 3 to 5 minutes.
- Fruit is done when it is lightly browned and tender but not mushy.
- Fruit can burn easily because of its sugar content, so watch it closely.
- Cut fruit, such as apples, pears, mangoes, pineapples, and peaches, into chunks and brush lightly with canola oil before grilling. Put pineapple or bananas sliced lengthwise directly on the grill.

2

I grill, therefore I am.
–Alton Brown

Appetizers & Snacks

CROWD-PLEASING NACHOS

PREP: 20 MIN. • GRILL: 15 MIN.

CARNE ASADA MARINADE

2 pounds flap meat (can substitute flank or skirt steak)

½ cup extra virgin olive oil

4 cloves garlic, roughly chopped

2 onions, thinly sliced

4 limes

2 lemons

1 orange

1 tablespoon chili powder

1 teaspoon cumin

1 teaspoon smoked paprika

12 ounces Mexican beer

FOR THE NACHOS

2 bags of your favorite tortilla chips

2 large avocados

4 limes

4 plum tomatoes, halved and seeded

1 bunch green onions

4 ounces can diced green chiles (can substitute sliced jalapeño for more heat)

14 ounces can vegetarian refried beans

1 tablespoon chili powder

½ teaspoon cumin

½ teaspoon cayenne pepper

1½ cups sour cream

1 small can diced chipotle in adobo sauce

16 ounces Monterey Jack cheese, grated

16 ounces medium cheddar cheese, grated

2 disposable aluminum sheet trays for grilling

Combine all of the marinade ingredients in a medium bowl and mix well. Put the carne asada meat in the very large zip top bag and pour the marinade over. Seal and place in a large bowl in the refrigerator for at least 2 hours or up to overnight.

Make the chipotle lime crema by combining the sour cream, 1–2 teaspoons of the chipotles in adobo (to taste according to your heat preference), and the juice of 2 limes. Stir well and set aside. For the guacamole, mash the avocado using a fork until you reach your desired chunkiness. Stir in the juice of 2 limes and a pinch of salt. Set aside. In a small bowl, combine the refried beans, chili powder, cumin, and cayenne pepper. Stir to combine and set aside.

Preheat your Professional TRU-Infrared Gas Grill over medium high heat for 10 minutes. During this time, drizzle the halved and seeded tomatoes and green onion with extra-virgin olive oil and sprinkle with salt and pepper. Spray the grates with non-stick grilling spray and put the green onions and the tomatoes, cut side down, on the grill. Cook for 2 minutes and flip, cooking for another 1 to 2 minutes. Remove from the grill, cool, dice, and set aside.

Back at the grill, give the grates another quick spritz with non-stick spray and add the meat. Grill, uncovered for 2–3 minutes per side. (If you choose use a thicker cut like flank steak, grill for 4 minutes per side.) Remove the meat from the grill and let stand 10 minutes before slicing against the grain, and then chopping to 1-inch bite-sized pieces.

Meanwhile prepare your nacho platter. Spread a nice layer of tortilla chips on each disposable sheet pan. Sprinkle a thin layer of cheese here so that the toppings have something to stick to once the cheese starts melting. Spoon dollops of the refried bean mixture over the top next, followed by a little more cheese. Sprinkle the diced green chiles or jalapeño slices over top, and cover with a little more cheese.

Divide the carne asada between the two platters and top with any remaining cheese. Place platter, one at a time, on the grill and grill over medium heat, closed, for 4 minutes or until the cheese has melted and some of the edges of the chips are starting to brown. Remove from grill and top with the Chipotle Lime Crema, guacamole, grilled tomatoes, and grilled green onions. Serve immediately.

GARLIC AND ROSEMARY BUTTER GRILLED BRIE

GRILL: 12 MIN.

2 tablespoons dried rosemary
  leaves, ground into a
  fine powder
½ teaspoon granulated
  garlic powder
½ stick of butter, melted
2 16-ounce wheels of
  Brie cheese
1 handful of Applewood chips

ESTABLISHING A 2-ZONE GRILLING SURFACE

Heat only one side of the grill, creating one hot direct heat zone and one cooler indirect heat zone. Target grill temperature of 450°F.

Gas 2-burner grill – Turn right side of the grill to high & leave the left side off. **3-burner grill –** Turn far right side of the grill to high, the middle to low-medium and the left side off. **4-burner grill –** Turn far right side of grill to high, middle right to medium, middle left to low, & leave the far left zone off.

2-Zone Grilling Surface on Charcoal: Ignite the charcoal in a chimney starter. When coals are glowing red, dump coals onto the grill floor. Rake coals, pushing ⅔ to one side of the grill, slanting the remaining coals to the opposite side of the grill, establishing high-piled 1 hot zone & 1 cooler zone. For every hour of cooking, add a half-stack of coals.

Hardwood Smoker Packs: Tear off 1 8" sheet of tin foil. Pour a handful of your favorite hardwood chips onto the foil in a mound. Wrap the tin foil around the chips creating a package-of-sorts. With a knife or fork, perforate the top of the packet allowing smoke to billow from the package when the chips are heated.

In advance of grilling, preheat grill to medium-high using the 2-zone cooking method. Wrap wood chips in an 8" sheet of tin foil, then perforate with a fork or knife. Apply wood packet in back corner of the direct heat-grilling zone.

Whisk together the melted butter, ground rosemary and garlic, then brush over entire surface of the Brie wheel.

Once woodchip packet is billowing with smoke, gently place cheese atop the direct heat grilling zone and sear with the grill lid open until char marks are well-defined, 60–90 seconds on each side. Then turn down the grill to low heat and transfer the wheel to the cooler, indirect heat zone to finish cooking—with the grill lid closed smoke the cheese for an additional 8–10 minutes.

Remove the Brie from the grill immediately. Plate alongside toasted artisan breads, an assortment of cured meats, fresh herbs, fruits and berries, pickled vegetables, and dry roasted nuts.

SMOKE-FLAVORED JERKY

Add wood chips for a smoky infusion. For a mild, sweet flavor, add apple or cherry woods. Hickory wood will add a hint of bacon. Mesquite wood is a traditional smoking wood, but it can be strong. To tone it down, add a little apple or cherry. Blending apple or cherry wood with hickory will help balance out sweet, bacony flavors.

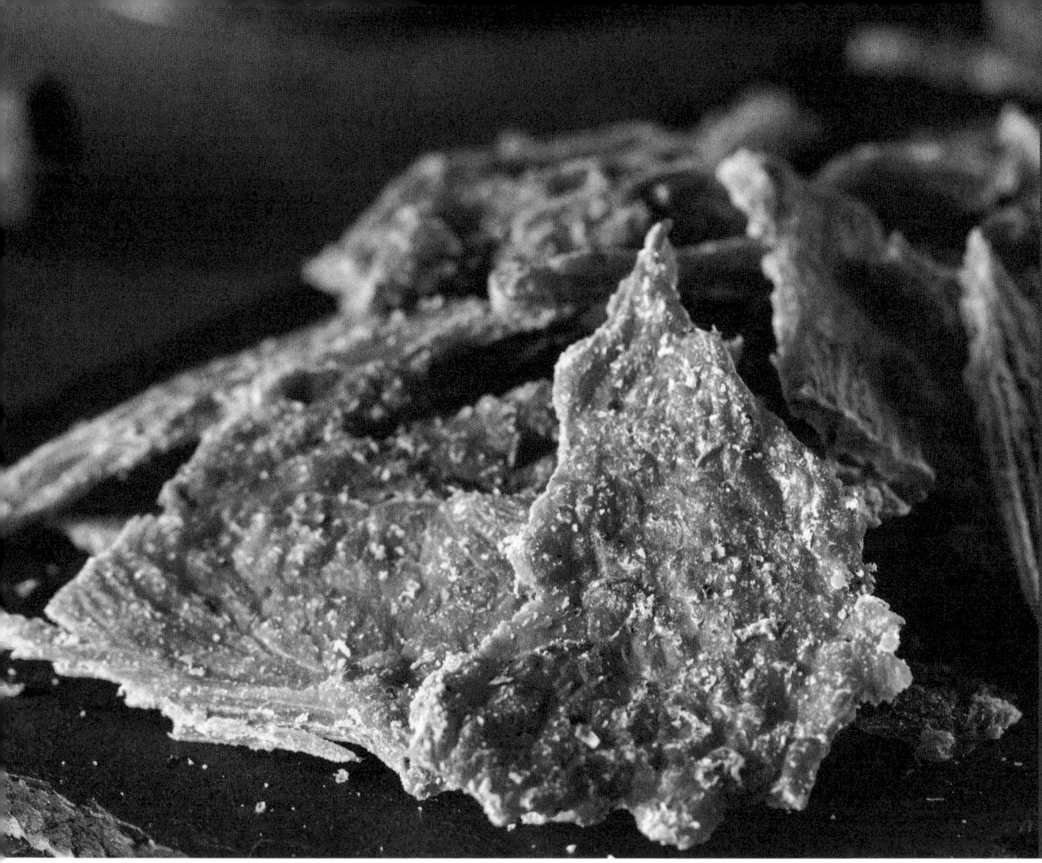

JERKY IN AN ELECTRIC SMOKER

GRILL: 4–6 HR. OR UNTIL MEAT IS FIRM

1 pound meat
½ cup soy sauce
2 tablespoons Worcestershire sauce
2 tablespoons honey
1 tablespoon red pepper flakes
2 teaspoons onion powder
2 teaspoons garlic powder
1 teaspoon black pepper

Along the grain of the meat, cut it into ¼" thick strips. Remove any fat as you slice. Thoroughly mix all your ingredients and marinate the meat overnight in the fridge.

Preheat your smoker at 165°F. Fill the water pan with water, and add your favorite wood chips. When your smoker has reached 165°F, add your meat. Either skewer the meat and hang the pieces from a rack, or lay them flat on the racks.

HOT tip! When placing the meat in your smoker, a little touching is fine, but don't overlap the meat. Use multiple racks instead of forcing all the pieces of meat onto one rack.

Smoke at 165°F for about 4–6 hours, or until the meat is firm. If you're not sure if the jerky is done, take a piece and lightly shake it between your fingers. If it's floppy or limp, put it back in the smoker and keep checking.

HOT tip! If you've made too much, homemade smoked jerky will usually last about 3 months in the freezer.

WOOD-FIRED PIZZA

GRILL: 10 MIN.

1 rolled pizza dough

Parchment paper cut into a
14" circle

8 thin slices provolone cheese

1 cup pizza sauce

8 ounces fresh Mozzarella, sliced,
shredded, or both

6 slices Genoa salami, halved
or quartered

16–18 slices pepperoni

6 sweet mini red bell peppers,
sliced and seeded

1 sweet onion, peeled and
thinly sliced

½ teaspoon Italian seasoning

¼ teaspoon kosher salt

3 tablespoons olive oil, divided
(see recipe steps 2 and 4)

Garnish: parsley, red pepper
flakes, grated Pecorino
Romano cheese

Preheat your grill to 450°F and set it up for indirect heat. For the Kamander kamado grill, load your lump charcoal on the coal grate and light it with both vents wide open. Once the grill reaches 300°F, place the drip pan and drip pan support in. Add the cooking grate and your pizza stone on top of that. Shut both vents to approximately the 2 setting. As the temperature approaches 375°F keep closing the vents more so that you "coast" up to 450°F. Remember, the vent number settings are just approximations and change based on the fuel, wind, air temperature, humidity, and a variety of factors. Go by your dome thermometer and adjust the vents to get the temperature you need.

Place the onion and bell peppers in an oven-safe pan. Drizzle with 2 tablespoons of olive oil, season with salt and Italian seasoning, and toss to coat. Place them on the grill, close the lid and let roast for 20 minutes. You can stir it halfway through the roasting. Remove from grill.

Turn it up. Open your lower vent a little to bring the cooking temperature up to 550°F.

Roll out your dough on a 14" piece of parchment paper. "Dock" your dough by jabbing it with a fork or docking tool. Brush the edges with 1 tablespoon of olive oil. Cover the dough, except for about ½ inch from the edge, with the provolone. Next, top that with sauce–use an amount to your liking but usually less is more. Add the salami, about half of the veggies, and top that with the mozzarella. Add the pepperoni and rest of the veggies.

Hold the edge of the parchment paper and slide your Char-Broil Pizza Peel under the paper. Carry it to your grill. Open the grill and then holding the parchment paper edge near the pizza peel handle, angle the peel toward the grill and carefully let the paper and pizza slide onto the stone (remember, the stone is HOT at this point). If it's off center, don't panic, just use the peel to adjust it back onto the stone. Close the grill and let cook for 5 minutes. Rotate the pizza about 180 degrees and cook until the crust is crisp and the cheese starting to turn golden brown, about another 4 to 6 minutes.

Carefully (HOT) slide the peel under the parchment paper and remove the pizza. Sit the pizza on a resting rack for about 3 minutes to let the pizza cool off just a touch. Move to a cutting board, slice, and serve.

SMOKY BABY BLEU ARTICHOKES

6 SERVINGS • PREP: 10 MIN. • PARBOIL: 4 MIN. • GRILL: 5 MIN.

12 baby artichokes
Nonstick cooking spray
Salt and pepper
½ cup bleu cheese, crumbled
Balsamic vinegar

To prepare the baby artichokes for cooking, snap off the lower petals until you reach the core. Trim each baby artichoke by cutting off the top ½-inch and the bottom stem. Place artichokes in a saucepan filled with water. Bring water to a boil, and parboil artichokes for approximately 3 to 4 minutes. Artichokes are done when a toothpick or knife tip will go into the base of the artichoke easily.

Preheat outdoor grill to medium. Directly spray either mesh grill basket or aluminum foil with nonstick cooking spray. Add artichokes to grill basket or foil, and cook over direct heat for 5 minutes or until artichokes are evenly browned.

Add salt and pepper to taste, and sprinkle bleu cheese on top of artichokes. Keep the basket on the grill for one minute or until the bleu cheese melts.

Remove the artichokes from the grill, and arrange them on a plate. Drizzle balsamic vinegar over the artichokes, and serve.

Make this dip while you get your main course going; just mix everything in a baking dish, and cook on the top rack.

HOT SWEET-ONION DIP

4 SERVINGS • PREP: 5 MIN. • GRILL: 30–50 MIN.

1 (4-ounce) package cream
  cheese, softened
½ cup mayonnaise
½ cup Parmigiano-
  Reggiano, grated
½ cup sweet onion (Vidalia or
  Maui), chopped
Black pepper to taste

Stir all ingredients together in a baking dish or aluminum pan. Place on top rack of grill that has been preheated to medium. Cook about 30 to 50 minutes, or until top is browned. Serve with crackers, vegetables, or toasted bread.

Grilling is much more relaxing when you are not trying to juggle a whole collection of plates and bowls as you do it. If your grill doesn't have enough workspace . . . set up a table right next to your grill.

–Bobby Flay

HOT CORN DIP

6 SERVINGS • PREP: 10 MIN. • GRILL: 10–20 MIN.

2 tablespoons unsalted butter

2 cups corn kernels (from 2 ears corn)

Salt and pepper to taste

½ cup yellow onion, chopped

¼ cup red bell pepper, chopped

¼ cup chopped green onions (green and white parts)

1 jalapeño, chopped

2 teaspoons garlic, chopped

¼ cup mayonnaise

½ cup Monterey Jack cheese, grated

¼ teaspoon cayenne

½ cup sharp cheddar, grated

Melt one tablespoon of the butter in a pan. Add the corn; season with salt and pepper; and sauté until the corn starts to turn golden brown, about 5 minutes. Remove from the pan, and set aside.

Melt the remaining tablespoon of butter in the same pan. Add the onion and pepper, and sauté until softened, about 2 minutes.

Add the green onions, jalapeño, and garlic; sauté until softened, about 2 minutes. Mix the corn, onions, peppers, mayonnaise, Monterey Jack, and cayenne in a bowl. Pour the mixture into an 8 x 8-inch baking dish or aluminum pan, and top with the cheddar cheese.

Place on the top rack of a grill that has been preheated to medium, and cook until bubbling and golden brown on top, about 10 to 20 minutes.

This warm, sweet dip is perfectly balanced by the heat of the jalapeños and the cayenne pepper. It's great served with tortilla chips.

GRILLED OYSTERS WITH BACON, TOMATO & TARRAGON

12 SERVINGS • PREP: 20 MIN. • GRILL: 10 MIN.

3 tablespoons unsalted butter

1 tablespoon shallot, minced

1 green onion, sliced thinly on the bias

2 tablespoons cider vinegar

2 tomatoes, peeled, seeded, and diced

2 teaspoons tarragon, minced

½ teaspoon ground black pepper

2 strips bacon, fried and crumbled

1 dozen oysters, shucked, shell reserved

TO SERVE THE OYSTERS

2 to 3 cups of coarse salt (kosher or rock)

Preheat one side of the grill to medium. (The oysters will be cooked over the indirect side.)

In a skillet over medium heat, melt the butter; add the shallot and green onion; and cook until they are softened, 4 minutes. Add the cider vinegar, and cook until bubbly and reduced, 3 minutes.

Add in the diced tomatoes, and stir gently to heat through, 2 minutes. Do not mash or break up the tomato chunks.

Remove from the heat, and stir in the tarragon and black pepper. Top each oyster with 1 to 3 teaspoons of the tomato mixture.

Grill over indirect heat, with lid closed, for 5 to 10 minutes. The oysters are done when the edges have curled and the topping is bubbly. Serve on a bed of coarse salt.

SCOTCH EGGS ON THE GRILL

4 SERVINGS • PREP: 25 MIN. • GRILL: 30–40 MIN.
OR UNTIL SAUSAGE IS COOKED TO 160°F

1 roll breakfast sausage, about
   1 pound
½ cup shredded cheese (cheddar
   or Monterey Jack)
½ cup crisp bacon, crumbled
4 eggs, parboiled for 4 to
   5 minutes

ADDITIONS
Chopped bell peppers, red
   pepper flakes, chipotle paste,
   seasoned bread crumbs,
   or any other condiment
   you prefer

Divide the sausage into four thin patties. Lightly sprinkle cheese, bacon bits, and any other fillings over the center of each patty. Peel the eggs, and place one on top of each patty. Wrap the sausage around the egg to cover evenly.

Preheat a grill or smoker set for indirect cooking to medium high. Place the sausage balls in a pan or directly on the grates over a drip pan on the side with indirect heat. Cook about 30 to 40 minutes or until the sausage is crispy on the outside.

SPICED CRANBERRY WINGS

4 SERVINGS • PREP: 30 MIN. • MARINATE: 3 HR.–OVERNIGHT • GRILL: 20–25 MIN.

3 to 4 pounds chicken wings
1 cup balsamic
    vinaigrette dressing
1 (14-ounce) can jellied
    cranberry sauce
2 tablespoons Tabasco sauce
½ teaspoon salt
¼ teaspoon pepper

Remove and discard tips from chicken wings. Combine remaining ingredients in a bowl, and whisk with a fork until smooth. Refrigerate half of the sauce to serve with the cooked wings.

Put the chicken and the remaining sauce in a resealable plastic bag; shake to coat well; and refrigerate from 3 hours to overnight.

Preheat grill to medium. Remove chicken from the marinade, and place on the grill skin side down. Discard marinade. Cook wings for about 10 to 12 minutes per side, basting often with the reserved sauce. Serve hot with remaining dipping sauce.

AVOCADO CHIMICHURRI BRUSCHETTA

6 SERVINGS • PREP: 5 MIN. • GRILL: 5 MIN.

2 ripe avocados
¼ cup parsley, chopped
¼ cup cilantro, chopped
½ shallot, finely diced
2 tablespoons red wine vinegar
1 tablespoon honey
Olive oil, enough to bring everything together
Salt and pepper to taste
6 slices thick Italian bread
1 garlic clove, peeled and cut in half

Cut the avocados in half; remove pits; and cut into cubes.

Combine avocados, parsley, cilantro, shallots, vinegar, honey, and olive oil. Season mixture with salt and pepper.

Brush olive oil on slices of bread, and grill on each side for a couple of minutes until toasted.

Rub the cut side of the garlic clove on grilled bread slices. Spread avocado mixture on bread, and serve immediately.

REUBEN DIP

8 SERVINGS • PREP: 10 MIN. • GRILL: 10–15 MIN.

2 pounds deli corned beef

1 pound Swiss cheese

1 jar Thousand Island dressing
   and dip

15-ounce can sauerkraut

4 tablespoons coarse
   Dijon mustard

2 packages party-size rye bread

Finely chop corned beef and Swiss cheese in a food processor. Add dressing, sauerkraut, and mustard to the processor, and pulse a few times to mix. Lightly butter one side of each bread slice, and wrap slices in aluminum foil to toast. Pour dip into a small aluminum pan, and place on the warming rack of a preheated grill. Close hood, and allow bread to toast and cheese to melt, about 10 to 15 minutes. Serve the dip with the toasted bread.

PEG-LEG CHICKEN DRUMS

12 SERVINGS • PREP: 30 MIN. • GRILL: 25 MIN. (UNTIL MEAT TEMP. IS 180°F)

This recipe is courtesy of competitive barbecue champion Mike "Pit Pirate" Hedrick.

12 chicken legs
12 strips thin-sliced bacon cut in
    half lengthwise
¼ cup brown sugar
Ground salt and pepper to taste
Favorite dry rub or
    poultry seasoning
Toothpicks as needed
Favorite barbecue sauce

Rinse drumsticks thoroughly under cold, running water; pat dry with paper towels. Using poultry scissors, remove skin by trimming all the way around the bottom of the drumstick. Peel off the lower skin and knuckle. (Sometimes you may need to cut around the knuckle, too.)

Place bacon strips on a clean, dry surface, and liberally sprinkle them on one side with brown sugar and freshly cracked salt and pepper. Coat the chicken with the dry rub.

Set a drumstick at the end of a bacon strip, seasoned side up. Wrap the bacon around the chicken several times, making sure the bacon strip does not overlap too much. Secure with heavy-duty plain toothpicks. Repeat until all the drumsticks are wrapped.

Place bacon-wrapped chicken legs on a standing grill rack so that they can cook using indirect heat. (They can also be smoked or fry-roasted in The Big Easy.)

When the bacon is almost crisp, insert an instant-read thermometer into one of the drumsticks to test for doneness (180°F). Lightly brush the drumsticks with barbecue sauce to glaze.

With this recipe from Barry "CB" Martin, you can eat these straight out of the smoker or over a green salad dressed with crispy bacon and vinaigrette dressing.

CB'S SMOKED EGGS

12 SERVINGS • PREP: 20 MIN. • SMOKE: 1 HR.

1 dozen large eggs in a
    cardboard carton, lid removed
Coarse salt

Place eggs in a saucepan in an even layer. Cover with cool water, and add salt. Bring to a boil over high heat on the side burner of the grill or on a stove. When the water begins to boil, cover the pan and remove from the heat. Let eggs sit for 10 minutes.

Remove the lid, and run hot tap water over the eggs. After a minute, pour out the hot water, and add lukewarm water. After another minute, pour this out, and add cold water. Repeat until eggs are cool, about 4 to 5 minutes. Roll eggs on a counter or cutting board to crack the shells, but don't remove them.

Preheat one side of the grill to low, and add your choice of wood chips. (For a more delicate smoke flavor, try apple or almond wood.) Poke a hole in the bottom of each section of the egg carton to allow smoke to penetrate, and then return the eggs to the carton. Place the carton over the unheated side of the grill; close the hood; and smoke for approximately 1 hour. Serve eggs immediately, or refrigerate in a sealed container for up to a week.

CB'S PROSCIUTTO-WRAPPED DATES

24 SERVINGS • PREP: 20 MIN. • GRILL: 20 MIN.

24 large pitted dates (Medjool is
a good variety)
1 cup cheese (manchego, feta,
goat, or bleu), crumbled
and chilled
1 (6 ounces) package prosciutto
24 plain wooden toothpicks

Slit the dates lengthwise, and stuff each one with about ½ teaspoon of cheese. Wrap a prosciutto slice completely around each cheese-filled date; secure with a toothpick. You can prepare these in advance and keep up to one day in the refrigerator.

Preheat one side of the grill to medium high. Arrange the dates about 1-inch apart in a disposable aluminum tray, and place on the unheated section of the grill. (You may want to use a wire rack to help prevent sticking and overcooking, or place a drip tray under the grates.)

Roast dates for about 10 minutes with the hood down. Use tongs to turn; then roast another 10 minutes or until the prosciutto is crispy and the cheese is slightly melted.

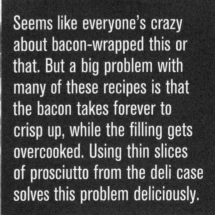

Seems like everyone's crazy about bacon-wrapped this or that. But a big problem with many of these recipes is that the bacon takes forever to crisp up, while the filling gets overcooked. Using thin slices of prosciutto from the deli case solves this problem deliciously.

THAI GRILLED SALT-AND-PEPPER SQUID

4 SERVINGS • PREP: 10 MIN. • GRILL: 5 MIN.

½ to ¾ pound cleaned calamari
    tubes (fresh or frozen)
1 tablespoon vegetable oil
¾ teaspoon ground white pepper
1 teaspoon salt
½ teaspoon cayenne pepper
½ teaspoon dried crushed chili
¼ teaspoon ground black pepper
1 teaspoon garlic powder
½ lime cut in wedges
¼ cup fresh coriander,
    lightly chopped
Thai sweet chili sauce (available
    in most supermarkets)
½ package prewashed
    baby greens
1 tablespoon Asian fish
    sauce, optional
Canola oil spray

Using a knife, cut open the calamari tubes so that they lie flat. Rinse and place the calamari on a clean kitchen towel. Dry them as thoroughly as possible to ensure that the spice mixture sticks.

Cut the calamari lengthwise into strips approximately 1 inch wide, and place in a mixing bowl. Drizzle the oil over the strips to coat them.

Mix the dry spices together in a cup or small bowl, and then sprinkle the mixture over the oiled calamari. Mix well until all of the strips are coated. Set aside to marinate while you heat the grill.

Preheat grill to medium. Place a piece of foil over the grill surface, and lightly spray with oil. Place calamari on top of the foil, and cook until edges curl. (Some strips may curl completely into a circle.) Cooking only takes 30 seconds to 2 minutes for each side, depending on the heat of your grill. Try not to overcook the calamari, because it will turn rubbery instead of tender.

Place the calamari on a serving platter over a bed of baby greens. Squeeze lime juice over calamari, and add salt and fish sauce if desired. Finish with a sprinkling of fresh coriander, and serve with Thai sweet chili sauce for dipping.

You can vary the size of the mushrooms to make bite-size hors d'oeuvres, or serve larger ones as a first course.

CB'S FETA-STUFFED PORTOBELLOS

6 SERVINGS • PREP: 15 MIN. • GRILL: 10 MIN.

6 large portobello mushroom caps (about 3 to 4 inches across)

¼ cup olive oil

¼ cup white balsamic vinegar

Salt and ground black pepper

½ cup feta cheese, crumbled

¼ cup sun-dried tomatoes, chopped

½ cup baby spinach leaves washed, dried, stems removed

1 teaspoon thyme

1 teaspoon curry powder

Place mushrooms in a large bowl. Add half of the oil and all of the vinegar, coating mushrooms on both sides. Season with salt and pepper, and set aside.

In the same bowl, add the feta cheese, tomatoes, and spinach. Add dry seasonings and remaining oil, and toss to coat.

Preheat one side of grill to medium high. Place the mushrooms on the heated side of the grill, and cook for 2 to 3 minutes on both sides. Remove the mushrooms to a pan on the unheated part of the grill.

Carefully spoon enough stuffing mixture into each mushroom to fill each cap. Close the hood, and continue to cook the mushrooms over indirect heat. When the cheese begins to melt, remove mushrooms using tongs, and place on a serving plate.

CB'S GRILLED SCALLOPS WITH PROSCIUTTO

4 SERVINGS • PREP: 25 MIN. • GRILL: 6–8 MIN. (UNTIL INTERNAL TEMP. IS 145°F)

12 jumbo sea scallops, about
    2 ounces each
6 slices prosciutto, cut into
    thin strips
12 plain wooden toothpicks or
    6 wooden skewers, soaked
    in water
Canola oil

OPTIONAL GLAZE
Melted butter, lemon juice, and
    touch of anchovy paste

If the scallops are still in their shells, have your fishmonger remove the shells and the tough side muscle. If desired, you can freeze these muscle pieces for making fish stock.

Wrap one slice of prosciutto around each scallop, and secure with a toothpick; or thread two scallops on each wooden skewer.

Preheat one-half of the grill to medium high. Spray the wrapped scallops with canola oil, and use tongs to place them on the heated grates. Sear for about 3 to 4 minutes per side or until grill marks appear, using tongs to turn.

When the scallops appear to be opaque in the center (about 145°F), set them in a holding tray placed on the unheated section of the grill.

Whisk together butter, lemon juice, and anchovy paste. You may glaze the scallops with this butter sauce before serving.

THE BIG EASY® YARDBIRD WINGS

4 SERVINGS • PREP: 4 HR. INCLUDING MARINATING
COOK IN THE BIG EASY: 10 MIN.

Around 24 chicken wings
½ cup canola or vegetable oil
½ cup or more lemon juice
½ cup favorite seasoning or rub
   for chicken wings
Salt and pepper to taste

Mix seasoning ingredients together in a nonreactive container. Wash and cut off the wing tips, and then the drum, from each 2-bone wing. Add prepped chicken parts to container, and allow them to marinate at least two hours or overnight.

Place all of the wings in The Big Easy cooking basket. (Use either the EZ-Out Cooking Rack or the Half Racks to fit all the wings in the basket.)

Place the loaded cooking basket into The Big Easy; cover with the lid; and set heat to high. Let wings cook for at least 5 to 10 minutes. Pay close attention to the wings, turning the basket and using tongs to move the wings around for even cooking. Serve wings with your favorite dipping sauce.

BBQ competitor Mike "Pit Pirate" Hedrick uses The Big Easy to prepare these crispy wings.

CB'S GRILLED MELON SALAD

4 SERVINGS • PREP: 10 MIN. • GRILL: 10 MIN.

1 cup balsamic vinegar
4 green onions
Extra-virgin olive oil
1 small melon (such as
    cantaloupe or honeydew),
    sliced into about 1-inch-
    thick crescents
1 head Boston or Bibb lettuce,
    washed and dried
¾ cup goat or feta
    cheese, crumbled
Sliced onions

On the grill's side burner or a stovetop, pour balsamic vinegar into a shallow saucepan, and over low heat, cook until liquid is reduced to about half. Reserve.

Preheat grill to high. Lightly oil the green onions, and place on grill, using tongs to turn as each is browned with sear marks. Remove onions, and cut into short diagonal pieces.

Use paper towel to blot surface moisture on each melon slice, and immediately place them on clean hot grates until sear marks appear. Keep an eye on each piece, and use tongs to turn them.

Remove sear-marked melon slices from the grill, and place two or three on each lettuce leaf. Top the warm melon slices with some crumbled goat cheese and sliced onions. Drizzle a thin line of the reduced balsamic vinegar over each in a single curving line. Drizzle in the opposite direction with a thin stream of extra-virgin olive oil.

CHICKEN SATAY WITH FIERY MANGO DIPPING SAUCE

4 SERVINGS • PREP: 15 MIN. • GRILL: UP TO 20 MIN.
(UNTIL INTERNAL TEMP. IS 165°F)

CHICKEN

14 ounces to 1 pound chicken
    breast, cut into strips
8 bamboo skewers
Salt and pepper to taste
Cooking spray as needed

DIPPING SAUCE

1 orange, juiced
1 lime, juiced
1 mango, ripe, peeled, pitted, and
    rough chopped
1 red jalapeño or Fresno pepper
½ cup roasted and chopped
    red onion
¼ cup fresh cilantro
Salt and pepper to taste

Preheat grill to medium. Weave the bamboo skewers through the chicken strips; season; and grill to an internal temperature of 165°F. In a blender, add all of the other ingredients, and purée until smooth. (You cannot overmix this.) Serve the mango sauce on the side of the grilled chicken.

GRILLED EDAMAME WITH SOY-MISO GLAZE

6 SERVINGS • PREP: 5–10 MIN. • GRILL: 5–7 MIN.

16-ounce bag frozen edamame, in
    their pods
½ cup red, yellow, or white
    miso paste
¼ cup sweet mirin (rice wine)
2 tablespoons brown or regular
    rice vinegar
1 tablespoon Dijon mustard
1 tablespoon minced garlic
1 tablespoon peeled and minced
    fresh ginger
1 tablespoon toasted
    sesame seeds
Cooking spray as needed

Preheat grill to medium. In a bowl, mix the miso, mirin, vinegar, mustard, garlic, and ginger. Toss the edamame in the dressing; spray the grill cooking surface; and grill the edamame to desired doneness. Serve immediately, garnished with the toasted sesame seeds.

GRILLED MUSHROOM LETTUCE WRAPS

4 SERVINGS • PREP: 10–12 MIN. • GRILL: 10–15 MIN.

14 shitake mushrooms
2 portobello mushrooms (large)
½ red pepper
4 ounces water chestnuts,
  chopped in chunks
6 cloves garlic, chopped
  in chunks
1 tablespoon oyster sauce
1 tablespoon fish sauce
1 tablespoon agave
2 tablespoons basil (fresh, about
  6–8 leaves), sliced in ribbons
12 Boston Bibb lettuce leaves
Cooking spray

Preheat grill to medium high. Grill the mushrooms and pepper until cooked, and take them off grill. Slice the shitake mushrooms and the peppers into strips. Dice the portobello mushrooms into ½-inch pieces.

Place a pan on the grill. (Make sure to spray the pan with cooking spray away from the grill.) Sauté the garlic and water chestnuts, and add agave, fish sauce, oyster sauce, and basil.

Place the mixture into a bowl, and mix with the mushrooms. Arrange the lettuce on a plate, and fill each leaf with the mushroom mixture. Garnish with some thin strips of red pepper.

PEPPER-AND-GARLIC HUMMUS

8 SERVINGS • PREP: 5–7 MIN. • GRILL: 15 MIN.

1 red bell pepper

2 cloves garlic, lightly oiled and
    wrapped in aluminum foil

1 15-ounce can of garbanzo
    beans, drained

¼ cup tahini

1 tablespoon extra-virgin olive oil

1 lemon, juiced

Salt and pepper to taste

Whole-grain crackers or
    vegetables (to dip) as needed

Preheat grill to high. Place both the aluminum-wrapped garlic and pepper on the grill. Char the outside of the pepper until black. Cook the garlic to the desired roasted amount.

Place the pepper in a paper bag or covered bowl, and let it cool until comfortable to handle. Remove the blacked skin, seeds, and stem from the pepper. In a food processor, blend all other ingredients with the pepper and garlic.

Serve with your favorite whole-grain cracker or vegetables.

Note: If the mixture is thicker than you desire, just thin it out with water.

GRILLED-AND-STUFFED POTATO SKINS

4 SERVINGS • PREP: 20 MIN. • GRILL: 40–50 MIN.

4 large red bliss potatoes
Cooking spray as needed
Salt as needed

STUFFING
½ cup sliced yellow
  summer squash
½ cup sliced zucchini
½ large red bell pepper, julienned
½ large green pablano
  pepper, julienned
1 small red onion, julienned
1 tablespoon olive oil
¼ cup balsamic vinegar
Salt and pepper to taste
¼ cup finely chopped parsley
¼ cup Parmesan cheese
  (optional)

Preheat one side of grill to high. Spray the potatoes with cooking spray; lightly coat with salt; and wrap in aluminum foil. Using indirect heat, cook the potatoes on the grill for 30 minutes or until fork tender.

For the stuffing, mix all of the vegetables, oil, vinegar, salt, and pepper in a bowl. Using a perforated grill basket, sauté the vegetables on the grill until al dente. Slice the potatoes in half; hollow the skins with a spoon; and stuff with the sautéed vegetables. (Optionally, you can top the stuffed potatoes with the cheese and return to the grill to melt.)

Serve on a plate, topped with the chopped parsley.

3

I love the culture of grilling. It creates an atmosphere that is festive but casual.

–Bobby Flay

Beef, Lamb & Veal

BACON-WRAPPED FILET MIGNON

4 SERVINGS • GRILL: 10 MIN. OR WHEN DESIRED DONENESS IS ACHIEVED

4 beef filet steaks, 2 inches thick
4 to 8 slices of bacon
3 tablespoons coarse sea salt
3 tablespoons freshly ground
   black pepper
2 tablespoons dried onion flakes

COMPOUND BUTTER

16 ounces butter, softened
2 tablespoons oregano
1 lemon zest
½ tablespoon hot pepper flakes
1 tablespoon minced garlic

Mix all of the compound butter ingredients in a bowl then spoon onto a parchment paper or plastic wrap. Roll into a log of about 2 inches in diameter and chill in the refrigerator for at least 1 hour.

Preheat your grill at maximum temperature. Season the steaks on both sides with the coarse sea salt, freshly cracked black pepper, and dried onion flakes. Wrap 1 or 2 slices of bacon around each steak and tie them securely using butcher string.

Grill the steaks over high heat for 4 to 6 minutes per side with the lid closed. Flip the steaks a quarter turn for the bacon to face the grate and grill for 15 seconds per side or until the bacon is brown and lightly crisp. Use an instant-read thermometer toward the end of cooking to achieve desired doneness: 120°F for rare, 130°F for medium rare. Remove steaks from the grill.

Cut four slices of compound butter up to ¼-inch thick and place them on each steak. Let the butter melt over the steaks for 8 to 10 minutes before serving.

BARBECUED BEEF SHORT RIBS

MARINATE: 4 HR. • REST 1 HR. • GRILL: UNTIL MEAT REACHES 195°F

3 pounds beef short ribs, trimmed

Olive oil

3 tablespoons chili powder

3 tablespoons finely ground
    coffee beans

1 tablespoon paprika

1 tablespoon onion powder

1 tablespoon granulated
    garlic powder

2 pinches sugar

Kosher salt and fresh ground
    peppercorn, to taste

Lager beer, for spritzing

Barbecue sauce, homemade
    or your favorite store-
    bought brand

Oak wood chunks

Pulse the olive oil and all the other spices in a food processor. Season to taste with salt and pepper. Set aside.

Trim ribs of fat atop the flesh, but leave silver skin on bottom side of the bone. Rinse the ribs with cold water, then pat entirely dry with paper towel. Brush with oil and massage a liberal degree of rub across all portions of the meat. Wrap ribs tightly with plastic and marinate in the refrigerator for 4 hours, up to overnight.

Rest ribs on counter at room temperature for 1 hour prior to grilling. Meanwhile, preheat grill to 225°F to 250°F, using the 2-zone cooking method and toss a few chunks of oak wood directly upon the smoldering coals (or, if using gas, place wood chunks in a perforated tin foil packet placed in the back corner of the direct-heat grill grates). When billowing smoke thins and turns bluish in hue, the grill is ready.

Lay ribs bone-side down over the cooler, indirect heat portion of the grill. Smoke the ribs with grill lid closed until the beef pulls back from the bone, intermittently spritzing with beer until internal temperatures reaches 195°F. At this juncture transfer ribs to the hotter direct-heat grill grates and begin slathering the ribs with barbecue sauce, caramelizing one layer upon another until the internal temperature reads 203°F. Remove the ribs from grill and tent with tinfoil for 10 minutes. Brush one final time with sauce, then plate and serve.

COWBOY-CUT T-BONE STEAK

REST BEFORE GRILLING: 1 HR. • GRILL: 10 MIN. AND THEN
WITHIN 5 DEGREES OF DESIRED DONENESS

2 T-bone steaks, butchered to a
    2" thickness
Olive oil
Onion powder
Granulated garlic powder
Kosher salt and fresh ground
    peppercorn, to taste
Ancho Chili-Honey Butter,
    recipe below
½ cup pine nuts
Maldon salt, to taste, to garnish
Fresh parsley, chopped,
    to garnish

ANCHO CHILI-
HONEY BUTTER

2 sticks unsalted butter,
    room temperature
1 tablespoon ancho chili powder
1 teaspoon honey
1 teaspoon kosher salt
1 teaspoon ground cumin
½ teaspoon paprika
½ teaspoon garlic powder
2 splashes hot sauce

Whisk together all the butter ingredients. Spoon over a sheet of plastic wrap, roll into a log, and tie off at the ends. Place in the refrigerator for 30 minutes before use.

Trim excess fat from steaks, rinse meat in cold water, pat dry, and liberally massage oil and seasonings across entire surface of the beef. Rest on counter for 1 hour prior to grilling.

Toast pine nuts in a heavy-bottom pan over medium heat until golden brown.

Preheat grill using 2-zone method (see notes on page 28). With grill lid open, lay steaks over hottest grill grates and sear 4–6 minutes per side. When charred upon both sides, turn down all burners to low and transfer steaks to the coolest grates. Top the steaks with a dollop of Ancho Chili-Honey Butter and close the grill lid. Remove steaks from grill when within 5 degrees of desired internal temperature in thickest part of the strip (e.g., to prepare a medium-rare steak at 135°F, remove from grill at 130°F). Pull steaks from grill, loosely tent with tin foil for 5–10 minutes, and allow carry-over energy stored in the steaks to finish the cooking.

To plate, cut the strip and filet from the bone. Slice both hunks of meat against the grain. Place bone and steaks back upon the serving dish. Season additionally with coarse maldon salt, to taste. Garnish with toasted pine nuts, a teaspoon of the chili butter, and fresh herbs.

GRILLED TRI-TIP SHISH KEBABS

MARINATE: 4 HR. • GRILL: 8 MIN. (OR UNTIL TEMP. REACHES 140°F)

MARINADE
¼ cup olive oil, plus additional
    for basting
¼ cup Worcestershire sauce
3 tablespoons balsamic vinegar
2 tablespoons soy sauce
2 tablespoons brown sugar
1–2 tablespoons garlic, minced
Fresh ground peppercorn, to taste

KEBABS
2 pounds tri-tip, trimmed
    and cubed
1–2 red onions, chopped
2 large bell peppers, chopped
Several white button mushrooms,
    rinsed and stems removed
4 cobs of corn, each chopped into
    6 rounds

Kosher salt and fresh ground
    peppercorn, to taste
Fresh parsley and green onion,
    chopped, to garnish

SKEWERS
6–8 12"–18" bamboo skewers,
    soaked in water for 30 minutes
    before grilling

Whisk together all marinade ingredients and bring to a simmer in pan until sugar is dissolved. Let the sauce cool entirely. Place steaks in a plastic bag and pour marinade over the steaks. Press all air from the bag and refrigerate for 4 hours, up to overnight.

Remove marinated beef from refrigerator, discard the marinade, and preheat grill to medium-high heat at least 20 minutes prior to cooking.

Load individual skewers with marinated steak and prepared vegetables. Place skewers over the hottest grill grates, searing the kebabs with grill lid open, turning the skewers a quarter turn every 2–3 minutes, until internal temperature of the steak reaches 140°F. Remove skewers from grill and place under aluminum foil tent for 5 minutes. To plate, garnish with chopped parsley and green onion. Season additionally to taste.

REVERSE-SEARED PRIME RIB

12 SERVINGS • REST BEFORE GRILLING: 1 HR.
GRILL: 3 HR. (OR UNTIL TEMP. REACHES 125–127°F

6-pound boneless beef rib roast,
tied and trimmed
1 ½ tablespoons beef base (a
jarred paste sold under the
brand name "Better Than
Bouillon")
2 cups beef stock

FOR THE BEEF SEASONING

2 tablespoons kosher salt
2 tablespoons coarse ground
black pepper
1 teaspoon granulated garlic
¼ teaspoon cayenne pepper
¼ teaspoon dried parsley

Thin the beef base with about 1 teaspoon of water and slather all over the beef roast. Mix together the beef seasoning and sprinkle all over the sides of the beef roast, leaving the ends not seasoned. Place on a rack and let sit at room temperature for 1 hour.

Fill your fire bowl with Char-Broil Center Cut Lump Charcoal. If you want a strong wood flavor, you can add wood chunks to the coal, but for beef rib roasts, the smoke from natural hardwood lump coal is the right amount for a balanced flavor. Light the coal and bring the grill up to 250°F, occasionally closing the vents as you approach 250°F. Insert the water pan/heat diffuser and the main grate. Keep the lid closed and let the fire get stabilized while the beef tempers.

Place the beef roast on the main cooking grate, centered over the water pan/heat diffuser, close the dome lid, and using a remote probe thermometer, cook until the internal temperature reaches 125°F to 127°F for medium rare (about 3 hours). Add 2 cups of beef stock to the water pan when the roast reaches an internal temperature of 90°F to 95°F.

This is a crucial step for the reverse sear and can't be rushed. The beef needs to be taken off the grill, placed on a cooling rack and allowed to rest. It will continue cooking and the internal temperature will rise 7–10 degrees. Once this has occurred and the temperature starts to decline, you can sear the beef. This rest should take anywhere from 15 to 30 minutes. Take out the water pan and pour the beef stock into a fat separator.

Your Kamander should now be set up for direct heat since you removed the water pan/heat diffuser. Open the vents and let the cooking temperature rise to 500°F. Sear the roast directly over the flames on all 4 sides for about 1 minute per side.

Once done searing, allow the roast to rest for 10 minutes. Meanwhile, pour out the beef stock from the fat separator, taste, and adjust seasoning with salt and pepper as desired.

Food, for me, has always been an adventure.
–Anthony Bourdain

ROASTED GARLIC BEEF TENDERLOIN

CHILL: 1 HR. • GRILL: 2–3 HR.

3½–4 pound beef tenderloin roast, trimmed

1 stick unsalted butter, softened but not melted

1 whole head of garlic

1 small shallot, minced

1 tablespoon Worcestershire sauce

1 teaspoon Dijon mustard

1½ tablespoons red wine reduction

2 tablespoons fresh rosemary, minced

1 tablespoon canola oil

1½ teaspoons salt

½ teaspoon fresh ground black pepper

Preheat the grill to around 400°F. Take an entire head of garlic and cut the top third completely off. Place the garlic on a piece of aluminum foil. Drizzle with extra-virgin olive oil and sprinkle with salt. Wrap tightly in foil and place over indirect heat on the grill for 35 to 40 minutes. Carefully remove and unwrap, and squeeze the softened cloves out of the bulb and into a bowl. Mash with a fork and set aside.

Meanwhile, in a small saucepan bring ⅓ cup red wine to a low simmer. Simmer uncovered until thickened and reduced to 2 tablespoons or so. With paper towels, pat the tenderloin dry. Fold the tapered ends of the tenderloin under itself then secure tightly with cooking twine. Continue to tightly tie the tenderloin in sections so it forms a uniform shape. This will guarantee even cooking.

Cream together the butter, roasted garlic, 1½ tablespoons red wine reduction, Worcestershire sauce, shallot, rosemary, Dijon mustard, salt, and pepper until well combined. Using cold, wet hands to keep the butter from sticking, pat the butter all over the tenderloin. Cover in plastic wrap and chill in the refrigerator for 1 hour or up to a day.

Let tenderloin come to room temperature while you heat the grill to 250°F. Remove the tenderloin from the plastic wrap and carefully wrap it in aluminum foil, making sure the juices and melted butter will not leak out when rotating while on the grill. Remember, you're basically making a buttery, herbaceous flavor packet for your tenderloin to slow roast inside.

Place the tenderloin in the Char-Broil Roast and Grill Rib Rack on the center of your grill, and slow cook for 2 to 3 hours until the desired internal temperature has been reached. Flip tenderloin every 30 minutes or so, for a flavorful butter-baste. Start checking at 2 hours, as ours was done at 2 hours and 20 minutes.

Remove at 125°F for rare or 130°F for medium rare. Keep in mind we are reverse-searing the tenderloin, so it will continue to cook a bit then. Let sit at room temperature for 10 minutes and increase the heat on the grill to medium-high heat. Carefully remove the tenderloin from the foil, reserving all of the juices that have collected inside. Sear tenderloin on the grill until the meat is well-browned on all sides. Transfer tenderloin to a cutting board and allow to rest for 5 minutes. Slice into ½-inch slices and drizzle with reserved cooking juices.

CB'S GRILLED NY STRIP STEAK

2 SERVINGS • PREP: 30 MIN. • GRILL: 10 MIN.

2 8-ounce New York strip steaks,
 approximately 1 inch thick
2 teaspoons kosher salt or
 sea salt
1 teaspoon freshly ground
 black pepper
2 tablespoons butter or oil

Trim steaks of any excess fat and allow to rest, covered loosely with wax paper, for 15 minutes at room temperature.

Preheat a gas grill to high or until coals are white hot on a charcoal grill. Season steaks with salt and pepper; then brush steaks lightly on both sides with melted butter or oil.

Grill steaks for approximately 5 minutes. Turn once using a spatula, and cook for an additional 2 to 5 minutes, depending upon thickness.

Check for doneness using an instant-read thermometer (145°F for medium rare). Remove steaks to a warm platter, and allow to rest for at least 2 minutes before serving.

TIPS & TRICKS FOR SMOKED BEEF BRISKET

Cooking brisket is more about technique than a recipe. Seasoning isn't as important as how you actually smoke the brisket. Yes, it affects the final result but not as much as the smoking process. When shopping, look for a whole brisket, which is comprised of two muscles—the point and the flat. You want even thickness from side to side on the flat end, as well as a flexible flat.

Looking at a top-down view of the brisket with the flat facing up, you should see the point sticking out from under the flat on the right side. Notice how the grain of the flat runs diagonally to the upper left

corner. Once cooked, you will slice perpendicular to the grain.

HOT tip! Some people either cut a notch or stick a toothpick in this corner, so that they know which direction to slice once cooked.

Make sure that you have planned for your brisket. Cooking a brisket takes time. Even at hotter cooking temperatures of 275°F to 325°F, it can still be 7–8 hours to cook with a 4-hour hold. Add that

> Weights can vary depending on the beef's breed, age and other factors, but we suggest looking for a 12- to 15-pound brisket.

> Whatever you use, you don't want a billowing, thick smoke. This will leave you with a brisket that tastes like charcoal. The smoke should be thin and very light in color.

to the 12-hour seasoning time and you have a full 24-hour process.

Preparing your brisket for smoking consists of trimming, injecting, and seasoning. We suggest having this done about 12 hours before the brisket goes onto the grill or smoker. Most whole briskets come with a fat cap on one side. Use a very sharp knife, trimming this to a quarter inch in thickness. Always inject briskets so that the needle is parallel with the grain of the beef.

Now it is time to season. Simple is better when thinking about rubs for brisket. Don't worry about using too much rub: it's a large piece of meat and can take it. Once prepared, keep the brisket well refrigerated until it is time to smoke. Your brisket needs to be cold when it hits the grates.

Set your grill or smoker up for indirect cooking. Your brisket will not be directly over the heat source. For the Charcoal Grill 780, the coal and wood are placed on the left. Notice the gap in the middle. This is where live coals will be placed. The brisket will go on the right side, away from the direct heat. Start a batch of live coals using a chimney starter. When adding live coals, they will provide initial heat and start the other coals and wood to for a sustained heat. If you are using a Kettleman™ grill, we recommend using a fuse-style burn set up like this to get longer, steady cooking temperatures. If you are lucky enough to have a Char-Broil® Digital Electric Smoker, it's super easy. Just preheat the unit as normal and put the brisket diagonally on one of the grates.

A key to a great brisket is moisture. Add moisture to the air by using a water pan in the cooker. For the Charcoal Grill 780, you can put a foil steam pan on the gates directly above the coals. For the Kettleman grill, you can just put a foil steam pan in the center of the fire ring. The Digital Electric Smoker comes with an integrated water pan. Add moisture directly to the brisket during the cook. Use a highly seasoned mop, dabbing the brisket every hour or so. This will also add layers of flavor. You can also use a squirt bottle with beef stock to spritz the brisket every hour or so as well.

Retain moisture toward the end of the cook using the "Texas Crutch." Wrap the brisket in foil or butcher paper. Add beef stock to the foil packet to finish your cook with a braise. This is a much gentler process than smoking. We suggest doing this when the "bark," or outer surface, is very dark, usually somewhere around an internal temperature of 160°F to 175°F.

Use a thermometer to monitor the brisket's internal temperature. There is no exact temperature at which you pull the brisket off the grill. After it hits an internal temperature of 200°F in the thickest portion, we suggest sliding either a temperature probe or BBQ skewer into the brisket to test its tenderness. When the probe or skewer slides in with little resistance, the brisket is ready to come off.

BEST NEW YORK STRIP STEAK

GRILL: 12 MIN. FOR MEDIUM RARE

1" thick New York strip steaks
Kosher salt
Freshly cracked black pepper
Butter

**Manage the heat,
let the meat cook,
and you'll get
fantastic results.
–Guy Fieri**

This method works with 1-inch thick steaks. If you have a ½" thick steak, you will end up overcooking it if you use this method. Most grocery store butchers will happily cut a steak to an inch for you. Also, most bulk warehouse shopping clubs sell steaks already cut to 1-inch thicknesses. As a rule of thumb, the thicker the steak, the longer you will need to cook it on the indirect side of the grill after the high heat sear. For example, a 1½-inch thick steak will require three minutes of searing over high heat on each side followed by approximately four minutes on each side for indirect grilling. As steak thickness increases, the amount of time required on the indirect side of the grill also increases.

Heavily rub both sides of the steaks with kosher salt and freshly cracked black pepper. It's just a simple enhancement of the flavors that are already present. No need to be crazy with flavors.

If you hold your hand 1" over the grill grates and you have to pull your hand away after two seconds because of pain, then you probably have a perfect heat for grilling steaks. If you can hold your hand there longer than that, add some more charcoal or crank up the gas. The Char-Broil® Kettleman™ was used for this recipe, so charcoal ruled the day. The idea is to sear the outside of the steak while leaving the inside soft, pink and juicy. To accomplish this, the key is to grill with high heat for the initial sear. Grill your steaks with a high-heat sear followed by some time on the indirect side of the grill. On a gas grill, an indirect cooking area can be the area where a burner is turned off. On a charcoal grill, the indirect heat area is where there is no charcoal.

Three is the magic number for a 1" thick steak. Grab a timer and place the steaks over high heat for three minutes. After three minutes, flip the steaks and let them sear over high heat for another three minutes. Then move the steaks to indirect heat. After another three minutes flip the steaks over the indirect heat. After this 12-minute cooking session, you should have a 1" thick New York strip steak that is medium rare. This results in a perfect, tender, juicy inside with a seared outside.

After the steaks are finished grilling, pile them on a plate and put some butter on each one. The steaks will be so hot that the butter will instantly melt. Serve each steak immediately with your favorite side dish. The simple salt and pepper flavors, with a little butter at the end, are all you need to grill the perfect New York strip steak.

GRILLED FLANK STEAK WITH LEMON & ROSEMARY MARINADE

2–4 SERVINGS • PREP: 5 MIN. • MARINATE: UP TO 4 HR.
GRILL: 6–10 MIN. (UNTIL MEAT TEMP. IS 145°F) • REST: 5 MIN.

This recipe is courtesy of Brys Stephens at www.cookthink.com.

1 flank steak, about 3 pounds
¼ cup olive oil
2 lemons, zested and juiced
2 tablespoons chopped
  fresh rosemary
2 cloves garlic, minced
1 teaspoon fresh ground
  black pepper
½ teaspoon coarse salt

Combine the marinade ingredients. Put the steak in a large plastic bag with the marinade, and seal. Turn several times to coat the steak. Refrigerate for 30 minutes to 4 hours.

Preheat one side of grill to high. Spray grates lightly with canola oil. Remove the steak from the marinade, and place directly on the high-heat side of the grill. Leave it alone until it develops a rich brown crust–3 to 5 minutes. Turn the steak, and repeat. Remove steak when it reaches 145°F for medium-rare. Cover loosely with foil, and let rest for 5 minutes. Carve into long slices at an angle, against the grain.

BBQ CHUCK STEAK

4–6 SERVINGS • PREP: 20 MIN. • MARINATE: 6 HR.–OVERNIGHT • GRILL: 15 MIN.

1½ pounds beef chuck, cut into
    ¾- to 1-inch-thick slices

MARINADE
1 cup finely chopped onion
1 cup ketchup
⅓ cup packed brown sugar
⅓ cup red wine vinegar
1 tablespoon
    Worcestershire sauce
⅛ teaspoon crushed red pepper

Combine marinade ingredients in a medium bowl. Place steak and 1 cup of marinade in food-safe plastic bag; turn to coat. Refrigerate remaining marinade.

Close bag securely. Marinate steak in refrigerator 6 hours or as long as overnight, turning occasionally. Remove steak; discard marinade. Place steak on the grill over medium heat. Grill, uncovered, 15 to 18 minutes for medium-rare to medium, turning occasionally.

Place refrigerated marinade in a small saucepan; bring to a boil. Reduce heat; simmer 10 to 15 minutes or until sauce thickens slightly, stirring occasionally.

Cut steak into serving-size pieces. Serve with sauce.

CB'S SLOW-GRILLED RIB EYES

2 SERVINGS • CHILL: 1 HR. • REST: 1 HR. • GRILL: 20–25 MIN.

2 rib-eye steaks, 8 to 12 ounces
    each, at least 1½ inches thick
Coarse salt
Canola, safflower, or peanut
    oil spray
2 teaspoons maître d' butter
    (see page 318)

Trim away excess fat from around steaks. Blot moisture from meat using a paper towel. Generously sprinkle both sides of steaks with salt. Refrigerate for at least 1 hour.

Remove steaks from the refrigerator about 1 hour prior to grilling. Lightly brush off remaining salt.

Preheat one side of the grill to high, and leave the other side off. Spray steaks lightly with the oil, and place on the cool side of the grill, as far from the heat as you can.

When steaks reach an internal temperature of 90°F, use tongs to place them on the hot side of the grill. Sear steaks over direct heat until they reach a temperature of 140°F (rare) to 145°F (medium rare). Turn steaks once, when sear marks appear on each side. Remove from the grill, and top each steak with a teaspoon of maître d' butter before serving.

CB'S RIB EYES WITH BALSAMIC-MUSHROOM SAUCE

2 SERVINGS • PREP: 30 MIN. • CHILL: 2 HR. • GRILL: 15 MIN. • REST: 15–20 MIN.

2 rib-eye steaks, cut 1 to 2
    inches thick
Coarse salt
Pepper
Canola oil spray

MUSHROOM SAUCE

8 ounces thinly sliced cremini or
    white mushrooms
¼ teaspoon salt
¾ cup balsamic vinegar
2 tablespoons butter
1 teaspoon crushed dried
    thyme leaves

Pat the steaks dry with a paper towel, and rub with salt. Refrigerate meat in a glass dish for 2 hours, removing it 30 minutes prior to grilling.

Trim ½ inch from the tip of each steak; mince and season with salt and pepper; and reserve.

Preheat grill to high; lightly spray steak with canola oil, and grill until the bottom edge begins to brown (about 3 minutes). Using tongs, turn over steaks and grill until that side of the meat begins to turn brown. Turn over the steaks again, and rotate them so that the grill grates are crossing the original sear marks. After 3 minutes, cross-hatch the other side. Finish steaks in an aluminum pan over indirect heat. Then let them rest at room temperature for 15 to 20 minutes.

Spray a sauté pan with canola oil, and place on the grill over medium heat. Brown the minced raw steak; then add the mushrooms and a pinch of salt. Sauté until mushrooms are tender.

Remove mushroom mixture, and set aside. Add balsamic vinegar to skillet; increase heat to medium high. Cook 7 to 10 minutes, stirring up any browned bits with a spatula. When the sauce is reduced to ¼ cup, stir in butter, thyme, cooked mushrooms, and a pinch of salt. Cook and stir until heated. Serve sauce with steaks.

MONTREAL GRILLED T-BONE

4 SERVINGS • PREP: 20 MIN. • GRILL: 15 MIN.

4 14-ounce T-bone steaks
½ cup beef stock
½ diced onion
½ teaspoon chili flakes
½ cup chicken broth
2 ounces bourbon
1 ounce port
¼ teaspoon Cajun seasoning
Salt and pepper to taste

Combine first six ingredients in medium saucepan. Bring to a boil. Simmer uncovered for 4 minutes.

Sprinkle steaks with Cajun seasoning, salt, and pepper. Cook steaks on high heat until desired doneness. Place steaks on plate. Serve with sauce.

The only time to eat diet food is while you're waiting for the steak to cook.
–Julia Child

FLANK-STEAK TOURNEDOS WITH GOAT CHEESE

2 SERVINGS • PREP: 10 MIN. • MARINATE: 45 MIN. • GRILL: 8 MIN.

4 2- to 3-ounce flank-steak slices, approximately 6 inches long and ½ inch or less thick

2 teaspoons coarse salt

2 teaspoons fresh ground black pepper

4 tablespoons extra-virgin olive oil

2 medium-size garlic cloves, minced

2 ounces goat cheese or other soft, creamy cheese

Butcher's twine

Place steak on cutting board or other hard surface, and cover with wax or parchment paper. Use mallet to flatten slightly.

Season meat with salt and pepper, and place in a shallow bowl. Cover with olive oil and minced garlic. Marinate for at least 45 minutes at room temperature. Lay the pieces of meat flat on a sheet of wax paper; spread softened goat cheese on each slice; roll up each one; and individually tie with string.

Preheat grill to high. Use tongs to place tournedos on grill, and allow them to sear for approximately 3 to 4 minutes. Turn meat; place on fresh section of grill; and sear for another 3 to 4 minutes.

Remove meat to a warming rack in a foil pan. Sprinkle additional crumbled goat cheese on tournedos, and allow to rest for a few minutes. Serve with cherry tomatoes, carrots, or other steamed vegetables.

Flank steak is a flavorful cut that lends itself quite well to this recipe.

GINGER-MAPLE STEAK WITH NAPA CABBAGE & GRILLED ONIONS

8 SERVINGS • PREP: 15 MIN. • MARINATE: 2 HR. • GRILL: 15–20 MIN.

2 boneless beef top-loin (strip) steaks, about 10 ounces each

¼ teaspoon black pepper

1 large red onion, cut into ½-inch-thick slices

4 cups thinly sliced Napa cabbage

GINGER-MAPLE MARINADE AND DRESSING

½ cup soy sauce

⅓ cup pure maple syrup

¼ cup lemon juice

2 tablespoons minced fresh ginger

1 tablespoon sesame oil

1½ teaspoons minced fresh garlic

1½ teaspoons Asian chile-garlic paste

Whisk marinade ingredients in a medium bowl. Place steaks and ½ cup marinade in a plastic bag; turn steaks to coat. Seal bag, and refrigerate up to 2 hours. Cover and refrigerate remaining marinade for dressing.

Preheat grill to medium high. Remove steaks from marinade; discard marinade. Sprinkle steaks with pepper. Place steaks in center of grill; arrange onion around steaks. Grill steaks, uncovered, 15 to 18 minutes for medium-rare to medium, turning occasionally. Grill onions 15 to 20 minutes, turning occasionally.

Carve steaks into slices. Cut onion into quarters. Toss cabbage, onion, and 2 tablespoons reserved dressing in a large bowl. Arrange beef on cabbage mixture. Drizzle with the remaining dressing.

CB'S GRILLED HANGER STEAK "MOUTARDE"

4 SERVINGS • PREP: 5 MIN. • MARINATE: 8 HR. • GRILL: 18 MIN. • REST: 5 MIN.

12- to 18-ounce hanger or flank steak
½ cup grainy Dijon mustard
2 tablespoons maple syrup
1 tablespoon cider vinegar
¼ teaspoon dried tarragon
¼ teaspoon hot sauce
Salt and pepper to taste
Canola oil spray

Combine the first 7 ingredients in a plastic bag; massage gently to coat. Marinate in refrigerator for up to 8 hours.

Preheat grill to high. Remove steak from bag; spray with canola oil; and grill on each side for about 4 minutes. Remove; place in an aluminum pan; and cover with foil. Place on warming shelf over indirect heat, and continue cooking for about 10 minutes. Remove from grill, and let steak rest, covered, for about 5 minutes. Slice into thin strips across the grain.

Several years ago, I had the opportunity to visit the Burgundy region of France, where I was delighted to see a grilled steak with "frites" (fries) on the menu at just about every restaurant! Here's my interpretation of those steaks.–CB

GRILLED TENDERLOINS WITH BLUE CHEESE TOPPING

2 SERVINGS • PREP: 10–20 MIN. • GRILL: 15 MIN.

2 tenderloin steaks, approximately
   ½ pound each
1 large clove garlic, halved
½ teaspoon salt
½ teaspoon chopped
   fresh parsley

TOPPING

2 tablespoons cream cheese
4 teaspoons crumbled
   blue cheese
4 teaspoons plain yogurt
2 teaspoons minced onion
Dash ground white pepper

Combine topping ingredients in a small bowl. Rub steaks with garlic halves.

Place steaks on hot grill, and cook 8 to 11 minutes, turning occasionally. One to two minutes before steaks are done, season with salt; then top evenly with cheese mixture. Remove from grill; sprinkle with parsley; and serve.

BLOODY MARY LONDON BROIL

6 SERVINGS • PREP: 20 MIN. • MARINATE: 30 MIN.–2+ HR. • GRILL: 15 MIN.

1 London broil (3½ pounds)
2 cups tomato juice
¼ cup Worcestershire sauce
3 tablespoons
    prepared horseradish
3 tablespoons dry sherry
2 teaspoons crushed
    dried marjoram
1 teaspoon crushed dried basil
1 teaspoon freshly ground
    black pepper

Combine tomato juice, Worcestershire sauce, horseradish, sherry, and seasonings in a bowl. Spread the steak out in a single layer in a baking dish. Spoon tomato-juice mixture over meat, spreading to cover. Turn meat to coat other side. Cover and refrigerate for at least 2 hours, or set aside at room temperature for 30 minutes.

Remove meat from marinade, and discard marinade. Grill steak over medium-high heat for 8 minutes. Turn and grill for 7 to 10 minutes longer for medium rare, or until desired doneness.

Let steak rest at room temperature for approximately 5 minutes. Slice steak diagonally into thin strips before serving.

PORTERHOUSE WITH SPICY PARMESAN BUTTER

2 SERVINGS • PREP: 30 MIN. • MARINATE: 2 HR.–OVERNIGHT • GRILL: 40 MIN.

1 Porterhouse steak,
    approximately 3 inches thick
¼ cup olive oil
8 garlic cloves, minced
1 tablespoon chopped
    fresh thyme
1 tablespoon salt
2 teaspoons ground black pepper
1½ teaspoons chopped
    fresh rosemary

SPICY PARMESAN BUTTER

3 tablespoons butter,
    room temperature
2 teaspoons grated
    Parmesan cheese
1 anchovy fillet, drained
    and minced
1 teaspoon paprika
½ teaspoon Dijon mustard
½ teaspoon Worcestershire sauce
¼ teaspoon ground black pepper
¼ teaspoon Tabasco sauce

Prepare butter by mixing all ingredients in a small bowl until blended. (Can be made 2 days ahead.) Refrigerate. When ready to use, remove from refrigerator and warm to room temperature.

Place steak in a glass dish. Whisk oil and next five ingredients in a small bowl to blend. Pour half of marinade over steak. Turn steak over, and coat with remaining marinade. Cover and refrigerate at least 2 hours and up to 24 hours, turning steak occasionally.

Preheat grill to medium. Remove meat from marinade, and grill to desired doneness or until internal temperature reaches 115°F to 130°F for medium-rare, approximately 18 minutes per side. Transfer steak to a platter; cover; and let rest for 5 minutes.

Cutting away from bone, slice each meat section into ⅓-inch slices. Spread Spicy Parmesan Butter over each portion, and serve.

PRIME RIB ROAST

GRILL: 3 HR. FOR MEDIUM RARE (OR UNTIL TEMP. REACHES
10°F LESS THAN DESIRED DONENESS)

BEEF RUB

1 tablespoon kosher salt
1 tablespoon coarse ground
   black pepper
1 teaspoon dried minced onion
1 teaspoon dried minced garlic
½ teaspoon dried parsley
½ teaspoon red pepper flakes

ROAST

4–6 pound bone-in beef rib roast
1–2 tablespoon vegetable oil
1 quart beef stock
1 ounce dried porcini mushrooms

Mix together the salt, pepper, onion, garlic, parsley, and pepper flakes. Remove the butcher's twine and lightly coat the roast and ribs with oil. Season on all sides (including the space between the ribs and roast) with the dry rub. Re-tie the beef roast and ribs back together. Let sit at room temperature for an hour.

Set up your grill for indirect heat and preheat to low (250°F–300°F). Place the roast, bone-side down, on a roasting rack and pan combination. Add enough stock to fill the pan about 1 inch deep. Add the dried mushrooms. Place the roast and pan on the grill on the indirect side where you don't have any burners on. Close the grill lid and cook until the rib roast hits 10°F less than your desired level of doneness. This should take about 3 hours for medium rare. It's a good idea to turn the roast around every 45 minutes or so. (For rare, pull at internal temperature of 115°F. For medium rare, 125°F. For medium, 135°F.)

Remove the roast and pan set up and let rest at room temperature until the internal temperature stops rising—about 20 minutes. Meanwhile, turn up the grill heat to high (500 °F). Taste the au jus (seasoned broth in the pan) and season with salt and pepper to taste. Keep warm. Fully remove the rib bones. Place the rib bones cut side down over the heat. Sear the roast 2–3 minutes on the cut side and 1–2 minutes on the other sides. Remove from the grill. You can let it rest for 5 minutes but it isn't needed—it already settled during the previous rest. Slice, top with some of the porcini au jus, and serve.

SIRLOIN TIP ROAST

4–6 SERVINGS • MARINATE: 4 HR. • GRILL: 1 HR. INDIRECT HEAT
AND ON HIGH DIRECT HEAT UNTIL TEMP. REACHES 120–130°F

½ cup Worcestershire sauce
¼ cup red wine vinegar
3 tablespoons minced garlic
1 tablespoon black pepper
1 tablespoon smoked paprika
1 tablespoon granulated onion
2 teaspoons kosher salt
1 sirloin tip roast, 2–3 pounds,
    trimmed and tied

In a small bowl, mix the Worcestershire sauce, vinegar, garlic, black pepper, paprika, onion and salt together. Place the sirloin tip beef roast in a 1-gallon resealable bag. Pour over the marinade to coat. Marinate the roast for a minimum of four hours or overnight in a fridge.

Create a 2-zone fire on your Char-Broil TRU-Infrared grill, turning one side of the grill on and leaving the other side off for indirect cooking. The temperature on the unlit side should be about 250°F.

Remove the roast, discarding the marinade and place it on the indirect side of the grill. Grill indirect for approximately one hour.

Remove the roast from the grill and increase the direct side of the grill to high. Grill each side of the roast until the internal temperature is 120°F–130°F for rare. Remove the roast from the grill and cover the roast with foil for 15 minutes. Slice thinly and serve.

THE BIG EASY® PRIME RIB

COOK: UNTIL TEMP. REACHES 135–145°F • REST: 20 MIN.

5-pound rib roast
1 tablespoon sea salt
1 tablespoon freshly ground
    black pepper

Place roast in the cooking basket. Insert a reliable oven-proof meat thermometer into the center of the meatiest part of roast.

Place the basket in The Big Easy cooking chamber and turn on the unit. Cook to an internal temp of 135°F for rare and 145°F for medium-rare.

HOT tip! To check the temperature, lift the roast occasionally and use an instant-read thermometer inserted into the roast so that it avoids fat and bone to check for doneness and even roasting.

When the internal temp is approximately 5–10°F below the target you desire, remove and place on a plate or tray, then cover with aluminum foil and a kitchen towel. Allow the roast to rest about 20 minutes while the internal temperature continues cooking the roast to the target temperature. The resting time is approximately 20 minutes before slicing.

THE BIG EASY® ROAST BEEF

COOK: 40 MIN.–1 HR. 10 MIN.

5–7-pound beef top roast
Salt and pepper to taste

Turn on The Big Easy® Oil-less Turkey Fryer. Salt and pepper the roast liberally. Place it in the basket. Then, place the basket in The Big Easy fryer.

Assume approximately 8–10 minutes per pound, checking the internal temperature of your meat 10 minutes before the end of your cook. This will help ensure that you don't overcook.

HOT tip! It should be about 30 to 45 minutes into your cook, depending on the size of your roast.

Remove the basket at an internal temperature of 130°F. Let the roast rest under foil for 10–15 minutes before slicing.

HOT tip! Allowing the roast time to rest allows the juices to redistribute. The internal temperature will continue to rise and even out.

SMOKED BEEF CHUCK POT ROAST

COOK: 1½ HR.

4-pound chuck roast, bone-in
    or boneless
3 medium-sized yellow onions,
    peeled and quartered
1 pound small butterball potatoes
1 large bunch carrots, stalks
    removed and peeled
Sea salt and black pepper
2 tablespoons chopped garlic
2 cups chicken stock

Prep the meat with salt and pepper and bring to room temperature. Prep the smoker or grill (set for indirect heat) and fill smoker box with dry wood chunks or chips. Place meat on rack in smoker and maintain constant level of light smoke at approximately 225°F, refilling smoker box with chips as necessary. The total smoke time is up to you, but at least 1½ to 2 hours is recommended. During the final hour of smoking, add the onion halves or quarters and maybe the potatoes.

The Braise: Place chopped onions (and other veggies like chopped carrots and celery if your recipe calls for them) in the slow cooker with 1 tablespoon of unsalted butter and 2–3 tablespoons of olive oil (or other cooking oil) and sauté on high until all are softened. Add smoked meat and 2 cups of chicken stock to the pot; cover and reduce heat to low. (Depending upon your slow-cooker settings, this may eventually bring the contents of the pot to slow boil. If so, reduce the temperature to warm.)

The Low & Slow Cook: After turning the control to the warm setting, add the rustic carrots, sliced potatoes (or whole if they are small ones), and 1 tablespoon of chopped garlic. Cover and cook at this temperature until such time as the potatoes and carrots are fork tender. Remove from heat and add additional tablespoon of garlic and place in fridge overnight. To serve, remove portion that you wish to re-heat, add to medium-size saucepan and simmer until warm. Spoon into serving bowls and garnish with chopped parsley and freshly ground pepper to taste.

LESS IS BEST

This recipe infuses extra flavor to the beef via your favorite wood smoke. Go light on the smoke—it will be in the broth and too much smoke flavor will overpower the unique tastes and textures of this tasty dish. Try a mix of lighter woods and your favorite stronger wood. A mix of Cherry-Apple-Mesquite gives a softer smokiness to the meat with a touch of bite from the mesquite. A heads-up: Because this meat will braise for several hours, the smoke is only there for flavor and the meat will not be fully cooked by smoking. Also, don't smoke all the veggies! Experiment with how many you smoke each time you prepare the dish. Too many smoked items in the final dish and every bite will taste the same.

CB'S BURGERS WITH CARAMELIZED ONION SPREAD

2 SERVINGS • PREP: 60 MIN. • GRILL: 10–20 MIN. (UNTIL MEAT TEMP. IS 160°F)

1 pound 80% lean ground chuck
1 tablespoon garlic powder
1 teaspoon cumin powder
1 teaspoon coarse salt or less to taste
1 teaspoon freshly ground black pepper or to taste
Chopped or shredded spinach leaves
1 medium tomato
2 sesame-seed burger buns

CARAMELIZED ONION SPREAD

1 large yellow onion
Canola oil spray
¼ cup ketchup
1 tablespoon mustard
2 tablespoons sour cream
1 teaspoon balsamic vinegar
1 teaspoon brown sugar or honey

Combine ground beef, garlic, cumin, salt, and pepper in a large mixing bowl. Gently form into two patties about ½–1 inch thick. Place in refrigerator for at least 1 hour prior to grilling.

While patties are chilling, heat grill to medium high. Slice onion into ½-inch disks; separate into rings; and spray with canola oil. Use tongs to place on the grill. When the onions are caramelized and soft, place them into a food processor or blender. Add ketchup, mustard, sour cream, balsamic vinegar, and brown sugar. Pulse until mixture is thick and chunky. Cover with foil, and place on warming rack while burgers cook.

Remove patties from refrigerator, and lightly spray with canola oil before placing them on the grill over medium-high heat. Cook for about 4 to 5 minutes per side, turning once with a spatula that has been sprayed with canola oil. Place patties in a foil pan on cooler section of the grill to continue cooking over indirect heat. Cook until meat reaches an internal temperature of 160°F.

While the patties are finishing, butter the buns, and toast on the grill. Add each burger to a bottom bun, and spread with spoonfuls of the caramelized onion mixture. Top with sliced tomatoes and spinach leaves and then with the top bun.

TOMATO-MOZZARELLA-POLENTA BURGERS

8 SERVINGS • PREP: 15 MIN. • GRILL: 15–20 MIN. (UNTIL MEAT TEMP. IS 160°F)

1½ pounds ground beef

⅔ cup balsamic vinegar

Salt and pepper

1 package (16 to 18 ounces) refrigerated polenta, cut into 8 disks

2 tablespoons olive oil

1 package (8 ounces) fresh mozzarella cheese, cut into 8 slices

2 medium tomatoes cut into 4 slices each

Fresh basil, thinly sliced

Bring vinegar to a boil in a 2-quart saucepan. Reduce heat; simmer uncovered for 9 to 10 minutes or until reduced to ⅓ cup. Set aside.

Preheat grill to medium high. Lightly shape ground beef into eight ½-inch-thick patties. Season burgers with salt and pepper. Brush polenta slices with oil.

Place patties in center of grill; arrange polenta disks around patties. Grill patties for 4 to 5 minutes per side, turning once and basting with 2 tablespoons reduced vinegar after turning. About 2 minutes before burgers are done, top each with a slice of mozzarella to warm and soften, taking care not to let cheese melt onto grill. Cook until centers of burgers reach 160°F. Cook polenta, turning once, until heated through and light grill marks appear on each side, about 9 to 10 minutes. For each serving, place burger on top of polenta and tomato slice. Drizzle with remaining vinegar, and sprinkle with basil to garnish.

CB'S SLIDERS

20 SERVINGS • PREP: 30 MIN. • GRILL: 10 MIN.

1 pound ground chuck
20 dinner rolls
American cheese (or other favorite), sliced into 20 1-inch squares
Canola oil spray
1 medium onion, diced

DRY SEASONING

½ teaspoon garlic powder
½ teaspoon freshly ground black pepper
½ teaspoon coarse salt
¼ teaspoon cumin

TOPPINGS

Butter pickles
Sliced cherry tomatoes
Mayonnaise
Ketchup
Mustard
Relish

Combine dry seasoning ingredients in a small bowl. In a large bowl, add the meat; sprinkle with the dry seasoning mixture; and incorporate gently, making sure not to overwork the meat.

Place the meat mixture in the center of a sheet pan that has been lined with parchment paper or foil. Loosely cover meat with plastic wrap. Using a rolling pin or bottle, evenly roll out the meat until it covers the surface of the pan and is about ¼ inch thick.

Using the parchment paper, lift the meat, and fold it in half lengthwise. Gently press the halves together, and re-cover with the plastic wrap. Refrigerate meat for at least 20 minutes to chill.

Slice each dinner roll in half, and arrange rolls on a large square of foil; loosely wrap and seal.

Preheat the grill to medium. Remove the meat from the refrigerator, and discard the plastic wrap. Using a pizza cutter or sharp knife, cut meat into 20 2 x 2-inch squares.

Use a pan or the griddle portion of your grill to cook the onions until lightly browned. Remove onions from the heat, and set aside.

Place foil packet containing rolls over indirect heat to warm. Add meat patties to grill, and cook approximately 3 minutes per side, turning once.

After turning the patties, top each with one square of cheese. Close the grill lid to melt. Place bottom halves of warmed buns on a serving plate. Using a spatula and tongs, remove cooked patties from the grill, and place one on each of the buns. Top with a teaspoon of grilled onions and the other half of the bun. Serve with condiments.

JAMAICAN JERK BURGERS

4 SERVINGS • PREP: 10 MIN. • GRILL: 15–20 MIN. (UNTIL MEAT TEMP. IS 160°F)

1 pound ground beef, pork,
  or turkey
2 tablespoons lime juice
2 tablespoons soy sauce
2 teaspoons ground ginger
4 tablespoons Jamaican
  jerk seasoning

CHIPOTLE-LIME MAYONNAISE

2 egg yolks
3 teaspoons lime juice
1 teaspoon chipotle puree
3 tablespoons cilantro,
  finely chopped
Salt and white pepper to taste
1 cup olive oil

For the meat: Whisk together all the ingredients except the beef. Then mix in the beef until combined, taking care not to overmix. Form into patties, and grill. Serve with Chipotle-Lime Mayonnaise.

For the mayo: Bring the egg yolks to room temperature. In a food processor, puree the yolks, lime juice, chipotle puree, cilantro, salt, and white pepper. Once fully incorporated, slowly drizzle in the olive oil while the food processor is still running.

Note: To avoid consuming raw eggs for health reasons, use pasteurized eggs, or substitute about 1½ cups store-bought mayonnaise for eggs and oil.

> **I still love making hamburgers on the grill. I guess whenever I eat them childhood memories come up for me.**
> **–Bobby Flay**

THAI-STYLE BURGERS

3–4 SERVINGS • PREP: 15 MIN. • CHILL: 1 HR.
GRILL: 10–15 MIN. (UNTIL MEAT TEMP. IS 160°F)

1 pound coarse-ground 80% lean beef

1 large shallot, finely chopped

2 green onions, coarsely chopped, including greens

4 to 7 garlic cloves, finely chopped

1 roasted poblano pepper, finely chopped (or use paste)

1 roasted habanero pepper, finely chopped (or use paste)

2 to 3 tablespoons ginger, freshly grated

2 to 3 tablespoons Thai green curry paste, plus additional for topping

Cayenne pepper to taste (optional)

Coarse salt

Black pepper

Bread crumbs (optional)

½ lime

Canola oil spray

½ bunch fresh cilantro or watercress sprigs

3 to 4 buns, toasted

Bean sprouts

Basil

In a large nonreactive bowl, thoroughly mix the 10 ingredients that follow the ground beef. Gently fold mixture into the meat, being careful not to overwork. If the meat is too loose, add bread crumbs until you can form 3 or 4 patties about 1 inch thick. Chill for at least 1 hour.

Preheat grill to medium high. Remove burgers from refrigerator, and lightly spray with canola oil before placing them on the grill. When you see some browning at the edges (about 2 to 3 minutes), spray a spatula with canola oil. Slip the spatula under the burger patty; away from the heat, spray the uncooked side; and then place it down on a clean section of grate. Grill over direct heat for another 2 to 3 minutes or until the meat is seared. Use the same method to lift patties and place them in a holding pan over indirect heat. Cook until internal temperature of patties reaches 160°F.

Before serving the burgers on toasted buns, squeeze a few drops of lime juice onto each one, along with some grated lime zest. Serve with cilantro or watercress and bean sprouts topped with a dollop of green curry paste if desired.

GRILLED BEEF TACOS WITH AVOCADO SALSA

6 SERVINGS • PREP: 45 MIN. • MARINATE: 15 MIN.–2 HR. • GRILL: 10–14 MIN.

4 beef top-blade (flat-iron) steaks,
    about 8 ounces each
18 small corn tortillas (6- to
    7-inch diameter)

MARINADE
1 cup prepared tomatillo salsa
⅓ cup chopped fresh cilantro
2 tablespoons fresh lime juice
2 teaspoons minced garlic
½ teaspoon salt
¼ teaspoon pepper

AVOCADO SALSA
1½ cups prepared tomatillo salsa
1 large avocado, diced
⅔ cup fresh cilantro, chopped
½ cup white onion, minced
1 tablespoon fresh lime juice
1 teaspoon garlic, minced
½ teaspoon salt

TOPPINGS
Minced white onion
Chopped fresh cilantro
Lime wedges

Combine marinade ingredients in a small bowl. Place steaks and marinade in a food-safe plastic bag; turn steaks to coat. Close bag securely, and marinate steaks in refrigerator for 15 minutes to 2 hours.

Remove steaks from marinade; discard marinade. Place steaks on grill over medium heat. Grill, covered, 10 to 14 minutes for medium rare to medium doneness, turning once.

Meanwhile, combine avocado salsa ingredients in a medium bowl. Set aside.

Place tortillas on grill. Grill until warm and slightly charred. Remove; keep warm.

Slice steaks, and serve in grilled tortillas with avocado salsa. Top with onion, cilantro, and lime wedges as desired.

SMOKY GRILLED MEAT LOAF

8–10 SERVINGS • PREP: 15–20 MIN. • GRILL/SMOKE: UP TO 1 HR.
(UNTIL MEAT TEMP. IS 160°F) • REST: 15–20 MIN.

1 pound ground pork
1 pound ground beef
1 pound ground turkey
1 pound center-cut bacon
¼ cup carrots, chopped
¼ cup celery, chopped
¼ cup white onion, chopped
3 large eggs, lightly beaten
¼ cup fine bread crumbs
5 large cloves garlic,
    roughly chopped
½ teaspoon ground cumin
½ teaspoon mustard powder
½ teaspoon
    Worcestershire sauce
½ teaspoon balsamic vinegar
¼ cup ketchup
Salt and pepper to taste

In a skillet, cook bacon until it starts to brown. Remove bacon, but reserve fat in the skillet.

Add carrots, celery, onion, and a pinch of salt to the bacon fat. Cover, and cook until the vegetables are softened and slightly browned, about 3 to 5 minutes. Remove from heat, and let vegetables cool.

In a large bowl, thoroughly mix the meat with the eggs, cooked vegetables, and all remaining ingredients except for the bacon. Place the meat mixture into a metal loaf pan, and weave bacon strips on top.

Preheat grill to high for about 10 minutes with hood closed. Turn center burner off, and reduce heat on outer burners. Temperature of cooking chamber with hood closed should remain steady at 350°F.

Put soaked wood chips in a smoker box or foil on the grill. Place meat loaf in center, and close the hood.

After about 30 minutes, check temperature inside grill. Add more wood chips if desired.

You can remove meat loaf from grill when a thermometer inserted in the center registers 160°F. Cover with foil, and let rest at room temperature for 15 to 20 minutes before serving.

CB'S SALTED MARGARITA FLANK STEAK

3–4 SERVINGS • PREP: 15 MIN. • "SALT CURE": 4 HR.–OVERNIGHT
MARINATE: 2 HR. • GRILL: 10–12 MIN. • REST: 5 MIN.

2 pounds skirt steak

Coarse salt

3 shots tequila

1 tablespoon Cointreau

2 tablespoons lime zest

2 tablespoons fresh
   cilantro, chopped

2 large garlic cloves, minced

2 tablespoons hot sauce

This dish benefits from an overnight "salt cure" to tenderize and flavor the meat.

Dry the meat with a paper towel. Liberally salt both sides of the steak; seal in plastic wrap; and place in refrigerator for at least 4 hours or overnight.

Mix together all remaining ingredients in a sealable plastic bag. Remove steak from plastic wrap; do not rinse off salt. Add steak to bag, and seal. Allow steak to marinate for up to 2 hours.

Preheat grill to high. Remove the steak from the marinade, and pat it dry. Spray the meat with canola oil. Cook until grill marks form, about 5 minutes. Use tongs to turn and sear the other side, about 5 minutes. Use an instant-read thermometer to check the temperature of the meat: 140°F for rare, 145°F for medium-rare, 160°F for medium.

Transfer steak to a cutting board, and let rest for 5 minutes. Cut the steak across the grain at an angle to expose more of the pink meat— about ⅛- to ¼-inch-thick slices. Serve with your favorite salsa on the side.

THE BIG EASY® COFFEE-BRINED BEEF ROAST

10–12 SERVINGS • PREP: 12 HR. (INCLUDES BRINING OVERNIGHT)
COOK IN THE BIG EASY: 1 HR. 30 MIN.

Recipe courtesy of Tommy Bommarito, Guest Chef for The Big Easy Users' Forum.

Sirloin tip beef roast
   (5 to 7 pounds)
1 tablespoon flour
½ tablespoon butter

COFFEE BRINE

4 cups warm water, or enough to
   cover roast
2 cups brewed coffee
½ cup salt
¼ cup white sugar
¼ cup brown sugar
3 tablespoons oil
2 teaspoons white pepper
2 teaspoons black pepper
¼ cup Worcestershire sauce
2 tablespoons onion flakes

Mix brine ingredients, and let mixture cool to room temperature. Place roast in a large pan or container; pour brine over meat. Cover meat, and refrigerate for a minimum of 8 hours.

Remove meat from brine about 1 hour before cooking; set in shallow pan or bowl to allow brine to drip off. Do not rinse.

Line the drip tray of The Big Easy with aluminum foil. Place meat vertically in the cooking basket (using skewers to hold it in place); lower basket into the cooking chamber; and cover with mesh lid. Set control knob to high; ignite.

After approximately 30 minutes, remove lid, and turn the control knob to about halfway between high and off. Continue cooking for approximately 1 hour or until meat reaches an internal temperature of 145°F for medium rare.

Lift cooking basket from cooker; carefully remove meat from basket; and wrap with foil. Place in shallow bowl or tray to rest for 30 minutes.

Pour drippings from the drip tray into a measuring cup. Skim off fat and solids, and add remaining juices to saucepan. Add one teaspoon of flour and ½ tablespoon of butter. Cook, stirring occasionally, until sauce is reduced by about half, approximately 5 minutes. Slice roast; arrange on platter; and serve.

CB'S CHILI-RUBBED RIBS

4 SERVINGS • PREP: 20 MIN. • MARINATE: 6 HR.–OVERNIGHT • GRILL: 2 HR.

4 pounds of pork ribs, trimmed of
    excess fat

SAUCE
6 ounces dark beer
18 ounces barbecue sauce
1 cup water
2 tablespoons honey
1 tablespoon instant
    espresso powder

CHILI RUB
2 tablespoons chili powder
2 tablespoons garlic powder
1 tablespoon ground ginger
1 tablespoon smoked paprika
1 tablespoon ground cumin
1 teaspoon salt
1 teaspoon ground black pepper

Combine sauce ingredients in saucepan, and simmer until it thickens. Cool slightly; then cover and refrigerate until needed.

Whisk chili-rub ingredients together in small bowl to blend. After drying ribs with a paper towel, rub chili mixture all over ribs. (Use food-safe gloves.) Wrap ribs in plastic wrap, and refrigerate for at least 6 hours or overnight.

Preheat grill, and set up for indirect heat to 200°F to 225°F (low). Add wood chips, if desired. Remove ribs from refrigerator, and unwrap. Place them on indirect heat side of the grill, bone-side down. Pour some of the sauce into a pan, and place over indirect heat. Close hood, and slow cook, monitoring temperature regularly. After 1 hour, brush ribs with sauce. Close hood, and allow ribs to cook 1 hour more, checking at 20-minute intervals and applying more sauce.

Ribs should be fully cooked after 2 hours. To keep warm on the grill for up to 1 hour, wrap ribs in 2 layers of heavy-duty aluminum foil (shiny side out) that has been sprayed on the dull side with canola oil. Add the remainder of the sauce before sealing.

CB'S TEXAS-STYLE BEEF RIBS

6–8 SERVINGS • PREP: 10 MIN. • CHILL: UP TO 4 HR. • GRILL: 2 HR. +

2 racks of beef back ribs (7 ribs
    per rack)
2 tablespoons black pepper
1 tablespoon smoked paprika
1 tablespoon ground
    mustard powder
½ teaspoon ground
    cayenne pepper

Combine all spices. Rub over surface of ribs to coat well. Wrap with plastic, and chill for up to 4 hours.

Set grill for indirect cooking, and preheat to medium-high with hood closed. Place ribs on rack in roasting pan. Add ½ inch of water to bottom of pan. Tent pan with foil, but leave sides open to allow smoke to enter. Place wood chips in smoker box or on grate. Cook ribs for about 2 hours. Remove ribs from pan, and place on grill over medium heat for 15 minutes. Cut between ribs to serve.

When I lived in Texas, I learned that a Texan's concept of barbecue is an appreciation of the meat—the flavors that evolve after careful preparation and attention to spices, heat, and smoke. So serve these ribs with sauce if you dare!—CB

CAESAR SKIRT STEAK WITH CHUNKY OLIVE TAPENADE

4–6 SERVINGS • PREP: 20 MIN. • MARINATE: 6 HR.–OVERNIGHT • GRILL: 15 MIN.

⅔ cup Kalamata and/or green pimento-stuffed olives, chopped

½ cup prepared non-creamy Caesar dressing, divided

2 teaspoons freshly grated lemon peel

1 teaspoon minced garlic

1 skirt or flank steak (1½ to 2 pounds)

Combine olives, 1 tablespoon dressing, lemon peel, and garlic in small bowl; season with pepper. Cover and refrigerate until ready to use.

Place meat and remaining dressing in a food-safe plastic bag; turn steak to coat. Close bag securely, and let marinate in refrigerator 6 hours or as long as overnight, turning occasionally.

Remove steak; discard marinade. Place steak on grill over medium heat. Grill, uncovered, 10 to 13 minutes, (17 to 21 minutes if using flank steak) for medium-rare to medium, turning occasionally.

Carve steak across the grain into thin slices. Serve with olive mixture.

STEAK & POTATO KEBABS

4 SERVINGS • PREP: 20 MIN. • GRILL: 15 MIN.

1 pound all-purpose potatoes
1 medium yellow or
    zucchini squash
1 pound boneless top sirloin
    steak, cut into 1-inch-
    thick cubes

SAUCE
¾ cup Heinz 57 Sauce
2 large cloves garlic, minced

Cut potatoes into 1½-inch pieces. Place in a microwave-safe dish; cover with vented plastic wrap. Microwave on high 6 to 8 minutes or until just tender, stirring once. Cool slightly.

Combine sauce ingredients in 1-cup measuring glass. Microwave on high 1½ minutes, stirring once.

Cut steak and squash into 1¼-inch pieces. Combine beef, squash, potatoes, and ⅓ cup sauce in a large bowl; toss. Alternately thread beef and vegetables onto metal skewers.

Place kebabs on grill over medium heat. Grill, uncovered, approximately 10 to 12 minutes for medium-rare to medium, turning occasionally. Brush kebabs with remaining sauce during last 5 minutes.

EASY MARINATED FLANK STEAK

4 SERVINGS • PREP: 20 MIN. • MARINATE: 4 HR.–OVERNIGHT • GRILL: 15 MIN.

1½-pound flank steak
½ cup any hickory-flavored
    barbecue sauce
¼ cup red wine

Place steak in a large zip-top plastic bag. Combine barbecue sauce with red wine; pour mixture over steak. Seal bag, and turn several times to coat steak. Marinate 4 to 24 hours in refrigerator, turning several times.

Discard marinade. Grill steak over medium heat to desired doneness, turning and brushing with additional barbecue sauce.

CB'S TAILGATE CHEESESTEAKS

4 SERVINGS • PREP: 10 MIN. • GRILL: 10 MIN.

2 onions, thinly sliced
1 pound sirloin steak (you
    can also use lamb, pork,
    or chicken)
4 cups shredded cheddar, jack, or
    havarti cheese
Salt and pepper
4 hoagie rolls
4 sheets heavy-duty foil

Preheat grill to medium high. Spray foil with nonstick cooking spray, and place one-quarter of the onion slices on each sheet.

Cut meat into strips ⅛ inch thick; season with salt and pepper. Add one-quarter of the steak strips, followed by one-quarter of the cheese to the onions on each foil sheet. Fold foil over mixture, sealing edges firmly. Leave some space for food to expand during cooking.

Grill 10 minutes on covered grill, turning once. Serve on hoagie rolls, topped with favorite BBQ sauce.

This is a great preparation method for picnics, tailgating, or any time you have a large group of folks to serve. Prepare the foil packets in advance, keep cool, and place on the grill as you need them.–CB

GRILLED LEG OF LAMB

PREP: 15 MIN. • MARINATE: 4 HR. • REST: 1 HR. BEFORE COOKING
TO REACH ROOM TEMP. • GRILL: 1 HR.

FOR THE LAMB

1 5–6 pound bone-in leg of lamb,
   frenched and trimmed (ask
   your butcher)
1 stick unsalted butter, melted

FOR THE MARINADE

¾ cup extra-virgin olive oil
½ cup minced fresh rosemary
¼ cup fresh mint, minced
1 orange, zest and juice
1 lemon, zest and juice
8–10 garlic cloves, minced
½ cup dry white wine
¼ cup brown sugar
½ teaspoon cumin
2 teaspoons salt
1 teaspoon black pepper

FOR THE TZATZIKI SAUCE

½ of a large English
   cucumber, grated
1½ cups plain Greek yogurt
2 garlic cloves, minced
2 tablespoons extra-virgin olive oil
1 tablespoon white vinegar
½ teaspoon salt
1 tablespoon fresh dill, minced

Combine all of the ingredients for the marinade in a medium bowl. Whisk to combine.

Fat side up, use a sharp knife to create 1-inch-long, ½-inch-deep cuts every 2 inches or so. Place the lamb in a shallow casserole dish, and cover with marinade. Use your hands to massage the garlic and herbs into the meat, making sure to tuck some down inside the cuts. Cover and let marinate at least 4 hours, up to overnight.

For the dipping sauce, drain all of the water you can from the grated cucumber by squeezing it tightly using cheesecloth or a clean dish towel. Combine the yogurt, garlic, oil, vinegar, and salt in a large bowl. Add the cucumber and dill. Stir to combine and set aside. This can be done the day before and kept in the refrigerator.

Take lamb out of refrigerator 1 hour prior to cooking to come to room temperature. Melt a stick of unsalted butter in a small saucepan. Pour marinade from lamb into the saucepan and simmer on low. You will use this butter/marinade mixture to baste the lamb as often as you turn it.

Turn all of the burners of your Signature Tru-Infrared Gas Grill to high heat for 15 minutes. After that, turn the middle burner(s) off and lower the heat of the outer burners to medium. Place lamb, fat-side up, in the middle of the grill over the indirect heat. Grill covered for approximately 1 hour, rotating and basting often. Start checking temperature at 45 minutes, and cook until an internal thermometer reaches 135°F–140°F. This is for medium-rare to medium. Continue to cook if you desire more doneness. Serve with tzatziki sauce.

HERB-CRUSTED LAMB CHOPS

4–8 SERVINGS • PREP: 10 MIN. • MARINATE: 1 HR. • GRILL: 8 MIN.

2 teaspoons fresh thyme
2 teaspoons fresh mint
2 teaspoons fresh rosemary
1 teaspoon fresh crushed garlic
1 teaspoon dried or fresh oregano
1 teaspoon steak spice
6–8 shoulder or baby lamb chops

Mix first six ingredients in small, flat dish. Place chops in marinade. Marinate for 1 hour. Grill over medium heat 6 to 8 minutes for medium doneness, turning frequently to avoid burning.

Instead of going out to dinner, buy good food.
Cooking at home shows such affection.

–Ina Garten

ROTISSERIE-ROASTED LEG OF LAMB

8–10 SERVINGS • PREP: 40 MIN.
GRILL: UNTIL INTERNAL TEMP. REACHES 140°F (RARE)

4-pound boneless leg of lamb
4 cloves of garlic, peeled and cut
    into slivers
3 tablespoons dried oregano
3 tablespoons dried rosemary
1 teaspoon dried thyme
5 tablespoons olive oil
Salt and freshly ground
    black pepper
Olive oil for basting
Juice of 2 lemons

Using a knife, create six to eight deep slashes at various points in roast, and insert garlic pieces. Combine the herbs, oil, salt, and pepper, and rub the meat with the seasonings. Allow meat to rest for 20 minutes.

Preheat the grill. Insert spit rod lengthwise through center of the lamb; secure with holding forks on each side.

Grill for 45 minutes to 1 hour, basting lamb with olive oil and lemon juice every 10 to 15 minutes. Allow the lamb to rest for 20 minutes; then carve and serve.

CB'S LAMB CHOPS WITH TOASTED CUMIN & ROSEMARY

2 SERVINGS • PREP: 5–10 MIN. • REST: 15 MIN.
GRILL: 20 MIN. (UNTIL MEAT TEMP. IS 135°F)

4 lamb chops
1 tablespoon toasted
    cumin seeds
1 teaspoon whole toasted
    mixed peppercorns
1 teaspoon coarse salt if desired
2 tablespoons fresh rosemary,
    finely minced

For the chops: Remove chops from package, and dry meat using paper towels. Trim off any excess fat or silver skin. Generously rub spice mixture into the meat using food-safe gloves. Let the meat rest at room temperature for at least 20 minutes. (If preparing a rack of lamb, cut it into two chops for even grilling.)

Preheat the grill to medium high. Spray the chops with canola oil. Place them on clean grates to sear, about 2 minutes per side. Use tongs to turn, and sear all sides.

When chops are seared, remove them to a holding pan away from direct heat to finish cooking (135°F internal temperature for rare). Remove from heat, and let rest for 10 to 15 minutes prior to serving.

For the rub: Toast the cumin seeds and peppercorns in a preheated, heavy skillet over medium-low heat, stirring to prevent burning. If desired, add the salt. It takes about a minute for the spices to toast, so remove them from the heat as soon as they release their aroma. Grind the toasted spices in a spice grinder, or smash them using a meat mallet. The spices should be coarsely ground, not fine. Add the minced rosemary, and set aside.

CB'S GRILLED LAMB SIRLOIN WITH RED-WINE SAUCE

3–6 SERVINGS • PREP: 10–15 MIN. • REST: 30 MIN.
GRILL: 15 MIN. (UNTIL MEAT TEMP. IS 135°F)

6 lamb sirloin steaks, about
   1 inch thick
Coarse salt and pepper to taste

RED-WINE SAUCE
2 tablespoons olive oil
¼ cup shallots, minced
¼ cup full-bodied dry red wine
   (such as Syrah or Zinfandel)
4 ounces chicken stock
2 tablespoons balsamic vinegar
1 tablespoon fresh thyme,
   finely chopped
½ tablespoon dark brown sugar
2 tablespoons unsalted butter

Trim off excess fat from the steaks, and reserve. Dry the lamb with paper towels, and season lightly with salt on both sides; then let meat rest for at least 30 minutes prior to grilling.

Preheat grill to high. Lightly spray both sides of the meat with canola oil, and sear on each side about 2 minutes or until sear marks appear. Remove seared lamb to a foil pan away from direct heat to finish cooking until rare (135°F internal temperature). Spoon sauce over lamb, and serve.

For red-wine sauce: Heat olive oil in a sauté pan over medium-high heat. Add the reserved fat and brown; discard solid bits. Add shallots, and cook until browned, stirring constantly 1 to 2 minutes. Add wine, broth, vinegar, thyme, and brown sugar, and cook, stirring, until liquid is reduced by half, about 3 to 5 minutes. Reduce heat to medium low, and add meat juices from the foil pan; swirl in butter. Season with salt and pepper, and serve.

FIVE-SPICE LAMB CHOPS WITH GRAPEFRUIT-FENNEL SALAD

4 SERVINGS • PREP: 20 MIN. • MARINATE: 20 MIN.–OVERNIGHT • GRILL: 10 MIN.

8 lamb shoulder chops, trimmed

MARINADE

1 teaspoon Chinese five-
 spice powder
1 tablespoon honey
1 tablespoon soy sauce
2 tablespoons red wine

SALAD

1 ruby red grapefruit, segmented,
 pith removed
1 small bulb fennel, white part
 only, finely sliced
½ bunch cilantro, chopped
1 bunch watercress
1 tablespoon olive oil
1 tablespoon lemon juice
Coarse salt and freshly ground
 pepper to taste

Place the lamb chops in a flat dish. Combine the five-spice powder, honey, soy sauce, and wine. Mix well. Pour over the chops, turning them so that they are fully coated in the mixture. Cover, and marinate 20 minutes to overnight.

Preheat the grill to medium, and cook the chops, turning occasionally, for 8 to 10 minutes or until cooked as desired.

To make the salad, combine the grapefruit, fennel, cilantro, and watercress in a bowl. Whisk together the oil and juice; season with salt and pepper to taste; and toss with the salad.

BUTTERFLIED LEG OF LAMB WITH CHINESE SEASONINGS

8–10 SERVINGS • PREP: 10 MIN. • GRILL: 20–30 MIN.
(UNTIL MEAT TEMP. IS 145°F) • REST: 5 MIN.

3- to 4½-pound leg of lamb, boned, butterflied, and trimmed of most fat
2 teaspoons cinnamon
2 teaspoons ground ginger
2 teaspoons brown sugar
1 teaspoon anise
½ teaspoon cayenne
1 large fresh clove garlic, minced
¼ cup peanut oil
1 teaspoon sesame oil
Salt to taste

Ask the butcher to bone and butterfly the leg for you. Mix seasonings and oil together, and rub into both sides of lamb, making sure all the nooks and crannies are coated. With the grill covered, cook lamb over medium-high heat, skin-side down to start, turning often. At its thickest point, the meat should register 145°F for medium-rare–thinner parts will be medium-rare to medium. Set lamb aside, covered loosely with foil, for about 5 minutes before slicing diagonally and serving.

LAMB BURGERS WITH FETA SPREAD

6 SERVINGS • PREP: 10 MIN. • CHILL: 2 HR. • GRILL: 8 MIN.

2¼ pounds ground lamb

½ cup shallots, minced

3 tablespoons fresh mint
   leaves, minced

1 tablespoon garlic, minced

1½ teaspoons salt

½ teaspoon cumin, ground

¼ teaspoon allspice, ground

¼ teaspoon cayenne pepper

¼ teaspoon cinnamon, ground

6 hamburger buns

Lettuce leaves

Sliced tomatoes

Sliced roasted red peppers

FETA SPREAD

⅛ teaspoon cayenne pepper

4 ounces feta cheese, crumbled

4 ounces cream cheese, softened

¼ cup mayonnaise

2 tablespoons green onion
   tops, minced

1 tablespoon plus 1 teaspoon
   olive oil

¼ teaspoon lemon zest,
   finely grated

For the feta spread: Stir together all of the ingredients in a mixing bowl. Cover with plastic wrap, and refrigerate for at least 1 hour.

In a mixing bowl, combine the lamb, shallots, mint, garlic, salt, cumin, allspice, cayenne, and cinnamon. Mix gently but thoroughly to combine. Using your hands and food-safe gloves, shape the mixture into 6 patties. Cover with plastic wrap, and refrigerate for at least 2 hours.

Preheat grill to medium high. Brush both sides of burgers with 1 tablespoon of olive oil. Cook for about 4 minutes on each side for medium. Transfer the burgers to a platter, and cover loosely with foil. Serve on toasted buns with feta spread and desired garnishes.

RACK OF LAMB WITH SOUR RED-PEPPER JELLY

4 SERVINGS • PREP: 20–25 MIN. • REFRIGERATE: OVERNIGHT
GRILL: 14–20 MIN. • REST: 5 MIN.

1 8-rib rack of lamb, frenched and
    fat cap trimmed
2 tablespoons extra-virgin olive oil
¼ cup Dijon mustard
Salt and pepper to taste

RED-PEPPER JELLY

½ pound red bell peppers,
    small, diced
1 tablespoon extra-virgin olive oil
1½ cups sugar
½ cup brown-rice vinegar
4 ounces liquid pectin
1 teaspoon salt
½ teaspoon freshly ground
    black pepper
1 teaspoon dried hot red pepper
    flakes (optional)
1 tablespoon chopped fresh mint
    (optional)

You should make the jelly a day before you plan to serve the dish. To do so, heat a saucepan over medium heat, and sauté the peppers in 1 tablespoon of oil until the peppers become soft. Add the sugar and vinegar, and reduce the liquid by one-half. Stir in the pectin, salt, pepper, and if desired, red pepper flakes and mint. Transfer the liquid to a bowl, and allow to cool overnight in the refrigerator.

Preheat grill to high. Remove any excess fat from the rib rack after frenching it; season with the other tablespoon of oil, salt, and pepper; and generously coat with mustard. Grill to desired doneness, 7 minutes or more a side, and set aside to rest for at least 5 minutes.

Cut the rack apart, serving two-rib portions topped with a tablespoon of the pepper jelly.

WASABI-SPICE RACK OF LAMB

4 SERVINGS • PREP: MIN. • GRILL: 14–20 MIN. • REST: 5 MIN.

1 8-rib rack of lamb, frenched and
   fat cap trimmed
1 tablespoon kosher salt
1 tablespoon whole
   pink peppercorns
1 tablespoon whole
   black peppercorns
1 tablespoon whole coriander
½–1 tablespoon wasabi powder
1 teaspoon ginger powder
¼ cup Dijon mustard
¼ cup sweet mirin rice wine
2 tablespoons extra-virgin olive oil
   or canola oil
Cooking spray as needed

Grind the salt, peppercorns, coriander, wasabi, and ginger together in a spice grinder or coffee grinder. Mix the mustard, mirin, and oil together in a bowl until blended. Add the spice mixture to the mustard mixture, and set aside.

Preheat grill to high. Remove any excess fat from the rib rack after frenching it; mist it with cooking spray to prevent sticking; and sear it, being mindful not to burn the bones too much, until it is well marked on the outside. When the rack is seared, reduce the heat and generously brush it with the wasabi-spice mixture. Continue to grill and baste the rack until it reaches your desired internal temperature, about 140°F to 150°F for medium. Let the rack rest for at least 5 minutes before cutting it apart.

CB'S LOW & SLOW LAMB ROAST

4–6 SERVINGS • PREP: 20 MIN. • CHILL: 12 HR.
GRILL: 3–4 HR. (UNTIL MEAT TEMP. IS 180°F) • REST: 30 MIN.

1 bone-in lamb shoulder roast, 3
    to 4 pounds
5 garlic cloves, finely minced
3 tablespoons thyme leaves,
    finely chopped
3 tablespoons sage leaves,
    finely chopped
1 teaspoon hot mustard, ground
1 teaspoon cumin, ground
Coarse salt and freshly ground
    black pepper to taste
¼ cup vegetable oil

Trim excess fat and silver skin from the lamb shoulder. Combine the garlic, thyme, sage, mustard, cumin, salt, pepper, and vegetable oil. Spread the paste all over the meat. Wrap roast in plastic wrap, and refrigerate overnight.

About 1 hour before cooking, remove the lamb from the refrigerator. Insert an oven-safe meat thermometer into the center of the roast. Preheat your grill to 225°F (low) for indirect cooking, or prepare a smoker. Place the lamb on the grill over a drip pan, and close the hood. Cook until the thermometer registers about 145°F. Turn up the heat to 325°F (medium). Wrap the roast in two layers of foil, and add some chicken stock or apple cider before sealing. Continue cooking until the internal temperature of the roast reaches 180°F. Remove, and let rest for at least 30 minutes before carving.

GRILLED LAMB & MANGO TOSTADAS

4 SERVINGS • PREP: 15 MIN. • GRILL: 15 MIN.

1 pound lamb shoulder chops, cubed (about 1½ inches thick), bones discarded

3¼ teaspoons coriander, freshly ground

¾ teaspoon kosher salt

1⅛ teaspoon black pepper, freshly ground

1 large red bell pepper

1 mango, peeled, pitted, and diced

1 small avocado, seeded, peeled, and diced

⅓ cup red onion, diced

1 tablespoon fresh mint, chopped

4 corn tostadas (4 to 5 inches in diameter)

Preheat grill to medium. Combine 3 teaspoons of coriander, ½ teaspoon salt, and 1 teaspoon black pepper in a small dish. Transfer spice mixture to a plate. Coat lamb well in spice mixture.

Slice the bell pepper in half, and remove the seeds and stem. Cook pepper halves and lamb cubes on grill over moderate heat, turning once or twice, until pepper is softened and lamb is browned. Remove both from heat; let lamb rest about 5 minutes. Transfer pepper to a cutting board, and dice. Combine diced pepper, mango, avocado, onion, and mint in a mixing bowl. Add remaining ¼ teaspoon salt, ⅛ teaspoon of pepper, and ¼ teaspoon coriander.

To serve: Place one layer of lamb on top of a tostada. Cover with a large spoonful of the mango mixture. Repeat with another layer of lamb and mango mixture. Garnish with sprigs of mint and a lime wedge.

CHEF ERIK'S LAMB KEBABS WITH MINT PESTO

4 SERVINGS • PREP: 15 MIN. • MARINATE: 4 HR. • GRILL: 6–10 MIN.

2 pounds boneless lamb leg or shoulder, cut into 1½-inch cubes (32 pieces)
½ cup extra-virgin olive oil
½ cup lemon juice
¼ cup honey
4 cloves garlic, minced
½ small onion, minced
¼ cup mint leaves, minced
¼ cup parsley leaves, minced
1 teaspoon rosemary leaves, minced

1 teaspoon oregano leaves, minced
16 skewers (if using wood, presoak for at least 30 minutes)
32 cherry tomatoes
32 pearl onions, or 4 medium onions, cut into 32 chunks
4 green bell peppers, cored, seeded, and cut into 1-inch squares (32 pieces)
16 fresh mushrooms
Salt and freshly ground black pepper

MINT PESTO
½ cup fresh mint leaves
1 tablespoon honey
Pinch kosher salt
2 tablespoons white wine vinegar
Freshly ground black pepper
¾ cup olive oil

In a nonreactive bowl, combine the olive oil, lemon juice, honey, garlic, onion, mint, parsley, rosemary, and oregano. Add the lamb, and toss to coat well. Marinate in the refrigerator for at least 4 hours.

Preheat the grill on high. On each skewer, thread tomato, lamb, onion, pepper, lamb, onion, mushroom, pepper, and tomato. Repeat until you have 16 prepared skewers. Season the skewers with salt and pepper. Grill to desired doneness, about 3 to 5 minutes per side for medium to medium-rare. Serve with the mint pesto.

For the pesto: Combine all of the ingredients, except for the oil, in a blender. Pulse until well pureed. With the blender running on low, slowly drizzle in the olive oil. Taste, and adjust seasonings.

GRILLED SAGE VEAL CHOPS

4 SERVINGS • PREP: 10 MIN. • MARINATE: 1–2 HR. • GRILL: 10 MIN.

4 veal chops (6 to 8 ounces each)
2 tablespoons olive oil
16 fresh sage leaves
White pepper and salt to taste

Brush chops evenly on both sides with olive oil. Season with salt and pepper to taste. Press 2 sage leaves on each side of the chops, and marinate in refrigerator for at least one hour.

Grill over high heat for approximately 5 to 6 minutes on each side.

CB'S VEAL CHOP FORESTIER

1–2 SERVINGS • PREP: 30 MIN. • GRILL: 10 MIN.

1 12–14 ounce veal chop,
    approximately 1 inch thick, or
    2 smaller chops
2 teaspoons olive oil
3 tablespoons unsalted butter
4 tablespoons rough-
    chopped shallots
1 teaspoon chopped garlic
2 tablespoons red port
2 tablespoons brandy or cognac
3 ounces chanterelle mushrooms,
    cut into bite-size pieces
Salt and pepper to taste
½ teaspoon flour (optional)

Allow veal chop to rest at room temperature for at least 20 minutes before cooking. Preheat grill to high. Season veal with salt and pepper, and brush lightly with oil or butter.

Reduce grill heat to medium. Place chop on hot section of grates, and turn down flames underneath meat. Sear for approximately 4 to 5 minutes; then turn and place on new section of hot grill, turning flame off beneath chop and relighting other side of grill. Sear for just a few minutes on this side.

Remove chop; allow to rest approximately 10 minutes before serving.

FORESTIER SAUCE

Heat butter in sauté pan on medium until it begins to bubble. Add shallots, browning slightly; then add garlic, making sure mixture doesn't burn. Add mushrooms, stirring to coat in mixture. When mushrooms begin to brown, stir in port. Let mixture reduce slightly before adding brandy. Stir in flour, and allow sauce to continue cooking for 3 to 5 minutes. Ladle over chop. Sprinkle with chopped parsley.

4

Grilling takes the formality out of entertaining.
Everyone wants to get involved.

–Bobby Flay

Pork

APPLE BUTTER BBQ RIBS

GRILL: 2 HR. INDIRECT HEAT, THEN 1 HR. WITH SAUCE
SEAR: 30 SEC. EACH SIDE ON DIRECT HEAT

2 full slabs of baby back ribs
2 tablespoons brown sugar
1 tablespoon paprika
1 teaspoon cayenne powder
½ tablespoon salt
½ tablespoon black pepper
1 teaspoon ground ginger
1 teaspoon dried thyme
Applewood chunks

APPLE BUTTER BBQ SAUCE

1 cup apple butter
½ cup ketchup
½ cup brown sugar
1 tablespoon apple cider vinegar
1 tablespoon yellow mustard
1 teaspoon Worcestershire sauce
Salt & pepper to taste

Preheat your grill for indirect: Place an aluminum foil pan filled with water under the grill grate and toss a chimney of hot coals alongside.

With a butter knife and some paper towels, remove the membrane under each slab of ribs by inserting the knife between the membrane and one of the bones. Pull the membrane with a paper towel to remove it completely.

Mix the brown sugar, paprika, cayenne powder, salt, black pepper, ground ginger, and dried thyme in a small bowl then apply the rub on both sides of the ribs with your hands so it penetrates the meat.

Place the ribs on the grill grate in indirect heat and toss a few applewood chunks onto hot coals. Close the lid and cook for 2 hours at 300°F. Add all the Apple Butter BBQ Sauce ingredients to a saucepan and simmer for 10 minutes.

After 2 hours of cooking, wrap the ribs in aluminum foil with 1 cup of the Apple Butter BBQ Sauce on top of each. Cook for another 1 hour at 300°F. You know the ribs are done when the meat has shrunk about 1 inch from the bones. Once fully cooked, remove from foil and sear over direct heat for 30 seconds per side to caramelize the BBQ sauce.

KANSAS CITY MOP RIBS

4–6 SERVINGS • PREP: 30 MIN. • MARINATE: 2 HR.–OVERNIGHT • SMOKE: 4 HR.

6 to 8 pounds pork spare ribs, long ends only

KANSAS CITY-STYLE BARBECUE SAUCE

1 small onion, chopped
2 cloves garlic, minced
1 tablespoon vegetable oil
1 cup ketchup
⅓ cup molasses
¼ cup distilled white vinegar
2 tablespoons chili powder
2 teaspoons dry mustard
1 teaspoon celery salt
1 teaspoon paprika
1 teaspoon ground cayenne chili
½ teaspoon freshly ground
    black pepper
¼ cup water or more if needed

KANSAS CITY DRY RUB

2 tablespoons brown sugar
2 tablespoons ground paprika
1 tablespoon white sugar
1 tablespoon garlic salt
1 tablespoon celery salt
1 tablespoon chili powder
2 teaspoons freshly ground
    black pepper
1 teaspoon ground cayenne chili
½ teaspoon dry mustard

For the sauce: Sauté onion and garlic in oil until onions are soft. Add remaining ingredients; simmer for 30 minutes or until thickened.

For the rub: Combine all dry rub ingredients in a bowl, and mix well. Store any unused rub in a sealed container in the freezer.

Sprinkle rub evenly over ribs, and let marinate for 2 hours at room temperature or overnight in refrigerator. Prepare smoker, and place ribs on grates. Smoke at approximately 200°F for 4 hours. Baste frequently with sauce during last 30 minutes of smoking. Serve with additional sauce on the side.

ASIAN-STYLE BABY BACK RIBS

4 SERVINGS • PREP: 20 MIN. • MARINATE: 1 HR.–OVERNIGHT • GRILL: 20–30 MIN.

2 racks baby backs or other
favorite ribs

ASIAN BARBECUE SAUCE

6 cloves garlic, minced

2 tablespoons ginger,
finely minced

8 serrano peppers, minced,
including seeds

4 small green onions, green and
white parts, minced

¼ cup cilantro, minced

1 tablespoon lime zest, grated

Juice from 3 limes

1 cup hoisin sauce

½ cup wine vinegar

¼ cup Thai fish sauce

¼ cup honey

2 tablespoons soy sauce

2 tablespoons canola oil

To make sauce, stir all ingredients together except ribs. Coat ribs evenly on both sides with one-half of the sauce. Reserve remaining sauce to serve with ribs. Marinate ribs, refrigerated, for at least 1 hour. For more flavor, marinate overnight.

Preheat grill to medium (325°F), and oil grill grates. Baste ribs occasionally with marinade during cooking, stopping 15 minutes before removing ribs from grill.

To serve, cut each side of ribs in half, or into individual ribs. Serve immediately with remaining sauce.

BEER-BASTED BABY BACK RIBS

4–6 SERVINGS • PREP: 60 MIN. • GRILL: 12 MIN.

6 cups beer
2½ cups brown sugar
1½ cups apple cider vinegar
1½ tablespoons chili powder
1½ tablespoons ground cumin
1 tablespoon dry mustard
2 teaspoons salt
2 teaspoons dried crushed
    red pepper
2 bay leaves
8 pounds baby back pork ribs, cut
    into 4-rib sections

Bring first nine ingredients to a boil in a large pot. Reduce heat, and simmer about 1 minute to blend flavors. Add half of ribs to sauce. Cover pot, and simmer until ribs are tender, turning frequently, about 25 minutes. Transfer ribs to baking dish. Repeat with remaining ribs. Boil barbecue sauce until reduced to 3 cups, about 40 minutes. Discard bay leaves. (Can be prepared 1 day ahead. Cover ribs and sauce separately, and refrigerate. Warm sauce before continuing.)

Preheat grill to medium, and oil the grill grates. Brush ribs with some of sauce; sprinkle with salt. Grill ribs until heated through, browned, and well-glazed, brushing occasionally with sauce, about 6 minutes per side.

MUSTARD-BOURBON
BABY BACK RIBS

4–6 SERVINGS • PREP: 20 MIN. • GRILL: 40–50 MIN.

3 racks baby back ribs (4 to
6 pounds)

SPICE RUB
2 tablespoons ground cumin
1 tablespoon chili powder
1 tablespoon dry mustard
1 tablespoon coarse salt
1½ teaspoons cayenne pepper
1½ teaspoons ground cardamom
1½ teaspoons ground cinnamon

SAUCE
1 tablespoon vegetable oil
2 bunches scallions, chopped
2 cups white onions, chopped
8 garlic cloves, chopped
2 cups brown sugar
1 cup ketchup
1 cup tomato paste
1 cup Dijon mustard
1 cup water
½ cup Worcestershire sauce

½ cup apple-cider vinegar
½ cup apple juice
1 large dried ancho chili,
stemmed, seeded, and cut into
small pieces
1 tablespoon ground cumin
1½ cups bourbon
Salt and pepper, to taste

Mix ingredients in medium bowl. Rub spice mixture over both sides of rib racks. Arrange ribs on a large baking sheet. Cover, and refrigerate overnight. Preheat grill to medium, and oil grill grates. Cut rib racks into four to six rib sections, and arrange on cooking grate. Grill until meat is tender, turning occasionally, for about 40 minutes. Cut rib sections between bones into individual ribs, and lay flat in baking dish. Transfer 3 cups sauce to small bowl; place remaining sauce in small saucepan, and reserve. Brush ribs with sauce from bowl. Return ribs to grill. Place pan of reserved sauce at edge of grill to warm. Grill ribs until brown and crisp on edges, brushing with more sauce from bowl and turning occasionally, about 10 minutes. Serve ribs with warm sauce.

For the sauce: Heat oil in large pot over medium-low heat. Add scallions, onions, and garlic; sauté until tender. Mix in remaining ingredients, adding bourbon last. Simmer sauce, stirring occasionally, until reduced to 7 cups, about 1 hour. Season to taste with salt and pepper. Refrigerate in covered container for up to 2 weeks.

"MEMPHIS IN MAY" RIBS

4–5 SERVINGS • PREP: 30 MIN. • MARINATE: 4–6 HR.
GRILL: 1½ HR. • SMOKE: 2 HR.

3 racks baby back ribs (4 to 6 pounds)
1 cup Memphis Rib Rub
1 cup Memphis-Style Finishing Sauce

FINISHING SAUCE

1 cup tomato sauce
1 cup red wine vinegar
2 teaspoons Louisiana-style hot sauce
1 tablespoon butter
½ teaspoon freshly ground black pepper
½ teaspoon salt
½ cup beer

MEMPHIS RIB RUB

¼ cup paprika
2 tablespoons garlic salt
1 tablespoon freshly ground black pepper
2 tablespoons brown sugar
1 tablespoon onion powder
1 tablespoon dried oregano
1 tablespoon dry mustard
1½ teaspoons ground cayenne

In a shallow dish, pour rub over ribs, massaging into both sides. Cover, and refrigerate for 4 to 6 hours. Remove ribs from refrigerator, and bring to room temperature. Preheat grill to 300°F to 350°F, and oil grill grates. Grill ribs, covered, for 1 hour, turning often. Continue cooking for 30 minutes, basting with finishing sauce. (If smoking ribs, maintain smoke at 200°F to 220°F, and smoke for 2 hours. Brush sauce over ribs several times during last hour of smoking, turning ribs occasionally.) Remove ribs from grill, and serve with sauce.

For the sauce: Place all ingredients in saucepan, and bring to a boil, stirring constantly. Reduce heat and simmer, uncovered, for 15 minutes. Serve warm with ribs.

For the rub: Combine all ingredients in bowl, and mix well. Freeze any unused rub in sealed container.

This recipe was a recent finalist in the annual Memphis in May World Championship Barbecue Cooking Contest.

MONTREAL JERK RIBS

2–4 SERVINGS • PREP: 20 MIN. • GRILL: 1½ HR.

2 racks baby back ribs

MONTREAL JERK RUB

2 tablespoons dried
   minced onions
1 tablespoon onion powder
4 teaspoons ground thyme
2 teaspoons salt
2 teaspoons ground allspice
½ teaspoon ground nutmeg
½ teaspoon ground cinnamon
1 tablespoon sugar
2 teaspoons black pepper
1 teaspoon cayenne

Rub dry ingredients onto all surfaces of ribs. Grill ribs over indirect heat about 1½ hours in covered grill, turning occasionally, until ribs are very tender. (Or roast ribs on rack in shallow pan in 350°F oven for 1½ hours.) Cut into one- or two-rib portions to serve.

For the rub: In a small jar with a tight-fitting lid, shake together all dry ingredients until blended.

TOMATO-BASIL RIBS WITH ZESTY RANCH DRESSING

3 SERVINGS • PREP: 20 MIN. • GRILL: 15–20 MIN.

6 boneless country-style pork ribs
½ cup margarine, softened
1 medium tomato, halved and thinly sliced
1 1-ounce package basil leaves
¼ teaspoon salt or to taste
⅛ teaspoon black pepper or to taste
1 cup ranch-style dressing
½ teaspoon hot pepper sauce
Butcher's twine

Preheat grill to medium-high. Slice each rib down center lengthwise, cutting halfway through. Spread equal amounts of margarine down center of each rib. Arrange tomato slices and basil leaves down center of each. Wrap each rib with butcher's twine in several places to hold rib together. Sprinkle evenly with salt and pepper.

Grill ribs 15 to 18 minutes or until no longer pink in center, turning frequently using spatula or tongs to handle easily. Watch closely for flare-ups. Margarine will melt and flames will occur. Move pieces to another area of grill when this happens. Combine salad dressing and hot pepper sauce in small bowl, and stir until well blended. Serve as dip for ribs.

EASTER HAM

GRILL: 2 HR. SMOKED, THEN INCREASE HEAT
UNTIL INTERNAL TEMP. REACHES 138°F

1 large bone-in cured spiral-cut ham
Canola oil
Cherry juice
Fresh ground peppercorn, to taste
Cherry-Spiced Maple Glaze
Fresh herbs, fruits, and berries,
    to garnish

CHERRY-SPICED MAPLE GLAZE

1 cup all-natural cherry reserves
½ cup light brown sugar, packed
½ cup maple syrup
¼ cup water
1 ounce honey whiskey
1 tablespoon Dijon mustard
2 dashes of cinnamon

1 pinch of ground cayenne pepper
1 pinch of ground cloves
¼ teaspoon of garlic powder
1 knob of butter
Kosher salt and fresh ground
    peppercorn, to taste

To make the glaze, pour all ingredients into a small, heavy-bottom pot. Place over medium heat and bring all ingredients just to a gentle simmer. Remove from heat and stir consistently for 2–3 minutes. Puree in a food processor until consistency is similar to a syrup. To thin, add water. Set aside.

Thirty minutes prior to grilling fill the chimney starter with charcoal and ignite. When coals are glowing red, pile into center of the grill floor. Place applewood chunks over and around the smoldering coals. Close the grill lid, open the top and bottom air damper all the way and wait 15 minutes until the wood is smoking. Once smoking, close both top and bottom dampers three-quarters of the way to minimize airflow and cool grilling temperature to 250°F–275°F.

Meanwhile, prepare the ham by scoring its exterior surface in a cross-hatch fashion, then drizzle with oil and liberally season with fresh ground peppercorn.

Gently place the ham atop the grill grates and smoke for two hours, brushing every 30 minutes with a 50/50 mixture of oil and cherry juice. In the third hour, slightly open air dampers to increase the temperature and begin intermittently brushing layer upon caramelized layer of the Cherry-Spiced Maple Glaze over the ham. Remove from the grill when internal temperature reaches 138°F in thickest part of the ham. Rest under a tinfoil tent for 5 minutes per pound, allowing the denatured proteins to reabsorb their natural juices (which have been pushed to the exterior of the ham during the smoking process). Brush one final time with the glaze and plate over a large dish garnished with fresh herbs, fruits, and berries. Carve and serve.

FRIED HAM

8 SERVINGS • PREP: 2 HR. • COOK: 4 HR.

14 pounds fresh, uncured ham
Brine for ham
Glaze for ham

Starting with a 14-pound fresh ham, we recommend removing the skin, but leaving as much of the fat intact as possible. Brine in basic brine for about 24 hours. Remove, rinse, and pat dry.

HOT tip! You may add a mustard and rub combo. But for this long cook, it might be best to limit the rub. It will mostly cook to carbon crust.

Place the ham into the basket and the basket into The Big Easy® Oil-less Turkey Fryer. Estimate about 10–12 minutes per pound for planning purposes. Be sure to monitor the internal temperature with a reliable meat thermometer until the temperature reaches approximately 150°F.

Add a honey, bourbon, and molasses glaze for the final 15–20 minutes of your cook. Once reaching the internal temperature of 150°F, remove the ham. Cover with foil and a towel. Place the covered ham in an insulated carrier or oven. This will allow to the ham to rest and finish cooking. Let the internal temperature rise to a USDA-recommended 165°F. This should take about 30 minutes.

HELPFUL HINTS FOR HAM

- When purchasing the ham, look for a product that has been naturally raised, is free of 12-syllable preservatives and chemical additives, has a healthy layer of trimmed exterior fat, and the face of the meat has a bright pinkish-red color. If smoking a bone-in ham, be sure to buy 10–12 ounces of meat per guest. If smoking a boneless ham, 8–10 ounces of meat per guest should work.
- Prepare the meat by scoring the ham's exterior with a sharp knife in a cross-hatch fashion. This not only increases the surface area of the ham, but aides presentation, texture, and taste as the browning, caramelizing, and encrusting processes occur throughout the smoke. Many Pit Masters will also inject marinades and juices into the ham to additionally flavor and assist in maintaining moisture throughout cooking.
- Finally, smoke the ham for approximately 3 hours. For the first 2 hours, smoke at 250°F–275°F, basting intermittently in a 50/50 mixture of oil and cherry juice. In the last hour, slightly increase the grill's temperature by opening up the air dampers and brush layer upon caramelized layer of the cherry-spiced maple glaze (page 122) over the ham, until the internal temperature has reached 138°F. The ham will continue to cook for a short time after it's been removed from the grill—this is called "carry-over cooking"—and the internal temperature will increase between 5–7 degrees in the 15–20 minutes during this period. The ideal serving temperature is between 140°F–145°F.

BROWN SUGAR MUSTARD-GLAZED SMOKED HAM

PREP: 30 MIN. • COOK: 6 HR.

HAM

5–10 pound bone-in, pre-cooked ham
2 teaspoons onion powder
1 teaspoon garlic powder
1 teaspoon dried thyme leaves
1 teaspoon dried rosemary leaves
2 teaspoons sweet paprika or smoked paprika
½ teaspoon kosher salt
½ teaspoon freshly ground black pepper
2 tablespoons brown sugar
1–2 tablespoons olive oil
Honey mustard, for brushing outside of ham

GLAZE

1 cup pineapple juice
1 cup orange juice
½ cup honey
¼ cup honey mustard
¼ teaspoon ground cloves
1 teaspoon ground ginger
Pinch ground cardamom
2 cups firmly packed brown sugar

Remove ham from refrigerator. Pat dry with paper towels, and place on baking sheet. In a small bowl, combine the onion powder, garlic powder, thyme, rosemary, paprika, salt, pepper, 2 tablespoons of brown sugar, and 1 tablespoon of olive oil. Whisk until you have a smooth paste. Add more oil if needed. Rub the outside of the ham with the paste, leaving the ham at room temperature for 1 hour.

In a small saucepan, combine the pineapple juice, orange juice, honey, mustard, cloves, ginger, and cardamom. Heat over medium-low heat. Stir often, until mixture is warmed through and blended. Reduce heat to low. Preheat smoker to 225°F. Add wood chips.

HOT tip! Because this will be a longer cook, refill the wood chips as needed. Timing will depend on your smoker and weather conditions.

Brush ham with honey mustard and place within your smoker. Cook for 1 hour without lifting the lid. After an hour, open the smoker, and baste ham with a little of the glaze. Close the lid and continue to cook for another 4 to 6 hours. Baste your ham lightly with glaze about every 45 minutes. To baste, drizzle a few tablespoons over the top.

When the internal temperature reaches 125°F to 130°F, combine 3 to 4 tablespoons of the remaining glaze with the brown sugar. This will make a paste about the thickness of honey. Whisk until smooth. Brush the paste over top of ham, allowing it to drip down the sides, covering most of the surface.

HOT tip! If you do not have any glaze left, just use pineapple juice instead.

Continue to cook until the ham reaches a final internal temperature of 145°F. At this time, there should be a sweet crust on the outside of the ham. Remove your ham from the smoker, letting it rest for at least 30 minutes before carving.

HAM WITH A BOURBON BROWN SUGAR GLAZE

8–10 SERVINGS

1 spiral-sliced ham, approximately 7 pounds

½ cup orange juice (plus additional 2 tablespoons)

½ cup dark brown sugar

2 tablespoons bourbon

2 tablespoons butter

1 tablespoon grainy mustard

Cherrywood chips (used in a smoker box)

Preheat the grill for indirect cooking (one side off) to 225°F as measured by an oven thermometer hung from the warming rack. Set the Char-Broil® cherry wood chips in smoker box on the lit side of the grill.

Remove the ham from its wrapping, and discard the pre-packaged glaze. Put a large sheet of heavy-duty aluminum foil in two aluminum half-pans stacked one inside the other. Set the ham on the foil, tucking any extra foil under the rims. Brush the ham, including inside each slice, with ½ cup orange juice to help the ham retain its moisture. Put the ham pan on the unlit side of the grill and shut the lid. Grill for one hour.

Meanwhile, make the glaze by combining the remaining 2 tablespoons of orange juice with the brown sugar, bourbon, butter, and mustard in a small saucepan. Heat the glaze over medium-high heat until it boils, and then simmer it to reduce by a third. Reserve.

After an hour, fold the foil over the ham and seal it completely. Continue grilling until the internal temperature of the ham is 130°F as measured by a digital probe thermometer inserted into the thickest part of the meat. Uncover the ham and liberally apply the glaze. Let the glaze set, with the grill lid closed, for about 10 minutes. Remove, slice, and serve.

GRILLED HAM WITH LEMON-ORANGE GLAZE

8–10 SERVINGS • PREP: 15 MIN. • GRILL: 1–1½ HR.

7-pound bone-in smoked ham
2 tablespoons brown sugar
1 tablespoon ground coriander
1 tablespoon paprika
1 teaspoon cumin
½ teaspoon cinnamon
¼ teaspoon cloves

LEMON-ORANGE GLAZE

¼ cup lemon marmalade
2 tablespoons orange juice

Preheat grill to medium (375°F to 425°F), and prepare for indirect cooking. Place drip pan in center, not over heat source. (For a gas grill, turn off the center burner; for a charcoal grill, bank coals on either side.) Score top and sides of ham with knife in a crisscross pattern. Mix remaining dry ingredients, and rub into surface of ham. Place ham, scored side up, in center of grill over drip pan. Cover, and grill for 1 to 1½ hours (add six to eight briquettes to charcoal grill if necessary to maintain heat), until internal temperature of ham is 140°F. While ham is grilling, prepare lemon-orange glaze. Brush glaze over ham, and grill for 5 more minutes. Remove ham from grill, and let rest 15 minutes.

For the glaze: Combine marmalade and orange juice in a small bowl; brush over ham during last 5 minutes of grilling.

HAWAIIAN HAM

4 SERVINGS • PREP: 15 MIN. • MARINATE: 30 MIN. • GRILL: 3–6 MIN.

Juice reserved from 1 8¼-ounce can sliced pineapple
1 to 2 tablespoons soy sauce
1 teaspoon ground ginger
1 clove garlic, minced
Fully cooked ham, sliced into 4 steaks (1 inch thick)
Canned pineapple slices

Blend together pineapple juice, soy sauce, ginger, and garlic. Score ham in diamond pattern. Put steaks into a plastic storage bag, and add liquid. Marinate at least 30 minutes. Remove ham, and reserve marinade. Preheat grill to high. Grill ham until heated through, brushing often with marinade. After about 3 minutes on one side, turn steaks, and put pineapple slices directly on grill or in grill basket. Place pineapple slices on top of ham slices before serving.

People want honest, flavorful food, not some show-off meal that takes days to prepare.
–Ted Allen

BOURBON-GLAZED ROTISSERIE HAM

10–12 SERVINGS • PREP: 45 MIN. • GRILL: 4–5 HR.

1 fresh ham, about 10 pounds
1 cup bourbon
1 cup brown sugar
½ teaspoon ground cloves
Zest of 1 orange
⅓ cup steak sauce

Skin ham and score in a diamond pattern. Mix remaining ingredients in a bowl. Tie ham every 2 inches with string. Thread ham on a rotisserie spit rod, and fasten forks. If desired, insert a meat thermometer in center of thickest part of ham, making sure not to touch a bone. Place drip pan in grill. Grill ham for 4 to 5 hours until meat reaches an internal temperature of 170°F. During the last hour of grilling, brush glaze over all sides of ham. Continue to brush with glaze every 10 minutes. Remove from spit rod, and cut into thin slices.

GRILLED BRATS

REST: 15–20 MIN. AT ROOM TEMP. BEFORE GRILLING • GRILL: 20 MIN.
THEN 20 MIN. MORE IN STEAM PAN

1 ¼ pounds bratwurst sausages

2 12-ounce light beers,
room temperature

1 large sweet onion, sliced
into wedges

2–3 tablespoons butter

1 teaspoon roasted garlic paste
or 2 cloves minced

½ teaspoon coarse ground
black pepper

Salt to taste

5 hard rolls or hot dog buns

Toppings of your choice

Preheat charcoal grill to 300°F–350°F. Place the onions, butter, roasted garlic (or minced garlic), beer, black pepper, and a few pinches of salt to taste in the steam pan.

Place the brats on the grill and grill for 20 minutes, flipping and shifting them around every five minutes.

Place the steam pan on the grill and place the brats in the steam pan, close the grill lid and cook for 20 minutes. Note: It should start simmering after 5 or so minutes, but not a full boil. If it starts to simmer too rapidly, reduce the heat. Remove pan from the grill. Serve with buns and choice of toppings.

TIPS FOR GRILLING BRATS

- Make sure that your grill grates are clean, preheated, and lightly oiled.
- Leave the brats at room temperature for about 15–20 minutes before grilling.
- Grill using medium heat, just 300°F–350°F.
- If your grill gets too hot, use the upper cooking grate.
- Do your best to avoid rupturing the casing of the sausages.

WISCONSIN-STYLE BRATS 'N KRAUT

6 SERVINGS • PREP: 45 MIN. • GRILL: 15–20 MIN. COMBINED

12 ounces beer
½ large onion, chopped
3 tablespoons brown mustard
½ teaspoon caraway seeds
½ teaspoon ground coriander
12 fresh bratwursts, (4
    to 5 ounces each),
    halved lengthwise

KRAUT RELISH
2 tablespoons butter
1 small onion, chopped
2 teaspoons caraway seeds
2 teaspoons brown mustard
2 cups sauerkraut, drained
Fresh ground black pepper
6 Kaiser or other large rolls
Additional brown mustard
6 thin slices Swiss or
    provolone cheese
Dill pickle, chopped

Prepare marinade by bringing first five ingredients to a boil in a saucepan; simmer mixture for 5 minutes. Add bratwursts to liquid; reduce heat to low; cover; and cook for 15 minutes. Remove pan from heat, leaving brats in liquid to steep.

Preheat grill to high. Prepare kraut relish by melting butter in a saucepan over medium heat. Stir in onion and caraway; cook 1 to 2 minutes until onion turns translucent. Add remaining relish ingredients, and heat through. Keep relish warm. Drain sausage, discarding marinade. Split halved brats in half again, lengthwise, resulting in four sausage spears. Grill brat pieces, uncovered, over high heat for about 2 minutes per side until well-browned. Toast rolls on edge of grill. To assemble sandwiches, spread both sides of each roll with mustard. To bottom of roll, add slice of cheese and build upward, topping each with eight brat pieces and a generous dollop of relish. Sprinkle chopped dill pickle over all; top with other half of roll. Repeat with remaining sandwiches, and serve.

PINEAPPLE TERIYAKI PORK BURGERS

4 SERVINGS • GRILL: 12 MIN.

BURGERS

1½ pounds ground pork
⅓ cup bread crumbs
4 pineapple slices, ¼ inch thick
4 burger buns

TERIYAKI SAUCE

1 cup water
1½ tablespoons cornstarch
¼ cup soy sauce
⅓ cup honey
1 clove garlic
½ teaspoon ground ginger

Preheat your grill for a 2-zone cooking: put two side-by-side burners at high and one at medium-low. In a saucepan, dissolve the cornstarch in 1 cup of cool water then mix in all of the remaining Teriyaki Sauce ingredients. Bring to a boil for about 4 minutes for the sauce to thicken.

Mix the ground pork and bread crumbs together then form 4 equal patties. Place the pork patties and pineapple slices on the grill. The pork patties go over the burners set to high and the pineapple goes over the one set to medium-low. Grill for 6 minutes.

Flip the burgers and pineapple slices then brush them with the Teriyaki Sauce. Close the lid for another 6 minutes. Serve on toasted buns with a slice of pineapple, lettuce and mayonnaise or your favorite choice of condiments.

GRILLED PORK BURGERS WITH APRICOT MAYONNAISE

6 SERVINGS • PREP: 15 MIN. • GRILL: 10–15 MIN.

1½ pounds lean ground pork
¼ cup minced onion
4 tablespoons cilantro,
　　finely chopped
½ teaspoon seasoned salt
¼ cup mayonnaise
¼ cup apricot preserves
1 teaspoon lemon juice
2 teaspoons fresh
　　cilantro, minced
12 slices Italian bread

In a large bowl, combine pork with onion, 4 tablespoons of cilantro, and seasoned salt; form into six patties, and set aside.

Preheat grill to medium-high. Combine mayonnaise, preserves, lemon juice, and 2 teaspoons of cilantro; set aside, or cover and refrigerate until ready to serve.

Grill burgers for about 5 to 6 minutes per side; remove and keep warm until an instant-read thermometer reads 160°F. Grill bread for 1 to 2 minutes per side until lightly toasted. To assemble sandwiches, spread mayonnaise mixture on one side of each slice of bread. Top with burgers and remaining bread sliced at an angle over burger. Pass around any remaining apricot mayonnaise.

| HOT tip! This tangy-sweet mayonnaise also makes a delicious spread for cold pork-roast sandwiches.

> Grilled veggies and sausage make this hearty soup a perfect meal for a cool fall day.—CB

CB'S GRILLED VEGETABLE & SAUSAGE SOUP

3–4 SERVINGS • PREP: 20 MIN. • GRILL: 30 MIN. (IT'S EVEN BETTER THE NEXT DAY)

2 tablespoons unsalted butter
1 teaspoon canola oil
1 medium yellow onion, chopped into bite-size chunks
1 large shallot, finely-chopped
4 inner stalks of celery, including leaves, roughly chopped into bite-size chunks

½ cup carrot slices or baby carrots
1 clove garlic, minced
Kosher salt to taste
Fresh ground black pepper to taste
2 tablespoons all-purpose flour
16 ounces chicken stock, unsalted
16 ounces vegetable stock, unsalted

1 cup baby zucchini squash
1 cup baby yellow squash
3 tablespoons extra virgin olive oil
1 medium-spicy sausage or bratwurst, precooked
1 cup of stale crusty bread, preferably ends

Preheat grill to high. On side burner, place large 8-quart stock pot on high heat. Add butter and canola oil to heated pot. Add onions and shallots, and stir, watching heat to ensure they caramelize but don't burn. Add celery after onions have begun to brown; let entire mixture sweat out excess moisture as celery cooks. Add carrots, and allow to cook until tender in remaining juices. Add garlic and salt and pepper to taste. Stir in flour, coating all vegetables; cook for 1 minute until vegetables begin to brown. Add both stocks to pot. (Make sure these are room temperature, as cold ingredients slow down the cooking!)

Place zucchini and squash in a large bowl; lightly toss with olive oil, salt, and pepper. Reduce grill heat to medium-high, and place vegetables on grill, turning as sear marks appear on veggies. (Note: you may wish to use a special stainless-steel grill plate that prevents veggies from dropping through grate, or place vegetables in a grill basket.) On the other side of grill, place precooked bratwurst or sausage, and brown until warm; remove to cutting board. Slice sausage into bite-size pieces, and add to soup, followed by grilled veggies. To serve, place a few chunks of bread in each bowl. (Note: you may wish to toast these on the grill first.) Ladle a generous portion of soup into each bowl, and serve.

MOJO CUBAN SANDWICHES

---

6 SERVINGS • PREP: 25 MIN. • MARINATE: 30 MIN.–2HR. • GRILL: 15–20 MIN.

---

1 to 1¼ pounds pork tenderloin

2 tablespoons prepared
    yellow mustard

6 Cuban or French rolls (buns)

Dill pickle slices, enough to cover
    each sandwich

12 thin slices ham

12 thin slices Swiss cheese

MOJO MARINADE

1 6-ounce can frozen orange juice
    concentrate, thawed

Juice of 3 key limes or 2
    regular limes, about 3 to
    4 tablespoons

¼ cup olive oil

3 large garlic cloves, chopped

1 tablespoon fresh oregano,
    minced, or 1½ teaspoons
    dried oregano

1 teaspoon kosher or sea salt

Several dashes of hot sauce
    (optional)

For the marinade: Whisk together first seven ingredients. Set aside ¼ cup plus 2 tablespoons of mojo. Place tenderloin in plastic bag, and pour rest of mojo over it. Set aside at room temperature for 30 minutes, or refrigerate for up to several hours, and let sit at room temperature for 30 minutes before grilling.

For the sandwiches: Preheat grill to high. Remove tenderloin from marinade. Grill meat over high heat for 5 minutes, rolling it on all sides. Reduce heat to medium and continue rolling meat occasionally to cook evenly. Pork is done when internal temperature reaches 155°F and center is barely pink. Let meat rest, covered with foil, for 10 minutes; then slice thinly.

Mix reserved mojo with mustard. Spread mojo-mustard mixture on both sides of bun. Layer pickles across bottom; add two ham slices, a layer of pork tenderloin, and two cheese slices. Top with remaining bun. Toast each sandwich at edge of grill. Press until lightly brown and cheese melts slightly. Serve immediately.

MA LANEY'S BARBECUE STEW

20 SERVINGS • PREP: 40 MIN. • COOK: 3–4 HR.

4 to 5 pounds smoked chicken
3 to 4 pounds barbecued
    Boston butt
2 large onions, chopped
3 cups chicken broth
2 12-ounce cans cream-style corn
2 12-ounce cans whole-
    kernel corn
1 12-ounce can baby lima beans
4 16-ounce cans diced tomatoes
1 14-ounce bottle ketchup
1 5-ounce bottle
    Worcestershire sauce
1 tablespoon vinegar
½ teaspoon red pepper powder
1 tablespoon dry mustard
Salt and Tabasco sauce to taste

Chop chicken and pork finely; mix with remaining ingredients. Preheat grill to medium-low. Simmer for 3 to 4 hours on grill or cooktop. If stew is too thick, add more broth; if consistency is too thin, thicken with potato flakes.

This recipe calls for leftover smoked chicken and pork butt. It's a modified version of Brunswick Stew, a classic country dish that often includes squirrel or rabbit.

Food is love.
–Rachael Ray

GRILLED PORK PANZANELLA

4 SERVINGS • PREP: 15 MIN. • MARINATE: 30 MIN.–OVERNIGHT • GRILL: 10–15 MIN.

4 boneless pork chops,
   ½ inch thick
⅔ cup Italian salad dressing
3 tablespoons balsamic vinegar
4 slices Italian bread, cut
   ½ inch thick
1 10-ounce package Italian
   lettuce mix
1 cup canned cannellini beans,
   drained and rinsed
1 cup ripe tomato, chopped
Freshly ground pepper
¼ cup Parmesan cheese,
   finely grated
Fresh basil for garnish

Combine Italian dressing and balsamic vinegar. Place ⅓ cup dressing mixture in zip-top bag along with pork chops. Seal bag, and refrigerate for at least 30 minutes or as long as overnight. Cover and reserve remaining dressing.

Preheat grill to medium. Remove chops from marinade (discarding marinade), and grill over direct heat for 5 minutes per side until browned. Remove from grill, and keep warm.

Grill bread slices 2 to 3 minutes per side until toasted. Remove bread from grill, and cut it into ½-inch cubes. Meanwhile, combine lettuce, beans, and tomato in a large bowl. Add bread pieces and reserved dressing mixture; toss to coat all ingredients. Distribute lettuce mixture on four plates. Slice pork chops, and fan one pork chop over each salad. Garnish with black pepper, Parmesan, and fresh basil.

SWEET & SPICY PORK AND PINEAPPLE KEBABS

PREP: 15 MIN. • MARINATE: 1 HR. • GRILL: 15 MIN.

FOR THE KEBABS

1½ pounds boneless pork chops,
  fat trimmed and cut into 1½–2
  inch cubes
1 cup low sodium soy sauce
1 tablespoon sesame oil
½ cup brown sugar
1 tablespoon honey
½ teaspoon ground ginger
½ teaspoon red pepper flakes
1 teaspoon–1 tablespoon sambal
  oelek (ground chili paste)
2 tablespoons ketchup
2 tablespoons cornstarch
2 cups fresh pineapple, cut into
  1½–2 inch cubes
1 red bell pepper, cored, seeded,
  and cut into 1½–2 inch cubes
1 red onion, cored, seeded, and
  cut into 1½–2 inch cubes

FOR THE CHIMICHURRI

1 bunch fresh flat-leaf parsley
1 bunch fresh mint
3 cloves garlic, minced
½ cup extra-virgin olive oil
2 tablespoons red wine vinegar
Pinch red pepper flakes
Salt and pepper, to taste

Combine soy sauce, sesame oil, brown sugar, honey, ground ginger, red pepper flakes, chili paste, and ketchup in a medium bowl. Add cubed pork and toss to coat. Cover and chill at least 1 hour, or up to overnight. When ready to cook, preheat your Char-Broil Patio Bistro Electric Grill to the highest heat setting.

Meanwhile, use a fine mesh sieve to strain the pork from the marinade, saving the marinade. In a small saucepan, bring the marinade to a boil and then reduce heat to low and simmer for 15 minutes. Mix 2 tablespoons of cornstarch with 2 tablespoons of water and stir well. Slowly drizzle cornstarch slurry into the saucepan, whisking the entire time, to create a nice sauce for basting and dipping. Remove from heat and set aside.

Use your Char-Broil stainless steel skewers to make your kebabs. Alternate pork, pineapple, red bell pepper, pork, pineapple, red onion, and repeat. Sprinkle each kebab with salt and pepper.

Make the chimichurri by combining all of the ingredients in the bowl of a food processor. Pulse until combined but still moderately chunky. Season with salt and pepper. Set aside.

Once temperature has reached 350°F, spray the grill grates with non stick spray and place kebabs on the grill. Grill on each side for 7–8 minutes, basting with the marinade at least once on each side. Remove from grill. Drizzle the chimichurri over the top of the kebabs and serve with remaining sauce.

PISTACHIO SAUSAGE

24 SERVINGS • PREP: 45 MIN.
MARINATE: 30 MIN.–SEVERAL HR. • GRILL: 15–20 MIN.

Janeyce Michel-Cupito of the Powderpuff Barbeque Team submitted this recipe.

3 pounds pork butt,
    coarsely ground
½ cup pistachios, shelled
1 clove of garlic, minced
1 tablespoon salt
1 tablespoon fresh
    parsley, chopped
1 teaspoon coarsely ground
    black pepper
½ teaspoon crushed red pepper
Additional black pepper to taste

Combine pork, pistachios, garlic, salt, parsley, black pepper, and red pepper in bowl; mix well. Divide into four portions. Shape each portion into a roll 1½ inches in diameter; wrap in plastic wrap. Store in refrigerator until just before cooking. Discard plastic wrap. Coat surface of sausage with black pepper to taste. Grill over high heat until cooked through and browned, turning frequently.

SPICY THAI PORK KEBABS

6 SERVINGS • PREP: 20 MIN. • MARINATE: 6 HR. • GRILL: 15–20 MIN.

1 large onion, chopped
1 clove garlic, minced
⅓ cup creamy peanut butter
3 tablespoons soy sauce
1½ tablespoons lemon juice
2 tablespoons brown sugar
1 teaspoon ground coriander
¼ cup chili sauce
1 teaspoon salt
1 teaspoon ground cumin
½ teaspoon red pepper
½ teaspoon freshly
   ground pepper
2 pounds pork tenderloin, cut into
   1½-inch cubes

Combine all ingredients except pork in blender, and blend well. Place pork into a sealable plastic bag; pour mixture over pork. Refrigerate about 6 hours. Preheat grill to medium. Thread pork on skewers, and grill about 20 minutes, turning frequently.

ASIAN SESAME TENDERLOIN

6–8 SERVINGS • PREP: 20 MIN. • MARINATE: 6 HR.–OVERNIGHT • GRILL: 30 MIN.

2 pork tenderloins, about ¾ to 1 pound each

MARINADE

6 tablespoons soy sauce
1 small onion, finely chopped
¼ cup brown sugar
2 tablespoons vegetable oil
2 tablespoons sesame oil
3 tablespoons water
2 cloves garlic, peeled and minced
2 teaspoons ground ginger
½ teaspoon black pepper
⅛ teaspoon cayenne pepper
1½ tablespoons sesame seeds

Mix marinade ingredients in a bowl. Trim any excess fat and skin from tenderloins. Pour marinade over tenderloins in large plastic storage bag or nonmetallic dish. Seal bag or cover dish with plastic wrap. Refrigerate for at least 6 hours or overnight, turning occasionally.

Preheat grill to medium-high. Remove tenderloins from marinade; discard marinade. Place tenderloins on cooking grate over indirect heat. Close lid, and grill for 10 to 15 minutes. Turn tenderloins; close the lid; and grill for 10 to 15 minutes more. Pork is considered done when internal temperature reaches 155°F and center is barely pink.

HONEY PORK TENDERLOIN KEBABS

4 SERVINGS • PREP: 20 MIN. • GRILL: 10 MIN.

1½ cup bourbon (or 2 tablespoons cider vinegar)

½ cup honey

½ cup mustard

1 teaspoon dried tarragon

3 to 4 yams or sweet potatoes, cut into 24 1-inch cubes

1½ pound pork tenderloin, cut into 24 1-inch cubes

4 ripe unpeeled peaches, pitted and quartered

4 green peppers, each cut into 8 2-inch pieces

8 yellow onions, each cut into 4 2-inch pieces

Olive oil for grilling

Mix first four ingredients in a bowl, stir well, and set aside. Steam or boil sweet potatoes until crisp-tender. Alternately thread sweet potato cubes, pork cubes, peach quarters, green pepper pieces, and onion pieces onto each of eight 10-inch skewers. Brush kebabs with honey mixture. Preheat grill to medium, and lightly oil grilling surface. Grill 5 minutes on each side, basting occasionally.

CHIPOTLE CHILI PORK TENDERLOIN

4 SERVINGS • PREP: 45 MIN. • MARINATE: 2 HR. • GRILL: 15–20 MIN.

5 canned chipotle chilies in adobo, stemmed, plus 2 tablespoons of sauce from can
5 garlic cloves, thinly sliced
1 strip of orange zest
¾ cup fresh orange juice
¼ cup lime juice
2 tablespoons red wine vinegar
1 tablespoon tomato paste
1 teaspoon dried oregano
1 teaspoon ground cumin
½ teaspoon freshly ground pepper
1½ pounds pork tenderloin

In saucepan, combine chipotles and their sauce with garlic, orange zest, orange juice, lime juice, red wine vinegar, tomato paste, oregano, cumin, and pepper. Simmer over high heat until reduced by one-third, about 3 minutes. Transfer sauce to food processor, and puree until smooth. Allow marinade to cool.

Trim any excess fat and skin from the tenderloin. Coat pork with ¼ cup of marinade, and refrigerate for 2 hours. Preheat grill to high. Grill pork, turning until cooked through, about 15 minutes. Pork is done when internal temperature reaches 155°F and center is barely pink. Let stand for 10 minutes before slicing and serving.

STUFFED PORK LOIN

PREP: 1 HR. • COOK: 45 MIN.

1 2-pound pork loin
Salt to taste
Pepper to taste
1 box pork stuffing mix
8 ounces sliced mushrooms
3 shallots
3 garlic cloves
2 tablespoons butter
¼ cup Madeira

Butterfly the pork so that it lays flat on a cutting board, fat side down. Season with salt and pepper. Prepare the stuffing according to the package directions. In a food processor, process the mushrooms, shallots, and garlic until minced. Sauté the mixture in the butter until browned. Deglaze the pan with the Madeira. Combine the mushroom mixture with half of the stuffing (reserve the rest for another use). Chill.

Spread the cooled mushroom mixture on the pork loin, leaving about a half inch at the edges. Roll the pork up. Tie with kitchen twine or silicone cooking twine. Salt and pepper the outside of the pork loin. Preheat the grill to medium. Put the loin on a roasting rack under a rimmed pan covered in foil.

Grill, lid down, until the internal temperature of the pork—with a digital thermometer inserted in the thickest part of the pork in the center of the roll—reaches 150°F. Let the roast rest for 20 minutes before removing the twine and slicing.

APPLEWOOD SMOKED PORK LOIN

4–6 SERVINGS

4 cups applewood chips
1 pork loin, trimmed
3 tablespoons canola oil
2 tablespoons garlic powder
2 tablespoons dried rosemary,
    finely chopped
¼ cup kosher salt
½ cup dry roasted pistachios,
    chopped plus additional
    for garnish
1 cup ground black peppercorns

Load the digital electric smoker with the wood chips and preheat it for 40 minutes. Set the temperature to 275°F. Pat the pork loin dry and brush with the oil.

Scatter the spices and nuts on a large rimmed baking sheet and shake it to create a level bed of the spices. Roll the pork loin in the spices to create an even layer. Smoke the pork loin until the internal temperature reaches 145°F as measured with the digital thermometer. Let the pork loin rest 10–15 minutes before slicing.

JUST THE FACTS . . . ABOUT PORK LOIN

The pork loin roast is a lean, budget-friendly cut harvested from the pig between the shoulder and rear leg. Often confused with the tenderloin, the loin roast weighs in between 2–5 pounds, while the tenderloin usually tips the scales below 2 pounds. When purchasing from the butcher look for pink, evenly colored meat that's slightly marbled and presented with a thick, fat cap.

Applewood is the perfect complement because of its sweet flavor, but any fruit or hardwood will do.

To help the smoking process, apply a liberal amount of spices to the pork's exterior. The thick application of salt, pepper, and herbs not only imparts tremendous flavor, but assists in the meat's capacity to absorb the wood smoke.

The "other white meat" is incredibly lean, lacking the fatty intramuscular marbling to keep the meat moist over longer cooking periods. So keep a close eye on the "low and slow" smoking method. Pork quickly transitions from a mouthwatering medium to overcooked well done in an instant. Turn your Char-Broil® Digital Electric Smoker to a well-balanced 275°F and use a digital thermometer to gauge the internal temperature until the pork loin reaches 140°F–145°F in its thickest part.

Immediately following the cooking process, allow 10–15 minutes of uncovered rest time before slicing and presenting. Plan for the loin to rise in temperature internally 5°F–7°F over the resting period. So, if you'd like to present the meat at 150°F, remove the pork at 145°F from the smoker.

PANCETTA-WRAPPED TENDERLOIN

4–6 SERVINGS • PREP: 20 MIN. • MARINATE: 20–30 MIN. • GRILL: 20–30 MIN.

2 pork tenderloins, about 1
    pound each
¼ pound pancetta (Italian-style
    bacon), thinly sliced
Cotton string

RUB
1 tablespoon garlic, minced
2 teaspoons fresh
    rosemary, minced
2 teaspoons kosher salt
¼ teaspoon freshly ground
    black pepper

Preheat grill to medium. Grill tenderloins over indirect heat about 25 to 30 minutes, turning once halfway through grilling time. Pork is done when internal temperature reaches 155°F and center is barely pink. Move tenderloins over to direct medium heat for last 3 minutes to crisp pancetta. Allow meat to rest for 10 minutes; then snip strings with scissors, and remove them. Cut tenderloins in thin slices on bias, and serve warm.

In a small bowl, combine rub ingredients. Trim any excess fat and skin from tenderloins, and spread them evenly with rub, pressing spices into the meat. Cut six 12-inch pieces of cotton string, three for each tenderloin. Wrap tenderloins with slices of pancetta, and secure pancetta with string. Allow to rest at room temperature for 20 to 30 minutes before grilling.

PESTO TENDERLOIN ON A PLANK

4 SERVINGS • PREP: 45 MIN. • MARINATE: 8 HR.–OVERNIGHT • GRILL: 60 MIN.

2 pounds pork tenderloin
1 plank (hickory, alder, or oak),
   soaked in water

GARLIC-SAGE PESTO
20 fresh sage leaves
4 large cloves garlic, chopped
Zest of 1 lemon
2 teaspoons salt
1 tablespoon olive oil

SUN-DRIED TOMATO PESTO
1½ cups sun-dried tomatoes,
   packed in oil, drained
6 garlic cloves, peeled
1 cup Parmesan cheese, grated
1 cup fresh basil leaves
½ cup olive oil
2 tablespoons balsamic vinegar

PARMESAN-BASIL PESTO
1⅓ cups basil leaves
1½ teaspoons garlic, chopped
¼ cup pine nuts, toasted
½ cup Parmesan cheese, grated
¼ cup olive oil
Salt and pepper to taste

In food processor, blend pesto ingredients for one of the pestos until smooth. Trim any excess fat and skin from tenderloin. Spread pesto over entire pork tenderloin, and seal in plastic storage bag. Marinate at least 8 hours or overnight in refrigerator.

Let stand at room temperature for about 15 minutes before grilling. Place marinated pork loin on prepared plank. Preheat grill to medium-high. Grill tenderloin for about 1 hour. Pork is done when internal temperature reaches 155°F and center is barely pink.

GREEK PORK LOIN ROAST

6–8 SERVINGS • PREP: 45 MIN. • MARINATE: OVERNIGHT • GRILL: 1–1½ HR.

3 pounds boneless
    pork tenderloin
1 cup plain yogurt
1 cucumber, peeled and chopped
½ teaspoon garlic, crushed
½ teaspoon coriander
    seeds, crushed
¼ cup red onion, minced
¼ teaspoon crushed red pepper

MARINADE

¼ cup olive oil
¼ cup lemon juice
1 teaspoon oregano
1 teaspoon salt
1 teaspoon pepper
6 cloves garlic, minced

Combine the marinade ingredients in a bowl.

Trim any excess fat and skin from tenderloin. Place pork tenderloin in large plastic storage bag. Pour marinade over tenderloin in bag. Seal bag, and marinate in refrigerator overnight. Remove from marinade; discard marinade.

Preheat grill to medium-high. Combine remaining six ingredients in a bowl; cover and refrigerate until ready to serve with pork roast. Place drip pan in grill under tenderloin. Grill 1 to 1½ hours over indirect heat in covered grill. Pork is done when internal temperature reaches 155°F and center is barely pink. Let meat rest 10 minutes before slicing thinly.

Try this with roasted-garlic mashed potatoes and grilled vegetables.

TERIYAKI PORK TENDERLOIN

4 SERVINGS • PREP: 20 MIN. • MARINATE: 30 MIN. MINIMUM • GRILL: 15–20 MIN.

1 fresh garlic clove
4 to 5 sprigs fresh rosemary
1½ cups teriyaki marinade
2½ to 3 pounds pork tenderloin

Chop garlic clove and fresh rosemary; then add them to the teriyaki. Trim any excess fat and skin from tenderloin. Add tenderloin to marinade, and allow to marinate for at least 30 minutes. (Tenderloin is better when marinated longer.) Preheat grill to high, and turn it down to medium-high just before cooking. Sear meat on both sides. After about 10 to 15 minutes of cooking, move tenderloin away from heat, and continue to cook over indirect heat for remaining time. Remove from grill, and let rest for 10 minutes. Slice tenderloin into medallions. Pork is done when internal temperature reaches 155°F and center is barely pink.

ASIAN-STYLE BBQ PORK TENDERLOIN

4 SERVINGS • PREP: 10–15 MIN. • MARINATE: 1 HR.–OVERNIGHT
GRILL: 20–26 MIN. (UNTIL INTERNAL TEMP. IS AT LEAST 145°F) • REST: 5 MIN.

¾–1 pound pork tenderloin, fat trimmed
Juice and zest of 1 orange
¼ cup low-sodium soy sauce
¼ cup brown-rice vinegar
¼ cup dark-brown sugar
2 tablespoons grated ginger
1 clove garlic, minced
1 tablespoon sambal oelek chili sauce
½ cup chopped cilantro
Carrot shavings and/or thinly sliced red pepper (optional garnish)
Cooking spray as needed

Combine the orange juice and zest, soy sauce, vinegar, sugar, ginger, garlic, and chili sauce in a bowl. Put the pork and the marinade you just made in a sealable plastic bag, and marinate for 1 hour to overnight.

Preheat grill to high. Mist the pork with the cooking spray to prevent sticking. Sear the pork on all sides; then lower the heat to medium, and cook the meat to an internal temperature of at least 145°F or more, according to taste. Remove the tenderloin from the heat, and let it rest for a minimum of 5 minutes. Slice and serve, garnished with the fresh cilantro and/or carrot shavings and thin-sliced pepper.

GRILLED PORK WITH AVOCADO SALSA

4 SERVINGS • PREP: 20–25 MIN. • GRILL: 14–20 MIN.
(UNTIL INTERNAL TEMP. IS AT LEAST 145°F) • REST: 5 MIN.

¾–1 pound boneless top-loin
   pork chops, thick cut (or pork
   tenderloin if unavailable)
½ cup rough-chopped
   Spanish onions
½ cup freshly squeezed lime juice
2 tablespoons extra-virgin olive oil
¼ cup seeded and chopped
   jalapeño peppers
2 teaspoons freshly ground cumin
1 teaspoon salt
1 teaspoon freshly ground
   black pepper
Water as needed

SALSA

1 Hass avocado, peeled, pit
   removed, and medium diced
1 cup halved cherry or
   pear tomatoes
½ cup seeded and medium-
   diced cucumber
¼ cup finely diced red onion
¼ cup chopped cilantro
1 tablespoon extra-virgin olive oil
1–2 tablespoons freshly
   squeezed lime juice
Salt and pepper to taste

Create a marinade by combining the Spanish onions, ½ cup of lime juice, 2 tablespoons of oil, jalapeño, cumin, and 1 teaspoon each of salt and pepper in a blender and blending on high until smooth. If the marinade does not blend properly, add water, a little at a time, until the mixture purées. Put the pork and the marinade in a sealable plastic bag, and marinate for 1 hour to overnight.

Preheat grill to high. Mix all of the salsa ingredients together in a bowl close to the time you will serve the dish to prevent browning (enzymatic oxidation) of the avocado. Mist the pork with the cooking spray to prevent sticking. Sear the pork on all sides; then lower the heat to medium, and cook the meat to an internal temperature of at least 145°F or more, according to taste. Remove the tenderloin from the heat, and let it rest for a minimum of 5 minutes. Slice and serve with a generous serving of the salsa.

PHILIPPINE-INSPIRED PORK LETTUCE WRAPS

4 SERVINGS • PREP: 25–30 MIN. • GRILL: 20–26 MIN.
(UNTIL INTERNAL TEMP. IS AT LEAST 145°F) • REST: 10 MIN.

½–¾ pound pork loin roast,
    fat trimmed
1 onion, finely diced
1 red bell pepper, finely diced
2 cloves garlic, minced
1 cup cooked brown rice,
    cooled overnight
½ cup chopped cilantro
1 jalapeño pepper, seeded
    and chopped
1 tablespoon extra-virgin olive oil
½ cup brown-rice vinegar
Salt and pepper to taste
Cooking spray as needed
1 Boston bibb or iceberg lettuce
1 lime, wedged

Preheat grill to high. Mist the pork with the cooking spray to prevent sticking, and season it with the salt and pepper. Sear the pork on all sides; then lower the heat to medium or low, and cook the roast to an internal temperature of at least 145°F or more, according to taste. Remove the tenderloin from the heat, and let it rest for at least 10 minutes.

Chop the pork into ¼- to ½-inch cubes, and add them to a bowl. Add all of the other ingredients, reserving the lettuce as a wrap. Place a generous spoonful of the mixture into a lettuce leaf, and serve with a lime wedge.

MEDITERRANEAN GRILLED PORK ROAST

4–6 SERVINGS • PREP: 15 MIN. • GRILL: 1–1¼ HR.

4-pound boneless pork loin roast

Zest of 2 lemons

5 garlic cloves, peeled

⅓ cup fresh rosemary leaves

¼ cup fresh sage leaves

¼ cup coarsely ground
   black pepper

Salt to taste

Pat pork roast dry. In bowl of food processor, place remaining six ingredients and process until fairly smooth. Pat seasoning mixture over all surfaces of roast. Place roast on medium-hot grill over indirect heat. Close grill lid, and grill for about 1 to 1¼ hours or until internal temperature reaches about 155°F. Remove pork from grill, and let rest about 10 minutes before slicing to serve.

SMOKED BBQ BOSTON BUTT

COOK: 6–7 HR. UNTIL INTERNAL TEMP. REACHES 200–210°F

10–12 pound Boston butt
Hickory, apple, or pecan
    wood chips

DRY RUB
⅓ cup smoked paprika
¼ cup kosher salt
¼ cup ground black pepper
¼ cup brown sugar
¼ cup chili powder
3 tablespoon ground cumin
2 tablespoon ground coriander
1 tablespoon cayenne pepper

MOP
1 cup apple cider
1 cup apple cider vinegar

Trim excess fat from top and sides of butt. Then, using a knife, make three or four long, shallow slices in alternating directions (six to eight in total) on the fatty, bottom area of butt, like a tic-tac-toe board. This process is called "scoring" the "fat cap" and will help with flavor and tenderness.

Fill the water box in the smoker up to the recommended level. Add the wood chips to the chip box and preheat the smoker for 40 minutes. Combine rub ingredients in a medium-size bowl. Rub the butt liberally with the dry rub on all sides. Once preheated, set the smoker for 225°F. Place the Boston butt fat side up in the smoker.

HOT tip! You can combine apple cider and apple cider vinegar into a spray bottle to spray the Boston butt every hour with the vinegar/juice mixture for the first four hours.

After five hours of smoking, remove the butt from the smoker and place on a large sheet of aluminum foil (enough to wrap the butt). Mix the cider and vinegar together and spray a healthy coat of it on all sides, sprinkle another coat of dry rub over the butt, seal tightly with aluminum foil and return the wrapped butt to the smoker.

HOT tip!
Caution: The butt will be HOT!

Insert the temperature probe into the butt through the foil. Continue to cook in smoker for six to seven hours or until an ideal internal temperature of 200°F–210°F. Remove the butt from the smoker and allow the finished product to rest for one hour before serving.

SMOKED PORK CHOPS WITH POLENTA & CRANBERRY CHUTNEY

6 SERVINGS • PREP: 45 MIN. • GRILL: 10 MIN.

6 cups water

1 pound coarse-ground cornmeal

2 teaspoons salt

1 cup Parmesan cheese, grated

5 tablespoons butter

12 ounces spinach

12-ounce pork chops, cured
    and smoked

CRANBERRY CHUTNEY

1 onion, chopped

1 tablespoon oil

2 cups fresh cranberries

1 cup water

¾ cup sugar

2 tablespoons dry mustard

⅛ teaspoon ground cloves

⅛ teaspoon cinnamon

⅛ teaspoon mace

In a heavy, large saucepan, whisk together 6 cups of water, cornmeal, and salt; bring to a boil; then reduce heat to low and simmer, stirring often, for 5 to 8 minutes or until polenta becomes thick, soft, and creamy. Stir in Parmesan and 4 tablespoons of butter. Cover, and keep warm.

In a medium pan, sauté spinach in 1 tablespoon butter for 3 to 4 minutes until softened. Set aside. Grill chops over medium-high heat about 10 minutes, turning once. Serve with spinach, polenta, and Cranberry Chutney.

For the chutney: Sauté 1 chopped onion in 1 tablespoon oil; stir in 2 cups fresh cranberries, 1 cup water, and ¾ cup sugar. Boil 1 minute; stir in 2 tablespoons dry mustard and ⅛ teaspoon each ground cloves, cinnamon, and mace.

Because the chops are already smoked and need just a few minutes on the grill, prepare the other ingredients in this recipe first. The cranberry chutney can be made a day in advance.

GARLIC & ORANGE-MARINATED GRILLED PORK CHOPS

4 SERVINGS • PREP: 5 MIN. • MARINATE: 4–24 HR. • GRILL: 15 MIN.

4 pork chops, boneless
    or bone-in, about 1¼
    inches thick
½ cup orange juice
½ tablespoon olive oil
½ crushed garlic clove
½ teaspoon ground cumin
¼ teaspoon coarsely ground
    black pepper

Place chops in large, self-sealing plastic bag. Combine remaining ingredients in small bowl, and pour over chops. Seal bag, and refrigerate 4 to 24 hours.

Preheat grill to medium. Remove chops from marinade (discarding marinade), and grill 12 to 15 minutes, turning to brown evenly. Serve chops immediately.

SPIT-ROASTED PORK CHOPS

6 SERVINGS • PREP: 20 MIN. • GRILL: 25–35 MIN.

2 tablespoons olive oil
8 center-cut pork chops,
   ¾ inch thick

BBQ RUB
¼ cup kosher salt
¼ cup paprika
½ teaspoon cayenne pepper
⅓ cup brown sugar
1 tablespoon garlic powder
2 teaspoons celery salt

GLAZE
¼ cup fresh lime juice
½ cup honey
2 teaspoons dried thyme
Pinch of cayenne
⅛ teaspoon ground cumin
¼ cup fresh cilantro
   leaves, chopped
2 limes, each cut into 8 wedges

Pour olive oil into shallow dish, and mix with barbecue rub ingredients. Dip chops into spice mixture, turning to coat evenly. Preheat grill to medium-high. Coat rotisserie basket with nonstick cooking spray; lay chops in basket; and close lid tightly. Load basket onto spit rod.

Combine glaze ingredients. When chops have cooked for 10 minutes, stop rotisserie and baste chops with glaze. Restart rotisserie, and continue to grill chops another 25 minutes or until thickest part reaches 160°F, stopping rotisserie three more times to baste. Remove chops from basket; garnish with cilantro and lime wedges. Serve.

DRUNKEN PORK CHOPS

6 SERVINGS • PREP: 20 MIN. • MARINATE: 8 HR.–OVERNIGHT • GRILL: 12–16 MIN.

2 cups dry red wine

5 bay leaves

2 tablespoons fresh
    rosemary, minced

1½ teaspoons ground coriander

½ teaspoon nutmeg

½ teaspoon ground cloves

6 pork chops, 1½ inches thick

Salt and pepper to taste

Olive oil for grilling

Combine red wine, bay leaves, rosemary, coriander, nutmeg, and cloves in a glass dish. Place chops in marinade mixture. Marinate overnight in refrigerator, turning occasionally.

Drain chops and pat dry; discard used marinade. Season with salt and pepper, and lightly brush with olive oil. Preheat grill to medium-high. Grill chops 6 to 8 minutes on each side.

ARUGULA-AND-ROQUEFORT-STUFFED PORK CHOPS

4 SERVINGS • PREP: 15–20 MIN. • GRILL: 14–20 MIN.
(UNTIL INTERNAL TEMP. IS AT LEAST 145°F) • REST: 5–10 MIN.

4 4–5-ounce boneless
    pork chops
2 cups chopped baby arugula
½ cup julienned red onion
¼ cup Roquefort or other
    blue cheese
1 Bosc pear, diced small
¼ cup roasted pine nuts
2 tablespoons olive oil
Salt and pepper to taste
1 teaspoon fresh lemon juice
Cooking spray as needed

Gently mix the arugula, onion, cheese, pear, nuts, and olive oil in a bowl. Adjust the seasonings.

Using a paring knife, create a pocket in the pork chops by inserting the knife into the side of the chop and working around the interior, making sure not to pierce the edges. Using your fingers, stuff the chops with the arugula mixture.

Preheat grill to high. Mist the stuffed chops with the cooking spray to prevent sticking, and season the top of each one with salt and pepper. Sear the chops on both sides to create grill marks; then lower the heat to medium or low, and cook them to an internal temperature of at least 145°F or more, according to taste. Remove the chops from the heat, and let them rest for 5–10 minutes. Cut each chop into thick slices, and serve topped with a squeeze of lemon juice.

PULLED SMOKED PORK

8–10 SERVINGS • COOK: 8 HR.

5–7-pound Boston butt bone-in pork shoulder
1 cup BBQ rub of your choice
7–8 pounds of charcoal

MOP SAUCE
2 cups distilled white vinegar
1 tablespoon black pepper
1 tablespoon cayenne pepper

The night before you smoke the butt, rub it with your favorite rub. Place in the refrigerator. Before cooking, soak wood chips for at least 30 minutes. Mesquite or hickory wood chips are good choices.

Start about 20 briquettes in a chimney starter or with lighter fluid. When they have ashed over, rake them into opposite ends of the charcoal grate. You can also place an aluminum drip pan in between the coals to catch the drippings from the meat. Place some wood chips onto the hot coals.

Load the meat in the middle of the grill onto the cooking grate between the coals. Maintain a temperature in the firebox of 220°F–250°F by adding additional charcoal throughout the day. Typically, 3 to 4 pieces per side are added every hour to maintain that temperature. When you open the lid to add more charcoal, mop the meat to keep it moist and to add flavor.

When the internal temperature reads around 185°F, wrap the pork shoulder in aluminum foil and continue cooking until the internal temperature reaches 193°F–195°F. The bone should now be separating from the meat. The total cook time for this recipe is 8 hours. Pull the bone out of the meat. With your fingers, tear the meat into thin, tender shreds.

SMOKED PORK CHOPS WITH APPLE ONION COMPOTE

4 SERVINGS • COOK: 40 MIN.

PORK
4 boneless pork chops, each
    about 1" thick
Favorite BBQ rub

COMPOTE
1 tablespoon canola oil
2 tablespoons water
1 large Spanish onion
2 tart apples, such as
    Granny Smith
2 tablespoons butter
¼ teaspoon cinnamon
¼ teaspoon dry mustard
¼ teaspoon nutmeg
Salt to taste

Preheat your electric smoker with the applewood chips in the smoke box for 40 minutes. While the smoker preheats, season your pork chops with the BBQ rub. Line a rimmed baking sheet with heavy-duty aluminum foil. Place a baking rack on top and add the chops.

When the smoker has preheated, set the smoker to 225°F. Insert the digital probe in the thickest part of one of the pork chops, setting the internal temperature to 145°F. Place baking sheet with rack and chops in smoker.

HOT tip!
Elevating the pork chops will help all sides smoke evenly.

Smoke the chops for about 40 minutes or until the targeted internal temperature is reached. Remove the chops from the smoker and let them rest for 10 minutes.

HOT tip! Smoke time will vary based on the size of your pork chops and weather conditions.

While the chops smoke, make the compote. Slice the onion thinly. Add the oil to a skillet over low heat. Then add the onion, cooking until completely soft and pale and golden in color. This should take about 30 minutes. Remove from pan and reserve. Remove the skin and core from the apples, cutting them into ¼ inch pieces. Melt the butter in the same pan used for the onions. Add the apples, cinnamon, dry mustard and nutmeg. Sauté until the apples are softened. Add the onions back into the pan with the apples. Mix to combine and season with a little salt to taste.

HOMEMADE CANADIAN AND PEAMEAL BACON

PREP: 30 MIN. • COOK: 2 HR.

1 gallon cool water

6 teaspoons pink salt (Prague Powder #1)

1 tablespoon juniper berries

1 tablespoon black peppercorns

2 bay leaves

1 teaspoon whole cloves

1 teaspoon allspice

1 cup brown sugar

¾ cup pickling salt

5-pound pork lion, divided in half

Combine the cool water with brine cure ingredients. Stir to dissolve salts and sugar. Trim fat from pork loin. Divide loin in half and submerge in the brine cure. Weigh the loin down with a plate if needed to make sure it is submerged. Cover and let the loin cure for 10 days under refrigeration.

Tie the loin with butcher's twine for uniform size. Sprinkle the loin with cracked black pepper. Place the loin inside of the Grill Top Infuser with smoking chips added. Smoke the bacon covered for one hour. Remove the Grill Top Infuser lid for the second hour of cooking. Smoke with indirect heat until the bacon reaches an internal temperature of 150°F, about 2 hours. The bacon is ready to eat or use in recipes.

JUST THE FACTS . . . ABOUT BACON

If you haven't tried making homemade bacon, you're missing out on a real treat. The hardest part of making bacon is waiting for it to cure. Traditional Canadian bacon is different from the American version in that the Canadian way is to roll the bacon in peameal before cooking (cornmeal is an easily obtained substitute). The American version of Canadian bacon omits the peameal and is usually smoked.

This recipe uses a back pork loin (not tenderloin). After the cure is complete, you have a few options: you can coat the cured bacon loin with peameal, or yellow cornmeal, for Canadian peameal bacon. This Canadian peameal bacon is ready to cook whole, slice and grill, or fry in butter and serve on a hot biscuit. It's great for breakfast!

Another tasty option for the uncooked bacon is kebabs! Cube the bacon and combine it with your favorite veggies. Just brush the kebabs with oil and sprinkle with pepper before grilling. Maybe the best way to prepare the American version of Canadian bacon is smoked, as in this recipe. There are many options for using both kinds of bacon. Let your imagination run wild!

TIPS

- Curing: The bacon cures for 10 days.
- Smoking Time & Temp: Smoking to an internal temperature of 150°F in the Grill Top Infuser takes about 2 hours.

5

I love grilling. Grilling is an incredible way to keep healthy. And you can marinate both with a dry rub and also wet marinades.

–Curtis Stone

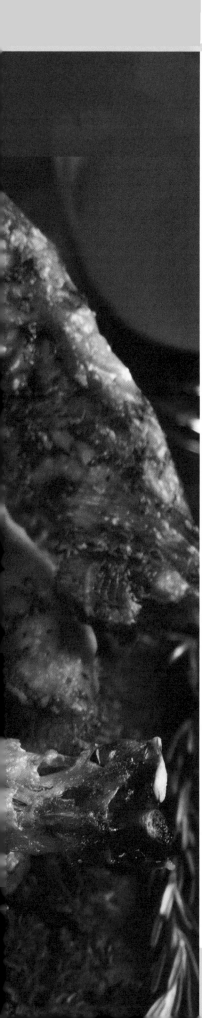

Poultry

CAJUN CHICKEN THIGHS AND DIRTY RICE

8 SERVINGS

8 chicken thighs, skin on, bone-in
2 tablespoons Cajun seasoning

"BUTTER" BASTE

1 cup squeeze "butter"
1 teaspoon coarse ground
    black pepper
1 teaspoon granulated garlic
¾ teaspoon dried thyme leaves
½ teaspoon kosher salt
½ teaspoon celery salt
½ teaspoon onion powder
½ teaspoon cayenne pepper

DIRTY RICE

½ pound spicy breakfast sausage
¼ cup diced bell pepper
¼ cup diced onion
¼ cup diced celery (optional)
1 cup long grain rice
2 cups chicken broth
½ tablespoon Cajun seasoning
Salt to taste

Set up your grill for indirect heat and preheat your grill to 350°F–400°F (medium high).

Mix the "butter" baste ingredients together. You can just mix a cup of squeeze "butter" and a tablespoon or so of the same Cajun seasoning that you use for the chicken. Trim off any excess skin or fat. Season all over with the Cajun seasoning, enough to lightly coat the chicken, and place skin side up in either a half-sized aluminum steam pan or a grill-safe casserole dish. Spoon the "butter" baste mixture over the thighs.

Place the steam pan over indirect heat on the grill. Close the grill lid and let cook for one hour. At 30 and 45 minutes, baste the chicken with the melted "butter."

Place the skillet on your side burner on medium-low heat. Brown the sausage and remove to a plate. Sauté the bell pepper, onion, and celery in the rendered fat until tender, about 4–5 minutes. Add the rice and stir to coat, cooking until the rice becomes fragrant and starts to turn light golden brown, about 1–2 minutes. Stir the cooked sausage in, add the stock, ½ tablespoon Cajun seasoning, and bring to a simmer. Cover tightly and cook for 18 minutes. Remove from heat and let rest covered until the chicken is done.

Use a digital thermometer to make sure the chicken is about 180°F. Remove the chicken from the liquid and let rest on a rack. Carefully open the rice and fluff it with a fork. Serve this family-style, with the chicken thighs right on top of the rice in the skillet.

TO SUB OR NOT TO SUB?

- **Chicken thighs:** You can use breasts but will need to adjust your cooking times a little shorter. If you want to use boneless, skinless thighs, they will cook much quicker and you'll need less of the "butter" baste.
- **Squeeze "butter":** Why not just use real or clarified butter, right? Part of what makes the squeeze "butter" work is the texture and how it clings to the chicken for the first 15 minutes or so, constantly self-basting. If you use real butter, baste a few extra times.
- **Dirty rice:** This is not an authentic dirty rice but it is close for a quickie.

CHICKEN LOLLIPOP?!

Chicken lollipops are a cool way to take an ordinary, inexpensive piece of chicken and turn it into something impressive. These chicken lollipops are popping up on menus at trendy food trucks and gastro pubs.

When it comes to Chicken Lollipops, size matters. Keep in mind that these weight variances among the chicken legs will drastically affect your cooking times. Always rely on internal temperature to know when to take them off the grill.

SMOKED CHICKEN LOLLIPOPS WITH COLA BBQ SAUCE

MAKES 24

24 chicken legs
1 cup hickory wood chips

WET RUB

5 tablespoons cayenne hot sauce
5 tablespoons olive oil
½ cup brown sugar
¼ cup garlic powder
4 teaspoons black pepper
3 tablespoons oregano
2 teaspoons salt

COLA BBQ SAUCE

1 cup cola
1 cup ketchup
¼ cup Worcestershire sauce
3 tablespoons steak sauce
1 teaspoon onion powder
½ teaspoon black pepper

Preheat the smoker at 250°F. Using a sharp chef's knife, cut and remove the skin that covers the bone of each chicken leg to shape them like a lollipop.

Mix all of the Wet Rub ingredients in a bowl, then dip each chicken leg into the mixture to give them an even coating.

Place the chicken lollipops in your smoker and add about 1 cup of hickory wood chips for smoking. Smoke until internal temperature of the chicken reaches 165°F.

Mix all of the Cola BBQ Sauce in a saucepan and simmer for 10 minutes.

Serve the chicken lollipops with Cola BBQ Sauce.

GRILLED & SHREDDED JERK CHICKEN SANDWICHES

GRILL: 5–7 MIN. PER SIDE ON DIRECT HEAT, THEN ON INDIRECT HEAT
UNTIL INTERNAL TEMP. REACHES 160°F • REST: 5–10 MIN.

4–6 chicken breasts, trimmed
Canola oil
Jerk chicken seasoning, premade or
    store bought
2 tablespoons garlic, minced
Kosher salt and fresh ground
    peppercorn, to taste
Pineapple-Kiwi Salsa
Onion-poppy seed hamburger
    buns, toasted

2 cups of peach wood chips,
    soaked in water for 1 hour

PINEAPPLE-KIWI SALSA
½ whole pineapple, trimmed and
    petite dice
4 kiwis, peeled and petite dice
1 small red onion, petite dice
1–2 jalapeños, seeds removed
    and minced

½ teaspoon garlic, minced
1 tablespoon lime juice
1 tablespoon lemon juice
½ cup cilantro leaves, stems
    removed, chopped and
    loosely packed
1 pinch sugar
Kosher salt and fresh ground
    peppercorn, to taste

SALSA

Prepare all ingredients per instruction above. Toss together in a large bowl, cover with plastic and refrigerate for 1–2 hours. Drain excess liquid and serve immediately.

CHICKEN

Preheat Char-Broil's TRU-Infrared Grill™ to medium-high using the 2-zone cooking method. Brush the grates with a cloth doused in canola oil. Wrap woodchips in a sheet of tinfoil, then perforate tinfoil several times with a fork or knife. Apply wood packet in back corner of the direct-heat grilling zone. Once wood packet is billowing with smoke, the grill is ready. Meanwhile, prepare the chicken by drizzling with oil and seasoning liberally with the jerk spice blend, minced garlic, salt and pepper.

Gently place the chicken breasts atop the direct-heat grilling zone and sear with the grill lid open for 5–7 minutes per side. Then transfer to the cooler, indirect-heat zone and close the grill lid, basting intermittently with oil until juices run clear and internal temperature reaches 160°F in thickest part of the breast.

Once the chicken is finished, remove and tent with tinfoil, resting for 5–10 minutes before shredding with two forks. Season additionally with jerk spice blend, to taste, and toss to coat evenly. Load shredded chicken on toasted onion-poppy seed buns, top with the Pineapple-Kiwi Salsa and finish with a squeeze of lime.

CHICKEN LOLLIPOPS WITH HABANERO LIME BUTTER

GRILL: 30 MIN. THEN ADD SAUCE AND COOK 5–15 MIN. MORE
UNTIL INTERNAL TEMP. REACHES 180°F

10 chicken legs

SEASONING

1 teaspoon seasoned salt
1 teaspoon lemon pepper
1 teaspoon chili powder
1 teaspoon turbinado sugar (aka Sugar in the Raw)
½ teaspoon black pepper

HABANERO LIME BUTTER

1 stick unsalted butter
1–2 ounces habanero sauce
1 teaspoon lime juice
1–2 pinches kosher salt

Preheat your grill to medium high (400°F–450°F).

French the chicken legs. Mix the dry rub ingredients together and evenly sprinkle it all over the drumstick meat.

Place the drumsticks on the upper rack of your grill and cook with the grill lid closed for 15 minutes. Flip the legs and cook another 15 minutes.

Meanwhile, make the butter (see note on sauce, below). Place the butter, habanero sauce, lime juice, and salt in a small pot and cook over low heat, whisking frequently, until the butter has melted. Remove from heat.

Sauce the drumsticks after they have been grilling for 30 total minutes. Let finish cooking until the sauce is cooked onto the legs and the internal temperature is 180°F, another 5 minutes for small drumsticks and up to 15 minutes for large ones.

Remove and serve with remaining sauce on the side.

TIPS

- **Upper grill rack:** If you have an adjustable coal tray (Charcoal Grills 580, 780, CB940X), set the charcoal tray to one of the lower positions. If your grill doesn't have an upper grill rack (Kettleman), you can just cook with indirect heat.
- **Spiciness of the sauce:** Habanero sauces vary in intensity, but in general, use 1 ounce of sauce to a stick of butter for mild to medium heat level. We like to use 2 ounces for a bit more of a sting. As always, start with less, taste, and add more hot sauce as needed.

GARLIC PEPPER CHICKEN WITH ASPARAGUS AND PURPLE CAULIFLOWER

PREP: 45 MIN. • MARINATE: 4 HR. • COOK: 15 MIN.

CHICKEN

3 chicken breasts, butterflied and halved into 6 cutlets
2 heads of garlic, plus 5 cloves
½ cup extra-virgin olive oil, plus more for roasting garlic
1 lemon, juiced
1 teaspoon Dijon mustard
1 teaspoon salt
1 tablespoon coarsely ground black pepper
½ teaspoon cayenne pepper

ASPARAGUS

1 bunch asparagus
¼ cup extra-virgin olive oil
1 tablespoon red wine vinegar
1 teaspoon Dijon mustard
1 tablespoon dried dill
1 teaspoon salt
½ teaspoon black pepper

CAULIFLOWER

1 head purple cauliflower
1 tablespoon extra-virgin olive oil
Salt and pepper to taste

Preheat the oven to 350°F. Trim ¼" off the top of each garlic head. Place both garlic heads on a sheet of aluminum foil large enough to fully wrap around both of them. Drizzle with extra-virgin olive oil, covering exposed garlic cloves. Sprinkle with salt and pepper to taste and wrap up into a little aluminum foil package. Place on the oven rack and roast for 45 minutes.

Meanwhile, prepare chicken marinade. Combine ½ cup extra-virgin olive oil, juice of one lemon, one teaspoon Dijon mustard, salt, pepper, and cayenne pepper. Whisk to combine.

Mince the five remaining garlic cloves and remove the roasted garlic from the oven once completed. Using tongs to keep from burning your hands, squeeze the entire head of garlic and the cloves will slide right out. Add minced and roasted garlic to the marinade. Stir to combine and pour over chicken inside a gallon-sized zip-top bag. Chill for at least 4 hours or overnight.

Just before grilling, wash and prep the asparagus and cauliflower. For the asparagus, trim the ends and place in a shallow casserole dish. Whisk together remaining ingredients and pour over asparagus. Set aside. For the cauliflower, cut the entire head in half and then cut into ½-inch-thick steaks. Drizzle cauliflower steaks with extra virgin olive oil and sprinkle with salt and pepper. Set aside.

To grill chicken, first spray the grates of the Char-Broil Signature™ 3 Burner Gas Grill with nonstick cooking spray and preheat to medium-high for 5 minutes. Place each chicken breast on the grill and cook for 3 to 4 minutes. Flip and repeat. These cutlets cook quickly since they are so thin, so be careful not to overcook. The internal temperature should reach 165°F. Remove from grill and set aside.

Carefully place the asparagus and cauliflower on the grill. Grill for 3 to 4 minutes, turning approximately halfway through. Veggies should be tender, but not limp. Remove asparagus and drizzle with remaining dill vinaigrette. Remove cauliflower to the cutting board and cut into florets. Serve garlic pepper chicken with grilled veggies and enjoy!

HONEY BBQ WINGS

GRILL: 22–27 MIN.

10 whole chicken wings
¼ cup dry BBQ rub

HONEY BBQ SAUCE
1 cup ketchup
½ cup local honey
½ cup brown sugar
2 tablespoons apple cider vinegar
1½ tablespoons
    Worcestershire sauce
¾ teaspoon kosher salt
¾ teaspoon black pepper
¾ teaspoon chili powder
¼ teaspoon dried minced garlic
¼ teaspoon dried onion flake

TO SUB OR NOT TO SUB

- **Homemade sauce:** This BBQ Sauce is a winner but if you don't have the time or inclination to make it, you can just add ¼ cup of honey to your favorite store-bought sauce.
- **Dried minced garlic:** You can substitute ¼ teaspoon of garlic paste or finely minced fresh garlic.
- **Dried onion flake:** You can substitute ½ teaspoon of finely minced sweet onion.
- **Local honey:** You can use store bought but studies have shown that most "honey" on the shelves contains no trace of pollen and may not actually be honey. Also, buying local honey supports beekeepers who are leading the fight against the declining honey bee population and colony collapse disorder.
- **Fire roasting:** To do this recipe as fire roasted on the Kamander, preheat to the same temperature but put the drip pan in. Roast the wings top down for 25 minutes. Flip them and cook another 25 minutes. Sauce and cook until the sauce is set on the wings, 5 to 10 minutes.

Take the wings out of the packaging and wipe them dry. Place the wings on a rack and place in the refrigerator to air dry for one hour. This step is optional but gives you the crispiest crust.

Preheat the grill to 375°F–400°F (medium high). Stir together all the Honey BBQ Sauce ingredients in a medium pot over medium high heat. Bring to a simmer and cook for 5 minutes to let the flavors blend. Taste for seasoning and add a pinch or two of salt and pepper as desired.

Season the wings on all sides with the dry BBQ rub. Place the wings top side down on the grate and cook, flipping every 5 minutes, until the wings reach an internal temperature of 180°F, about 20–25 minutes. Keep the lid closed when you aren't actively handling the wings.

Brush some of the Honey BBQ Sauce on all sides of the wings. Cook just long enough for the sauce to "set" on the wings, about 1 minute per side. The sauce will burn so keep a very close watch at this point. Using the upper rack of your grill (if equipped) makes this a bit easier so you can see when it's time to flip and the heat is less intense. Remove and serve with the remaining Honey BBQ Sauce on the side.

LEMON HERBED CHICKEN AND BALSAMIC VEGGIES

PREP: 5 MIN. • COOK: 22 MIN.

2 boneless, skinless chicken breasts, butterflied and halved into 4 cutlets

½ teaspoon salt, plus more to taste

½ teaspoon black pepper, plus more to taste

½ teaspoon dried basil

½ teaspoon dried dill

½ teaspoon dried oregano

1 teaspoon garlic powder

1 teaspoon onion powder

1 teaspoon lemon zest

1–2 lemons, thinly sliced into 8 rounds

1 pound baby red potatoes, diced into 1-inch pieces

6 ounces green beans, stems trimmed, diced into 1½-inch pieces

8 ounces cherry tomatoes

2 tablespoons extra-virgin olive oil

2 tablespoons balsamic vinegar

Preheat your Char-Broil Signature Tru-Infrared Grill over high heat for 10 minutes. In a small bowl, combine the dried herbs, salt, pepper, and lemon zest. Set aside.

In a medium bowl, toss potatoes, cherry tomatoes, and green beans with extra-virgin olive oil, balsamic vinegar, and salt and pepper until evenly coated. Set aside.

Lay out four 12x12 sheets of nonstick foil on a flat surface. Divide potato, tomato, and green bean mixture evenly between the four sheets, keeping it as close to the center as you can. Top each vegetable mixture with a chicken cutlet. Sprinkle cutlet and vegetables with a quarter of the dried herb mixture each. Top chicken with two lemon slices.

Seal foil packets by folding over and scrunching ends together. Be careful not to break the foil while making sure each packet is well sealed so the juices stay inside. Place the packets on the grill and lower the heat to medium. Grill for 15 minutes and then flip and grill for another 5 to 7 minutes.

Carefully open one packet using tongs and heatproof mitts, and check chicken for doneness. It should have an internal temperature of 165°F. Serve each packet on a plate and enjoy!

PINEAPPLE HABANERO CHICKEN WINGS

2–4 SERVINGS AS A STARTER

---

2 pounds chicken wings
¼ cup olive oil
1 tablespoon paprika
1 tablespoon onion powder
½ tablespoon salt
1 teaspoon black pepper

PINEAPPLE & HABANERO SAUCE

1¼ cup pineapple, diced
¼ yellow bell pepper
1 habanero pepper
2 garlic cloves
½ cup brown sugar
⅓ cup white vinegar
½ teaspoon salt
2 tablespoons butter

Preheat your grill for indirect cooking. Mix the chicken wings with the olive oil in a bowl then add the paprika, onion powder, salt, and pepper. Mix until all of the wings are equally coated with seasonings.

Cook the wings in indirect heat for 25 to 30 minutes at 350°F.

Add all the pineapple and habanero sauce ingredients, except the butter, in a blender, and blend until you get a nice smooth consistency. Add to a saucepan over medium heat with 2 tablespoons of butter and simmer for 10 minutes.

Once close to fully cooked, place the chicken wings in the sauce to give them a generous coating, then sear over direct heat for 30 seconds per side.

SWEET & SPICY PINEAPPLE CHILE WINGS

MAKES 16 WING PORTIONS

8 chicken wings, cut into drummettes and wingettes

1 tablespoon all-purpose chicken seasoning

PINEAPPLE CHILE SAUCE

¼ cup pineapple jelly/preserves (see Tips below)

¼ cup thick teriyaki sauce (see Tips below)

¼ cup chicken stock

1 teaspoon rice wine vinegar

½ teaspoon soy sauce

½ teaspoon crushed red pepper flakes (see notes/ substitutions)

[Optional] Place wing pieces, uncovered, on a cooling rack over a sheet pan in the refrigerator for one hour. This will dry the surface of the wings out, making them brown easier and providing a crispier wing texture.

Place all the sauce ingredients into a small saucepan and heat until almost boiling. Reduce heat and let the sauce simmer until slightly thickened, about 10–15 minutes.

Preheat a grill to medium-high heat (400–450°F). Season the wings all over with the rub and toss to coat. Place the wings on the grill, close the lid, and let cook for 15 minutes.

Flip the wings, close the lid, and let cook another 15 minutes. Use an instant-read thermometer to check that the wings have reached an internal temperature of 180°F. If not, continue grilling until they do.

Reduce the heat to medium-low (300°F), sauce the wings, and let them cook until the sauce is set on them, about 5–10 minutes.

TIPS

- **All-purpose chicken seasoning:** You can make a quick, all-purpose seasoning with 1¼ teaspoon kosher salt, 1¼ teaspoon coarse ground black pepper, and ½ teaspoon of granulated garlic.
- **Pineapple jelly/preserves:** Use jelly for a thinner sauce. Use preserves for a chunkier and thicker sauce. Preserves will only take about 10–12 minutes while jelly tends to run 15 minutes. If you can find pineapple habanero jelly, you can use that and skip the red pepper flakes.
- **Teriyaki sauce:** Teriyaki sauces vary a lot. While at the grocery store, tilt the bottle and watch the liquid to see how thick or thin it is. Use a thicker teriyaki sauce or glaze.
- **Red pepper flakes:** You can substitute a heaping ¼ teaspoon of cayenne pepper. If you really want to kick it up, try using some of the designer dried chile flakes.

ASIAN CHICKEN WINGS

MARINATE: 1 HR. • SMOKE: 1 ½ HR. UNTIL INTERNAL TEMP.
REACHES 160°F • FRY: 1–2 MIN.

1 cup soy sauce

½ cup mirin (Japanese rice wine)

½ cup orange juice

¼ cup brown sugar

1 teaspoon five-spice powder

2 pounds chicken wings, trimmed
    to drumettes and flats

Orange, pecan, or cherry
    wood chips

Vegetable oil (for frying)

Add wood chips to the wood chip box of the Digital Electric Vertical Smoker. Add water to the recommended level in the water pan. Preheat the smoker for 40 minutes. Combine the soy sauce, mirin, orange juice, brown sugar and five-spice powder in a bowl. Add the wings and marinate in the refrigerator for one hour.

HOT tip! Marinate in a zip-top plastic bag to seal out air and to protect wings from contamination.

Once the smoker has preheated, set it to 225°F. Put the wing pieces in a disposable aluminum pan and put in the smoker. Smoke for about 1½ hours or until a digital thermometer registers 160°F internal temperature in the meatiest part of the wings. Remove the wings from the smoker. Heat about three inches of vegetable oil in a high-sided skillet to 350°F. Add the wings in batches and fry for one to two minutes until the skin is crisp. Drain on a wire rack and serve.

EASY BBQ CHICKEN

4 SERVINGS

2 tablespoons paprika
2 tablespoons cumin
1 tablespoon kosher salt

1 tablespoon chili powder
½ tablespoon allspice
4 chicken thighs, bone-in, skin-on

½ cup barbecue sauce

Mix the paprika, cumin, salt, chili powder and allspice together and liberally coat the chicken on both sides. Let it sit in refrigerator for 1 hour or more. Preheat your gas grill on high, with the lid down, for 10–15 minutes. This is an important step that many people miss. Preheating gets the grates hot enough to sear the meat and allow it to release from the grill grates when it's ready. This recipe was tested on a two-burner Quantum TRU-Infrared grill, one of the best grills for beginners because it really doesn't flare up.

Once preheated, turn down the burners to medium-high. Place the thighs on the grates and grill on one side for about seven minutes or until the meat naturally releases from the grill. This is another key part of the grilling process. Enough collagen will seep out of the meat that it will let go from the grill on its own. You can check if the chicken is ready by lifting up a corner of the thigh. If it resists and sticks, then let it grill for another few minutes before you try again. Once you can easily lift the chicken off the grill, flip and repeat the process on the second side, but with the lid closed.

After seven minutes or so, once the chicken releases easily from the grill, move all the thighs onto one half of your grill. Turn off the burner directly under the chicken, but leave the other burner or burners on. Close the lid. This is called indirect grilling because the flame is not directly under what you are cooking. Cook the chicken for another 10 minutes, then lift the lid and brush the tops lightly with barbecue sauce.

Cook for another 10 minutes until your chicken is done—when it reads at least 165°F on your thermometer. Cooking on a TRU-Infrared grill will help you avoid flare ups when the grease hits the flame. If you do get a flare up, turn off the burners and close the lid to smother the fire. Use the rack above the grill to put your chicken on if it's cooking too fast or too hot.

THE BIG EASY® THAI-INSPIRED ROTISSERIE CHICKEN

PREP: 4 HR. • COOK: 2½ HR.

CHICKEN

1 5–6 pound roaster chicken
1 teaspoon salt
¾ teaspoon black pepper

BRINE

2 quarts water
5 tablespoons salt
1 teaspoon red pepper flakes
1 teaspoon dried minced garlic

COMPOUND BUTTER

1 stick unsalted butter, room temperature
1 tablespoon sambal oelek
1 teaspoon ginger, minced
1 teaspoon cilantro, chopped
2 cloves garlic, peeled and chopped
8 basil leaves, sliced into strips

Mix the brine. Stir 1 quart of water, salt, red pepper flakes, and dried garlic together in a pot large enough to hold your bird. Bring to a boil and allow it to sit for 5 minutes. Add the remaining cool water and place in the fridge. Chill the brine to 40°F before using. Once chilled, place the chicken in the brine. Let it sit for 2–4 hours.

While the bird brines, make the compound butter. Stir together the butter, sambal oelek, ginger, cilantro, garlic and basil. Keep refrigerated until ready to use. Preheat The Big Easy® Oil-less Turkey Fryer. Remove the chicken from the brine, rinse and pat dry. Work the compound butter under and on top of the chicken skin. Season the chicken with salt and pepper. Then place the chicken into The Big Easy® basket.

Lower the chicken and basket into the fryer. Allow it to cook until it reaches an internal temperature of 165°F in the breasts and 175°F in the thighs. If desired, you can use the mesh screen top in the last few minutes to help crisp up the skin. Remove and let rest for 10 minutes. Slice and serve.

HOT tip! Cook time should take about 10 to 15 minutes per pound, but that is just an estimate. Timing varies based on weather conditions and the exact size of your chicken.

SMOKED CHICKEN BREAST WITH CARAMELIZED ONIONS

BRINE: 1 HR. • SMOKE: 2 HR. • GRILL: 15 MIN.

4 chicken breast halves, bone-in
4 tablespoons olive oil
1 onion, medium, sliced
Salt and pepper to taste
Your favorite brine recipe
Your favorite dry rub recipe

Brine the chicken. Remove 1 hour prior to cooking and rinse. Add rub on and under skin and work into meat. Preheat the smoker to 225°F–230°F. Add the wood chips.

Place chicken in smoker and cook about 2 hours. Set up for indirect heat and preheat the grill to 375°F. Place a cast-iron skillet on the non-heated side. Let the skillet warm with the grill. Add olive oil and onions to the skillet and cook about 15 minutes, or until onions are slightly translucent.

Remove the chicken from the smoker and add to the skillet. Carefully cover with foil (the skillet is hot!) and let roast about 15 minutes until the onions become brown and caramelized. Remove from heat, serve with pan drippings, and enjoy.

TASTY TIPS

- Use a sweeter wood like apple or cherry instead of a more earthy wood like mesquite.
- If using bone-in chicken, serve the chicken as is, or slice the meat off the bone before eating.
- Try adding sweet potatoes and zucchini with the onions for more variety of caramelized vegetables.
- Serve with all vegetable and chicken drippings to be sure all of the sweet flavor makes it to the plate.

Use a meat hook or grilling gloves to safely remove the chicken from the smoker.

GARLIC HERB SMOKED WHOLE CHICKEN

SMOKE: 3–4 HR. UNTIL INTERNAL TEMP. REACHES 165°F • REST: 15–20 MIN.

1 5-pound whole chicken
6 cups applewood or
    cherrywood chips
1 can amber beer
2 tablespoons extra virgin olive oil
20 garlic cloves
2 finely chopped rosemary sprigs
2 lemon peels
Coarse sea salt
Coarse pepper

In your sink, rinse the chicken exterior and cavities with cold water. Using a towel or paper towel, dry well. Set the chicken aside and allow to come to room temperature. Fill up your water pan with amber beer to the suggested amount. Add the wood chips to the chip box. Preheat your digital electric smoker for 40 minutes.

While your smoker is preheating, rub the chicken skin with olive oil. Remove the paper skin from garlic cloves (if necessary). Fill the chicken cavity with the garlic, half of the chopped rosemary and the lemon peel. Season the chicken's exterior with salt, pepper and the remaining chopped rosemary.

HOT tip! Mix your spices in a separate bowl before applying to keep the spice containers sanitary.

Once the digital smoker is preheated, set it to 250°F. Add the chicken to the middle rack, breast side up. Insert the thermometer probe into the bird between the thigh and breast. Set the digital thermometer for 165°F internal temperature. Smoke the chicken for three to four hours or until the internal temperature of the chicken has reached an ideal internal temperature of 165°F and the juices run clear. Do not cut until the bird has rested for 15–20 minutes.

BBQ-STYLE SMOKED CHICKEN LEGS

SMOKE: 2 HR. OR UNTIL INTERNAL TEMP. REACHES 165°F

Chicken legs
Oil
Dry rub
BBQ sauce

Preheat the smoker to 225°F. Add wood chips. Prepare the chicken by lightly coating with oil and BBQ dry rub. Place the chicken in the smoker.

Use a BBQ sauce to baste the chicken while cooking and rotate it a few times. Smoke for about 2 hours or until the chicken reaches an internal temperature of 165°F.

When I want to kick it up, I like to add hardwood chips or chunks to the grill; it adds bold, smoky flavors.

–Emeril Lagasse

TIPS

- **Chicken legs:** Whole legs are a combination of the drumstick and thigh.
- **Added flavor and moisture:** Use whole legs with the skin and bone, as the additional fat will provide flavor and moisture to the meat while it smokes.
- **BBQ sauce:** Prepare a large amount of BBQ sauce to keep the chicken coated while cooking and to serve once the chicken is done.

JAMAICAN JERK SMOKED CHICKEN THIGHS

6 SERVINGS

6 chicken thighs
4 tablespoons soy sauce
1 teaspoon sesame oil
3 garlic cloves
3 scallions
½ tablespoon thyme
1 teaspoon allspice
1 teaspoon black pepper
½ teaspoon cinnamon
½ teaspoon crushed red pepper

Mix soy sauce with sesame oil and lightly rub into chicken. In a food processor, combine garlic cloves, scallions, thyme, allspice, pepper, cinnamon, and red pepper until smooth. Rub onto and underneath skin of chicken thighs. Seal chicken in a plastic bag, place in fridge, and let marinate for at least 4 hours.

Preheat the smoker to 225°F and add cherry wood chips. Remove the chicken from the fridge 30 minutes prior to cooking. Remove it from the marinade and place the chicken in a smoker. Smoke for two hours, rotating throughout cooking. Chicken thighs will be done once the internal temperature of the meat has reached 165°F.

JUST THE FACTS . . . ABOUT CHICKEN THIGHS

Want a more flavorful and juicy piece of smoked chicken? Try smoked chicken thighs! Full of delicious dark meat, chicken thighs are incredible when smoked because they are naturally more moist than other white meat parts of the bird. The thigh has a higher fat content than breasts or wings. Putting chicken thighs in the smoker helps this fat to break down and naturally flavor the meat of the thighs. This cut of chicken is perfect when grilled, baked, or roasted in the slow cooker, but our favorite chicken thighs are slow smoked with Jamaican jerk seasoning. Create this homemade seasoning mix for smoked chicken thighs full of fresh island flavor.

CB'S GRILLED CHICKEN WITH BALSAMIC GARLIC SAUCE

5 SERVINGS • PREP: 15 MIN. • GRILL: 20–25 MIN. (UNTIL THIGH TEMP. IS 180°F)

5 chicken-leg quarters
Sea salt and fresh
    cracked pepper
Canola oil spray

SAUCE

2 tablespoons olive oil
1 tablespoon butter, softened
1 small shallot, chopped
3 cloves of garlic, minced
⅓ cup balsamic vinegar
1 cup chicken broth
2 tablespoons instant flour
Chopped parsley for garnish

Preheat one side of the grill to medium and the other side to low. Season the chicken with salt and pepper, and lightly spray all sides with canola oil.

Sear the chicken over medium heat, about 3 to 5 minutes per side; then remove it to a foil pan on the low-heat side of the grill. Keep the other side of the grill on medium, but shut off the burners under the pan. Close the lid. Cook until the temperature of the thick thigh meat is 180°F.

Sauce: Heat 1 tablespoon of olive oil and the butter in a saucepan over medium-high heat. Add the shallot, cooking until translucent, and then add the garlic. Combine with the vinegar and chicken broth, and bring to a boil.

In a small bowl, mix 1 tablespoon olive oil and flour. Drizzle it into the sauce mixture, whisking to prevent lumps. Bring to a boil; then simmer on low for 1 to 2 minutes, whisking as necessary. Serve with the chicken. Top with the chopped parsley.

CATALAN GRILLED CHICKEN LEGS

4 SERVINGS • PREP: 10 MIN. • GRILL: 10 MIN. • COOK: 20 MIN.

4 chicken-leg quarters
¼ teaspoon cayenne pepper
½ teaspoon cumin
½ teaspoon cinnamon
1 teaspoon salt
¼ teaspoon black pepper
2 tablespoons olive oil
1 medium size onion, chopped
4 cloves garlic, chopped
¾ cup chorizo or other spicy
    sausage, chopped
1 28-ounce can whole,
    peeled tomatoes, drained
    and chopped
½ cup full-bodied red wine
½ cup chopped pitted black olives
6 tablespoons pine nuts, toasted

Preheat the grill to high. In a small bowl, stir together the cayenne pepper, cumin, cinnamon, salt, and black pepper. Rub thoroughly over chicken-leg quarters. Reduce grill to medium. Place chicken on grill, and cook, turning until browned on all sides, about 10 minutes. While the chicken is grilling, warm the olive oil in a large pot over medium heat. Add the onions and garlic, and sauté until they begin to brown, about 4 minutes. Stir in the sausage, and continue to sauté for 3 more minutes. Stir in the tomatoes and wine, and bring the mixture to a simmer. When chicken is finished grilling, add it to the pot. Stir in the olives. Cover; reduce heat to medium low; and simmer for 20 minutes.

To serve, put one piece of chicken in each of four shallow bowls. Top with the sauce, and sprinkle with toasted pine nuts.

CB'S KOREAN-STYLE CHICKEN

6 SERVINGS • PREP: 1 ¾ HR. (INCL. MARINATING)
GRILL: 15–20 MIN. (UNTIL MEAT TEMP. IS 180°F)

3 pounds boneless, skinless
    chicken thighs

⅓ cup soy sauce

2 tablespoons sugar

1 tablespoon sweet rice wine

½ medium onion, grated

2 cloves garlic, mashed
    and minced

1 teaspoon grated ginger

1 teaspoon Chinese-style dry
    mustard powder

¼ teaspoon black pepper

1 teaspoon sesame seeds,
    toasted for garnish

Green onions or chives, chopped
    for garnish

GLAZE

¼ cup soy sauce

1 tablespoon sesame oil

1 tablespoon butter, melted

Mix glaze ingredients together in a small bowl and set aside.

Flatten chicken thighs. Mix the next eight ingredients in a large plastic bag. Add chicken, and seal. Place the sealed bag in the refrigerator for 1 hour.

About 30 minutes before grilling, remove chicken from marinade. Pat chicken dry, and cover loosely with plastic wrap. Preheat grill to high; then lower one side to medium.

Spray the chicken with canola oil. Sear one side of it over high heat. Then move the chicken, seared side up, to the medium side of the grill. When the chicken reaches an internal temperature just below 160°F, remove it to a foil tray or pan, and put it back on the medium side of the grill. Brush on the glaze, and loosely cover the pan with foil. Chicken is ready when it reaches an internal temperature of 180°F.

Arrange the grilled chicken on a platter, and drizzle with glazing sauce.

CB'S CHICKEN WITH ROSEMARY BUTTER & WHITE BBQ SAUCE

8 SERVINGS • PREP: 15 MIN. • BRINE: 8–12 HR.
GRILL: 40–50 MIN. (UNTIL THIGH TEMP. IS 180°F)

2 4- to-5-pound chickens, each
    cut in half along the back- and
    breast-bone
¼ cup kosher salt
¼ cup brown sugar
1 tablespoon apple cider vinegar
    (optional)
¼ pound unsalted butter, softened
Freshly ground sea salt to taste
Freshly ground black pepper
    to taste
½ cup finely chopped fresh
    rosemary, plus several sprigs
    for garnish

CB'S WHITE BBQ SAUCE

1⅓ cups mayonnaise
2 garlic cloves, finely minced
½ cup fresh lemon juice
2 to 3 tablespoons lemon zest
    (or very finely chopped
    lemon peel)
¼ teaspoon smoked paprika

Brine chicken, overnight if possible, in a mixture of ¼ cup kosher salt, ¼ cup brown sugar, vinegar, and water to cover. One hour before grilling, remove the chicken; rinse under cool water; and pat dry. Allow the chicken halves to air dry in the fridge for up to several hours if time permits.

Mix butter, salt, pepper, and all but about 2 tablespoons of the rosemary; insert under the skin. Set up your grill for indirect cooking with a drip pan under the grates on the side without heat. Turn on the direct-heat burner. The hood temperature inside the closed grill should read about 400°F.

Place the chicken halves skin side up on the indirect-heat side of the grill, and close the hood. After 15 minutes, move the chicken so that all of it is exposed equally to the "hot" side of the grill. Then turn it over (skin side down) to sear. Continue to cook chicken with the hood closed about another 15 to 20 minutes.

When chicken temperature reaches 160°F, finish cooking, indirectly until internal temperature is 180°F. Drizzle with CB's White BBQ Sauce.

For the sauce: In a nonreactive bowl, whisk together the ingredients in the order listed. Spoon sauce over hot pieces of grilled chicken or pork.

CB'S GRILLED CHICKEN CACCIATORE

4 SERVINGS • PREP: 25 MIN. • GRILL: 3–4 HR.

2 to 3 pounds chicken thighs
    and drumsticks
Kosher salt and freshly ground
    black pepper
3 tablespoons canola oil or spray
1 yellow onion, sliced
2 medium shallots, diced
2 cups diced red, yellow, and/or
    green peppers
3 cloves garlic, minced
3 tablespoons flour
½ pound mushrooms, quartered
1 cup baby carrots
15-ounce can diced tomatoes
2 cups chicken broth
⅓ cup red wine
2 tablespoons chopped
    fresh cilantro
2 tablespoons chopped
    fresh parsley
1 tablespoon dried thyme
¼ teaspoon red pepper flakes
Dash Tabasco sauce
Sliced black olives, if desired

Preheat grill to high. Season chicken with salt and pepper. Brush or lightly spray chicken with oil. Place on hot grill skin-side down. Cook until browned on one side; then turn and brown the other side, but do not cook completely. Set aside.

Turn grill's side burner to high. In a large, non-reactive pan over the burner, heat the oil. Then reduce heat to medium, and add onion. Sauté for 2 to 3 minutes; add shallots. Continue to cook for 1 minute before adding bell peppers. When shallots and onions begin to caramelize and peppers soften, add garlic, making sure that mixture does not burn.

Add the flour to mixture 1 tablespoon at a time. Add mushrooms and the remaining ingredients.

Reduce heat to low, and add chicken. Cover and cook over indirect heat on grill for 3 to 4 hours.

HOT tip! Grilling the chicken adds a rich flavor that's even better if you use some wood chips to impart a bit of smoke. To get a head start, grill the chicken the day before.–CB

Georgia is known as the "peach state" because the commercial peach industry originated there with the introduction of the delectable–and shippable–Elberta peach in 1875.

PEACH-BARBECUED CHICKEN

4 SERVINGS • PREP: 5 MIN. • GRILL: 15–20 MIN. (UNTIL MEAT TEMP. IS 165°F)

4 boneless, skinless
   chicken breasts
2 teaspoons onion salt
⅓ cup peach or apricot preserves
3 tablespoons barbecue sauce

SERVE WITH
Store-bought buttermilk biscuits
Carrot salad

Sprinkle chicken with 1 teaspoon onion salt. Combine peach preserves, barbecue sauce, and remaining teaspoon of onion salt in a small bowl.

Grill chicken over medium-low heat, turning and brushing frequently with peach barbecue sauce, for 15 to 20 minutes or until the internal temperature is 165°F.

I think many cooks are afraid of undercooked meats. A good thermometer is a cook's best friend.

–Emeril Lagasse

BEER-CAN CHICKEN

4–6 SERVINGS • PREP: 15 MIN. • MARINATE: 1 HR.–OVERNIGHT • GRILL: 1½–2 HR.

1 whole chicken (4 to 5 pounds)
2 teaspoons vegetable oil
1 16-ounce can beer

RUB 1

1 teaspoon dry mustard
¼ cup minced onion
1 teaspoon paprika
1 teaspoon kosher salt
4 small cloves garlic, minced
½ teaspoon ground coriander
½ teaspoon ground cumin
½ teaspoon freshly ground
   black pepper

RUB 2

3 tablespoons paprika
2 tablespoons sugar
1 tablespoon salt
2 teaspoons coarsely ground
   black pepper
1 teaspoon onion powder
1 teaspoon garlic powder
1 teaspoon ground red pepper
   (cayenne)

In a small bowl, combine the rub ingredients. Wash the chicken, and pat it dry. Coat the entire chicken with vegetable oil and season it with the rub, inside and out.

Preheat the grill to medium. Pour half of the beer out of the can, and carefully place the half-full can inside the cavity of the chicken. Note: The can will be almost completely covered by the chicken. Transfer the bird to the grill, keeping the can upright. Grill for 1½ to 2 hours or until the internal temperature reaches 180°F in the thickest part of the thigh and the meat is no longer pink. Carefully remove the chicken with the can from the grill using protective mitts. Let the chicken rest for about 10 minutes before lifting it from the can. Discard the beer. Cut the chicken into serving pieces.

CB'S BEER-BRINED CHICKEN QUARTERS

4 SERVINGS • PREP: 15 MIN. • BRINE: 8 HR. • CHILL: 1 HR.
GRILL: 45 MIN. (UNTIL MEAT TEMP. IS 180°F)

4 chicken quarters (legs
   and thighs)
1 quart water
¼ cup kosher salt
¼ cup packed brown sugar
12 ounces beer

RUB
1 tablespoon smoked paprika
1 tablespoon kosher salt
1 teaspoon garlic powder
1 teaspoon ground ginger
1 teaspoon powdered mustard
½ teaspoon pepper

Thoroughly mix together all rub ingredients, and set aside. Brine the chicken in the water, salt, sugar, and beer, adding the water last to ensure that the chicken is covered. Store in the refrigerator up to 8 hours.

Remove chicken from brine; rinse; and pat dry with paper towels. Refrigerate uncovered about 1 hour to air dry. Remove chicken from the refrigerator, and apply the rub, massaging it into the skin using your hands in food-safe gloves.

Preheat half of grill to medium high. Spray chicken lightly on all sides with canola oil. Cook chicken pieces on the hot section of the grill until they lift easily and sear marks appear. Turn and sear the other sides.

Move chicken to an aluminum pan on an unheated section of grates; loosely cover with foil; and close grill hood. Reduce the heat to low on the section furthest from the chicken. Cook, covered, until chicken reaches an internal temperature of 180°F.

HOT tip! Brining is usually done with salted water, in which sugar and assorted flavors have been added. Brining helps the chicken stay moist when grilling.—CB

SESAME-CRUSTED CHICKEN WITH WASABI CREAM SAUCE

4 SERVINGS • PREP: 20 MIN. • MARINATE: 12 HR.
GRILL: 15 MIN. (UNTIL MEAT TEMP. IS 165°F)

4 boneless, skinless
   chicken breasts
1 cup bottled teriyaki sauce
½ to 1 teaspoon
   prepared wasabi*
½ cup light sour cream
2 teaspoons lemon juice
½ teaspoon grated lemon rind
¼ cup black sesame seeds**
¼ cup white sesame seeds
1 egg white, lightly beaten

Wasabi is Japanese horseradish. It is green and spicy. Prepared wasabi is a ready-to-use paste that comes in a tube. Add more or less wasabi depending on your desire for heat.

**Black sesame seeds are available at Asian grocery stores. If you prefer, use ½ cup of white sesame seeds instead.*

Pound chicken until slightly flattened. Marinate chicken in the teriyaki overnight in the refrigerator.

Stir wasabi, sour cream, lemon juice, and rind until smooth. Cover and refrigerate until serving time. Preheat the grill to medium. Mix black and white sesame seeds on a plate. Remove chicken from teriyaki sauce; pat it dry using paper towels.

Dip each piece in beaten egg white; then coat with sesame seeds, pressing the seeds into the chicken. Transfer chicken to a wax-paper-lined pan to stand for 10 minutes to allow the coating to set. Grill for 5 to 7 minutes per side with the lid down or until a meat thermometer reads 165°F. Serve immediately with wasabi cream sauce on the side.

COFFEE & COCOA GRILLED CHICKEN THIGHS

4 SERVINGS • PREP: 10 MIN. • REST: 1 HR.
GRILL: 30–40 MIN. (UNTIL MEAT TEMP. IS 180°F)

8 pieces skinless chicken thighs,
    bone-in
1 tablespoon plus 2
    teaspoons paprika
1 tablespoon chili powder
½ teaspoon sea salt
½ teaspoon sugar
½ teaspoon ground cumin
½ teaspoon ground coriander
½ teaspoon freshly ground
    black pepper
½ teaspoon garlic powder
1 tablespoon finely ground dark-
    roast coffee
1 tablespoon cocoa or a dark hot-
    chocolate mix

Combine spice ingredients in a sealable plastic bag. Add chicken pieces, and shake to coat. Massage spices into the chicken through bag. Allow the chicken to rest for at least 1 hour so that the spice flavors can set. Preheat grill to medium high. Grill, turning often, until a thermometer inserted into the chicken pieces reads 180°F.

Note: Use this easy barbecue rub to fully seal chicken pieces to yield the juiciest chicken. Use a strong, dark, powdered coffee, such as espresso, and a high-quality cocoa or hot chocolate.

> I love Marsala sauce, but the traditional version is packed with fat. This lighter recipe has so much creamy, wine-y, mushroom flavor.—CB

Grilled Stuffed Tomatoes Caprese, page 258

GRILLED CHICKEN MARSALA

4 SERVINGS • PREP: 30 MIN. • GRILL: 20 MIN.

Recipe courtesy of www.danicasdaily.com

4 4-ounce boneless, skinless chicken breasts
16 small carrots, peeled
2 teaspoons extra-virgin olive oil
8 ounces sliced fresh mushrooms
2 shallots, chopped
3 cloves garlic, minced
12 ounces Marsala wine or low-sodium chicken broth, or 6 ounces of each
1 teaspoon cornstarch (optional)
4 tablespoons nonfat yogurt
Chives, chopped for garnish
4 sprigs fresh rosemary

SPICE MIXTURE

1 teaspoon chopped fresh rosemary
1 teaspoon sea salt
¼ teaspoon freshly ground black pepper
½ teaspoon red pepper flakes

Combine spice mixture, and sprinkle over the chicken. Boil carrots for about 8 to 10 minutes; drain.

Add the oil to a large skillet, and heat over medium heat. Add mushrooms, shallots, and garlic. Season with salt and pepper. Cook until the mushrooms are slightly brown and soft. Add wine or broth. If thicker sauce is desired, stir in cornstarch, and simmer until liquid thickens and reduces to one-third, about 20 minutes.

Preheat grill to medium high. Grill chicken for 8 to 10 minutes on each side or until cooked through. Grill carrots for about 5 minutes, rotating until charred.

Once the mushroom sauce has reduced, remove from heat, and whisk in yogurt. Divide carrots among four plates, and top each with chicken, sauce, chives, and rosemary.

GRILLED STUFFED CHICKEN BREASTS WITH ARTICHOKES & ITALIAN CHEESES

4 SERVINGS • PREP: 20 MIN. • MARINATE: 2 HR.–OVERNIGHT • GRILL: 10 MIN.

4 large, boneless, skinless chicken breasts

1 bottle Italian salad dressing

2 tablespoons olive oil

1 teaspoon thyme, dried or fresh

¼ teaspoon red pepper flakes

2 cloves garlic, minced

2 tablespoons chopped fresh basil

1 small jar (6 or 7 ounces) artichoke hearts, rinsed and drained

¼ teaspoon salt

A few grinds of pepper

1 cup shredded Italian cheese such as Parmesan, Romano, mozzarella, provolone, or a blend

8 toothpicks

Using a sharp paring knife, create a 2- to 3-inch pocket in each breast. Marinate the chicken in the salad dressing in the refrigerator for 2 hours to overnight.

To prepare stuffing, combine olive oil, thyme, and pepper flakes in a saucepan over medium heat. Cook until the spices release their fragrance. Stir in the garlic, basil, artichoke hearts, salt, and pepper. Cook for about 3 minutes. Add the cheese, and blend well. Cook for another minute or two, until the cheese is partially melted. Remove from heat, and cool.

Spoon stuffing into each breast pocket, securing each one using 2 toothpicks.

Preheat the oven to medium high. Cook the chicken for 4 to 5 minutes on each side. Meat should be medium brown, with its juices running clear. Let the chicken rest before removing the toothpicks.

CB'S GRILLED GINGER CHICKEN TENDERLOINS WITH SPICY PEANUT SAUCE

4 SERVINGS • PREP: 1 HR. • MARINATE: 1–4 HR.
GRILL: 20 MIN. (UNTIL MEAT TEMP. IS 165°F)

1 pound chicken tenderloins or
    boneless, skinless chicken
    thighs, cut into large chunks
3 garlic cloves, minced
2 tablespoons minced
    fresh ginger
2 teaspoons dark brown sugar
½ teaspoon cumin
½ teaspoon turmeric
½ teaspoon salt
Safflower or peanut oil, as needed
Juice of 1 lime and 1 lemon,
    as needed

PEANUT SAUCE

1 cup creamy peanut butter
½ cup ginger tea, hot
Hot sauce to taste
1 tablespoon garlic powder
1 tablespoon brown sugar
1 tablespoon soy sauce
1 tablespoon peanut oil

In a large bowl, whisk together all of the ingredients except the chicken. Add to sealable plastic bag. Rinse and pat the chicken dry, and place in bag with marinade. Refrigerate for at least 1 hour and up to 4 hours before grilling.

Preheat grill to medium high. Remove chicken pieces from marinade; place on grill; and discard the contents of bag. Turn the pieces to form sear marks. When the chicken has seared on all sides and has an internal temperature of 165°F (180°F for thighs), it is done. Place on plate, and serve with peanut sauce for dipping.

For the sauce: In a microwavable bowl, heat the peanut butter until it is runny, not bubbling, about 1 minute. Mix in the ginger tea and the remaining ingredients, reheating as necessary. Pour into container, and cover to keep warm until ready to serve.

CB'S EASY SMOKY CHICKEN DRUMETTES PARTY PLATTER

4–5 SERVINGS • PREP: 15 MIN. • SMOKE: 20 MIN.

20 chicken wing drumettes
2 tablespoons garlic powder
1 teaspoon ground ginger
1 teaspoon ground mustard
1 pinch ground cumin
Coarse salt & pepper to taste
¼ cup peanut or canola oil
¼ cup white wine
¼ cup favorite BBQ sauce
    for dipping

Rinse and pat dry chicken drumettes, and place them in a large mixing bowl. Add the next five ingredients, and mix thoroughly. Drizzle oil onto drumettes, and mix until chicken is lightly coated with oil and spices.

Preheat grill to high. Place small packet of moist wood chips on grill; when they begin to smoke, reduce heat to medium.

Grill chicken approximately 8 to 10 minutes, turning to prevent burning. Keep lid closed between turns to ensure that the smoke permeates the meat. After drumettes have browned sufficiently, remove them from grill, and place them in the center of a large sheet of aluminum foil. Fold foil around the drumettes, leaving a small opening. Pour wine into opening, and loosely seal foil. Place foil packet with drumettes back onto grill until wine begins to steam. Remove drumettes, and garnish with lettuce, celery, or parsley. Serve with your favorite BBQ sauce.

TEQUILA LIME CHICKEN

4 SERVINGS • PREP: 5 MIN. • MARINATE: 30 MIN. • GRILL: 10–12 MIN.

Recipe courtesy of Marcia Frankenberg, Minneapolis, MN

4 split boneless, skinless
  chicken breasts
1 tablespoon fresh minced garlic
½ cup fresh-squeezed lime juice
½ cup gold tequila
1 teaspoon kosher salt
½ teaspoon fresh ground
  black pepper
1½ teaspoon ancho chili powder
1 tablespoon olive oil

Combine the chicken with remaining ingredients, and marinate for 30 minutes at room temperature. (The acid in the lime juice cooks the chicken, so be careful not to over-marinate.) Heat the grill to medium high, and spray the grates with oil to prevent the chicken from sticking. Grill the chicken over direct heat for about 5 to 6 minutes per side. Cook until nicely browned—it should feel firm and the juices should run clear. The sugars in the tequila and lime juice will blacken the chicken— so move them to a lower heat if it gets out of control. Serve hot off the grill with lime wedges and rice.

Cooking is a subject you can never know enough about. There is always something new to discover.

–Bobby Flay

CHEESY GRILLED CHICKEN QUESADILLAS

12 SERVINGS • PREP: 10 MIN. • GRILL: 5–8 MIN.

1 large grilled chicken
    breast, chopped
1 3-ounce package cream
    cheese, softened
1 cup shredded Monterey
    Jack cheese
⅓ cup crumbled feta cheese
½ teaspoon dried oregano
4 large flour tortillas
⅓ cup chopped pitted ripe olives
2 tablespoons diced pimento
2 tablespoons thinly sliced
    green onion

For filling, stir together cream cheese, Monterey Jack, feta, and oregano. Spread ¼ of the filling onto half of each tortilla. Top with chicken, olives, pimento, and green onion. Fold plain side over; press gently to seal edges. Preheat grill to high; then reduce to medium. Place tortillas on grill, flipping once. When cheese has melted (about 5 to 8 minutes), remove and cut into three wedges. Serve immediately.

SOUTH-OF-THE-BORDER CHICKEN PIZZA

4 SERVINGS • PREP: 20 MIN. • GRILL: 4–7 MIN.

1½ cup shredded grilled
  chicken breast
Store-bought pizza dough
2 cloves garlic, minced
1 cup chopped fresh cilantro
⅓ cup grated fresh
  Parmesan cheese
6 tablespoons olive oil
Salt and freshly ground
  black pepper
1¼ cup grated Monterey
  Jack cheese
2 ripe plum tomatoes, sliced
  or chopped
½ cup chopped fresh
  green chilies
Crushed red pepper to taste

Prepare pizza dough, adding one clove minced garlic. Preheat grill to high. In food processor, pulse together cilantro, the rest of the garlic, and Parmesan. Slowly pour in oil until combined and mixture resembles pesto. Add salt and pepper to taste. Reserve for pizza assembly.

When grill is hot, place first pizza crust directly onto oiled grill grates; cook 1 to 1½ minutes until crust becomes somewhat firm. Flip crust over onto baking sheet, with cooked side up. Spread half of pesto mixture on top; then sprinkle with half of Monterey Jack cheese, chicken, tomatoes, green chilies, and crushed red pepper.

Slide pizza off baking sheet back onto grill, placing it so half is over high heat and other half is over medium to low heat. Cook pizza 3 to 4 minutes, rotating frequently to get uniformly brown, crisp crust. Slide pizza onto a serving board, and slice into wedges. Repeat process for second pizza.

CB'S GRILLED CHICKEN MEATBALLS

8 SERVINGS • PREP: 20 MIN. • CHILL, DRAIN: 12 HR. • GRILL: 20 MIN.

2 pounds ground chicken
1 cup fresh bread crumbs
1 cup Parmesan cheese
2 onions, finely diced
1 medium carrot, finely chopped
1 tablespoon ketchup
1 tablespoon Worcestershire
    sauce
Your favorite hot sauce to taste
Kosher salt and freshly ground
    pepper to taste
1 egg, beaten
¼ cup roughly chopped cilantro

SERVE WITH
Marinara sauce
Toasted baguette or sub roll
Shredded mozzarella cheese

The night before, place ground chicken in a colander over a dish, cover, and refrigerate overnight to drain excess moisture.

The following day, combine chicken with remaining ingredients in a large nonreactive bowl using your hands. (Food-safe gloves are recommended.) Form ping-pong-ball-size meatballs, and spray them lightly with canola oil.

Preheat grill to medium high. Use tongs to place meatballs on grill, and turn as searing occurs. If meatballs are seared on all sides and internal temperature has not reached 165°F, use tongs to place meatballs in a disposable aluminum pan; loosely cover with foil; and finish cooking over indirect heat. Close hood.

To make a meatball sub, add your favorite marinara sauce to the aluminum tray while meatballs are finishing. When sauce is warm, serve meatballs on toasted baguette or sub rolls, along with additional sauce. Top with shredded mozzarella cheese.

DO-AHEAD MINCED BBQ CHICKEN

24 SERVINGS • PREP: 25 MIN. • MARINATE: 2 HR. • GRILL: 1 HR.

12 chicken-leg quarters
1 quart apple cider vinegar
⅓ cup low-sodium chicken broth
⅓ teaspoon onion salt
1 teaspoon coarsely ground
    fresh pepper
2 bay leaves
24 sandwich buns
1 cup Dijon mustard

In a large saucepan, mix together the vinegar, chicken broth, onion salt, pepper, and bay leaves. Bring to a boil over high heat. Place the chicken in a bowl, and pour the hot vinegar mixture over it. Cover, and marinate in the refrigerator for at least 2 hours.

Preheat the grill to medium. Place the chicken on the grill, skin side up. Pour 2 cups of the marinade in a small saucepan, and bring to a boil on the grill. Grill the chicken, turning and basting with the boiled marinade every 10 to 15 minutes for about 1 hour or until the internal temperature reaches 165°F.

Remove the chicken from the grill, and let it cool for about 10 minutes. Cut the chicken from the bone, discarding the bones and skin. Place the meat, four quarters at a time, into a food processor and pulse 3 or 4 times until the chicken is coarsely chopped. (Chop with a knife if a processor is not available.) Repeat this with the remaining chicken. (There should be about 9 cups.)

Boil the remaining marinade to reduce it to 1¼ cups; pour over the minced chicken. Serve on toasted buns spread with mustard. Garnish with a dill pickle slice if desired.

HOW TO GRILL A WHOLE TURKEY

There's more than one way to cook a turkey. Grilling turkey on a gas grill is becoming a popular alternative for this holiday staple. No matter the occasion, your gas grill can produce a beautifully browned bird that's full of flavor. Did we mention that it is also fairly simple? Follow these steps to grill a whole turkey.

1 Start with a good brine. Drying out the turkey is a common faux pas for beginners. A brine is simple to make—it's just salt and water. You'll want to use 1 cup of salt for every gallon of water. Soak your turkey in a brine for an hour per pound. For example, if you have a 15-pound bird, let it brine for 15 hours. You can also try a dry brine with a variety of seasonings for extra flavor.

2 Let it thaw. Allow your turkey to thaw in the refrigerator before grilling. Otherwise, it won't cook properly. Plan ahead, because a 20- to

24-pound turkey can take up to 5–6 days in the fridge. Always place your turkey in a plastic bag for thawing. This will help prevent food contamination.

HOT tip! If you want to speed things up, you can try thawing it in cold water. It takes about 30 minutes per pound.

3 Spatchcocking helps. Spatchcocking is easy to do. Spatchcocking involves removing the spine and flattening the turkey out. It will cook more evenly.

4 Don't guess. You can't tell if a turkey is done just by looking at it. Use a digital meat thermometer to make sure it's cooked properly. Shoot for at least 160°F in the breast and 175°F in the thigh.

STEPS TO SPATCHCOCKING

Spatchcocking is the process of butterflying a whole chicken or turkey, bones and all. To spatchcock a chicken, turkey or really any bird, you are cutting it so that it will lay flat. A flattened chicken will cook evenly and faster than a whole chicken due to a similar thickness throughout. It will also be much easier to manage on the grill and have more surface area to absorb your marinade, seasoning and smoky flavors—if you're using charcoal or wood chips. All you need is a pair of meat shears, a sharp knife, a hard cutting surface, and a chicken or turkey.

1. Place the bird breast side down and grab the tail. Then cut up along the side of the backbone.

2. Cut down the other side of the spine.

3. Remove the backbone.

4. The bird still will not be completely flat. So flip the bird over and find the triangle of cartilage where the breastbone starts.

5. Take a sharp knife and cut down about a quarter inch through the cartilage. Cut so that you can see the breastbone.

6. Use your fingers to open it up. The breastbone will release. At this point, you can remove the breastbone or leave it in if you choose. It's up to you. Even with the breastbone, it will still lay flat.

7. Flip the bird back over. You have a spatchcocked chicken.

8. *Optional:* You can take it one step further and tuck the wings behind the bird, exposing the breast and creating a more flattened bird.

5 Use indirect heat. Even though you're not using your oven, you're transforming your grill into an oven, so to speak. Don't throw your turkey directly over a scorching hot burner like you would with a steak. The outside will be burnt to a crisp and the inside will be undercooked. You want to set up your grill for indirect heat and preheat it to 325°F, or medium heat. Place the turkey on the cool side of the grill to roast.

DIRECT-HEAT GRILLING

Direct heat grills your food right above the heat source. You can use direct heat for searing or for foods that cook quickly. It takes less time to grill with direct heat and foods can burn quickly if you're not careful. In fact, you'll need to keep a watchful eye on your foods with this method. Foods cook right above the burner or fuel. Temperatures in this region can be from 500°F and above. Thinner foods with less water and sugar content cook better with direct heat. For example, steaks, fish, veggies and other tender foods are good options for direct-heat grilling.

INDIRECT-HEAT GRILLING

Indirect heat is cooking on the cooler side of the grill. When the lid is lowered on your grill and you place your food away from the heat source, the grill acts like an oven. It's a great way to cook if your food has high sugar content, is thicker, or if you want to slow roast or barbecue your food. You can also start your foods in the direct zone and transfer them to indirect to finish them. Temperatures in this zone are usually around 225°F, so it will take longer to cook your foods, much like when you bake with an oven. Cook tougher and larger foods like roasts, ribs and whole chickens with indirect heat.

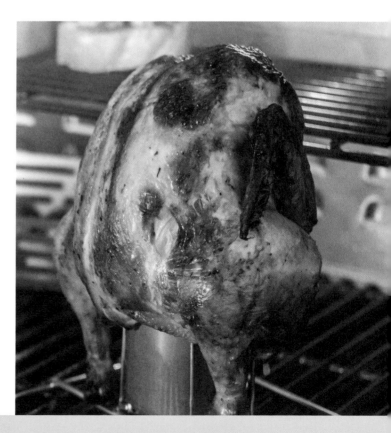

SMOKED TURKEY LEGS

BRINE: 12 HR. • SMOKE: 2½–3½ HR. OR UNTIL INTERNAL TEMP. REACHES 180°F

4 turkey legs
1 tablespoon kosher salt
1 tablespoon coarse ground
    black pepper

BRINE

3 quarts water
1 quart apple juice
1 cup coarse salt
1 cup turbinado sugar (aka Sugar
    in the Raw)
¼ cup bourbon
¼ cup pickling spice

TIPS

- A 16 mesh, dustless Malabar or Telicherry black pepper works very nicely. This will often be labeled as "restaurant grind."
- In this recipe, you can substitute brown sugar for the turbinado sugar.
- You can buy pickling spice at most grocery stores, but it might be with the canning supplies instead of where the other spices are sold.
- This would also be a good cook for the Kettleman, using a fuse burn pattern. If you're using one of the Char-Broil Digital Electric smokers, you'll need to cook them a little longer since their maximum temperature is 275°F.

Combine all of the brine ingredients together in a large pot and bring to a simmer. Stir until all of the salt and sugar has dissolved, about 5 minutes. Remove from heat and allow to cool for an hour and then refrigerate the brine until it is 40°F.

Place the legs into a container just large enough to hold the legs and brine, the legs need to be fully submerged. A 1½-gallon brining bucket works great for this. Refrigerate and let the legs brine for 12 hours.

Preheat your smoker to 300°F. For the Kamander, fill the fire bowl with Char-Broil Center Cut Lump Charcoal and strategically bury several chunks of hickory and cherry wood near the places where the coal is lit. On a warm day the vent settings would be 1½ to 2 for both the top and bottom vents. Place the heat shield/water pan in position with about 1 quart of water in it.

Remove the legs from the brine, rinse them off, and pat them dry. Mix 1 tablespoon each of kosher salt and black pepper together. Season the legs on all sides. Use about half of the seasoning for mild legs and use all of the seasoning for bolder flavored legs.

Place the turkey legs on the upper rack, close the dome lid, and smoke the legs until they reach an internal temperature of 180°F, about 2½ to 3½ hours depending on the size of your legs. Legs that weighed ¾ pounds each took 2 hours and 45 minutes.

GARLIC HERB-ROASTED TURKEY

COOK: UNTIL INTERNAL TEMP. REACHES 165°F • REST: 10 MIN.

TURKEY

10- to 16-pound turkey
1½ cup softened butter
2 tablespoons fresh
    thyme, minced
1 tablespoon fresh sage, minced
½ tablespoon fresh
    rosemary, minced
3 garlic cloves, minced
1 tablespoon lemon zest
1 tablespoon salt
½ tablespoon black pepper

GRAVY

½ cup turkey drippings
½ cup flour
4 cups chicken broth
1 teaspoon ground black pepper

Preheat The Big Easy® fryer at high temperature. Combine the softened butter with the thyme, sage, rosemary, garlic, lemon zest, salt, and black pepper. Mix well until all herbs are evenly incorporated.

Loosen the turkey skin with your fingers by working your hand between the breast and the skin. Place about 2 tablespoons of the seasoned butter under the skin of each breast, then brush the outside of the turkey with the remaining butter.

Place the turkey in The Big Easy® fryer and insert the instant read thermometer in the deepest section of the breast. Cook until the internal temperature of the bird reaches 165°F. Remove the turkey from The Big Easy® fryer and let rest for 10 minutes before serving.

GRAVY

Pour the turkey drippings into a fine mesh strainer to remove any chunks. Place ½ cup of drippings into a saucepan and slowly whisk in flour over medium/high temperature to get a roux. Gradually whisk in the 4 cups of chicken broth then add the black pepper. Simmer for 10 minutes and serve.

PICKY EATERS' THANKSGIVING

TURKEY TENDERS & CRANBERRY BBQ SAUCE

2½ pounds turkey breast tenderloin, cut into 1" thick strips

2 lemons, zest from 1, juice from both

½ cup extra-virgin olive oil

2 tablespoons fresh thyme, minced

2 garlic cloves, minced

¼ cup of your favorite BBQ sauce

½ can jellied cranberry sauce, smashed

1 tablespoon brown sugar

Combine lemon juice, zest, extra-virgin olive oil, garlic, salt, and pepper. Mix well and pour over turkey tenders. Let chill for one hour or up to overnight.

Mix ¼ cup BBQ sauce with smashed cranberry sauce and brown sugar. Season with salt and pepper to taste.

Preheat the grill over medium-high heat for 10 minutes. Grease the grill grates and reduce heat to medium. Put marinated turkey tenders on the grill and grill for 5 minutes per side, or until the internal temperature reaches 165°F. Serve with cranberry BBQ sauce.

SWEET POTATO WEDGES & MARSHMALLOW DIPPING SAUCE

3 similarly sized sweet potatoes, each cut into 8 wedges

2 tablespoons vegetable oil

2 tablespoons minced fresh rosemary

1 teaspoon salt

½ teaspoon black pepper

3 cups mini marshmallows

¼ cup heavy cream

Toss sweet potato wedges with vegetable oil, rosemary, salt, and pepper. Set aside.

Meanwhile, add marshmallows and heavy cream to a saucepan over medium-low heat. Slowly melt while stirring often to keep from burning. Once marshmallows are fully melted, remove from heat and put into serving dish. Set aside.

With the grill heated over medium heat and grates greased, carefully add the wedges and cook for 4 to 5 minutes per side, depending on thickness. If the wedges need more cooking but are becoming charred, toss into a grill-proof dish and set over indirect heat to continue cooking until perfectly soft. Serve wedges with marshmallow dipping sauce.

CANDIED BRUSSELS SPROUTS AND APPLE KEBABS

1 large red apple, cut into 1-inch pieces

½ pound Brussels sprouts, outer leaves removed, bottom trimmed, halved

¼ cup balsamic vinegar

¼ cup maple syrup

¼ cup brown sugar

Extra-virgin olive oil, for drizzling

Salt and pepper, to taste

In a small bowl, combine balsamic vinegar, maple syrup, and brown sugar. Set aside.

Using the Char-Broil stainless steel skewers, carefully alternate threading halved Brussels sprouts and apple pieces onto the skewer. Brush kebabs with maple-brown sugar glaze and sprinkle with salt and pepper.

Add kebabs to a preheated and greased grill over medium heat. Cook for 3 to 4 minutes per side, continuing the brush with glaze often. When the Brussels sprouts are cooked through, remove from grill and brush one final time with the glaze. Serve with any remaining glaze.

CREAMY MAC AND CHEESE

1 stick unsalted butter

½ cup all-purpose flour

2 cups half-and-half

2 cups milk

1 pound cavatappi pasta, cooked al dente

8 ounces sharp cheddar cheese, grated

16 ounces Colby Jack cheese, grated

½ teaspoon dry mustard

½ teaspoon grated nutmeg

1 teaspoon salt, plus more to taste

½ teaspoon black pepper, plus more to taste

Using your Char-Broil Signature Tru-Infrared Grill side burner, bring 8 cups of well-salted water to a boil in a large stock pot. Once boiling, add pasta and cook al dente according to package directions. Drain and set aside.

In the same pot, melt one stick of butter over medium heat. Add a half cup of all-purpose flour and whisk until dissolved and incorporated with no lumps. Slowly pour in half-and-half and milk, whisking continuously. Add dry mustard, nutmeg, salt, and pepper and stir. Let milk mixture thicken over medium-heat for four minutes.

Add shredded cheese and stir to combine and fully melt all of the cheese. Once completely melted and creamy, taste for seasoning. Add more salt and pepper to taste if necessary. Stir in cavatappi pasta and combine well. Keep covered over low heat until serving.

SPICED MAPLE-APPLE CIDER TURKEY

BRINE: 24–48 HR. • COOK: 2½ HR. UNTIL INTERNAL
TEMP. REACHES 160°F • REST: 30 MIN.

1 16-pound fresh turkey, cleaned, trimmed and giblets removed
Seasonal Turkey Brine
Spiced Maple-Apple Cider Glaze
Olive oil
Kosher salt and fresh ground peppercorn, to taste
Homemade or store-bought stuffing

SEASONAL TURKEY BRINE

2 gallons water
1 gallon chicken stock, low or no sodium
1 cup salt
1 cup sugar
2 bay leaves
1 handful of rosemary, sage, thyme sprigs
1 handful of peppercorns
1 head of garlic cloves, smashed

SPICED MAPLE-APPLE CIDER GLAZE

3 cups apple cider
½ cup apple jelly
½ cup maple syrup
3 tablespoons bourbon
2 tablespoons Dijon mustard
2 pinches garlic powder
Kosher salt, to taste

In a large stock pot, bring all Seasonal Turkey Brine ingredients to a rolling boil. Stir intermittently until salt and sugar are dissolved. Remove from heat and allow to cool completely, until brine is at room temperature. Submerge whole, entirely-thawed raw turkey into the brining liquid. Cover pot with a lid and place in refrigerator for 24–48 hours.

Four to six hours prior to cooking, remove the bird from its brine and discard brine. Thoroughly rinse the turkey inside and out with water and pat dry with paper towel. Liberally season every portion of the winged beast with olive oil, salt, and peppercorn, then tightly with plastic and rest at room temperature.

Meanwhile, prepare the Spiced Maple-Apple Cider Glaze by combining all ingredients in a saucepan over medium-high heat. Stirring intermittently, reduce concoction by ⅓. Set aside to cool. Pour reduced liquid into a spray bottle.

Preheat The Big Easy. Remove turkey from its plastic wrapping and set it in the basket, positioned sitting upright with legs-down. Cook the bird for approximately 2½ hours (or 9–10 minutes per pound), until internal temperature of the thickest, inner most portion of the thigh reads 160°F. During the cook intermittently spray the turkey with the Spiced Maple-Apple Cider Glaze, caramelizing one layer of the glaze upon another. Remove bird from The Big Easy, spay one final time with glaze and loosely tent with tinfoil. Rest the bird for 30 minutes before carving, allowing the bird's denatured proteins to relax and reabsorb their juices. Present the bird with a stuffing that was prepared outside of the bird's cavity. Carve the turkey tableside. Season additionally, to taste. Plate. Eat. Drink. Be merry.

Take time enough for your meals, and eat them in company whenever you can. There is no need for hurry in life—least of all when we are eating.

–Edward Everett Hale

THE BIG EASY® SOUTHERN THANKSGIVING TURKEY

10–12 SERVINGS

1 whole turkey, 12–13 pounds
2 tablespoons vegetable or
    peanut oil
1 cup herb seasoning or dry rub

WHICH OIL?

It does not matter which of the two you use—vegetable or peanut. Both are mild in flavor and also have higher smoke points, making them excellent for deep-frying. Avoid heavier oils like olive. These tend to be richer in flavor and will affect the taste of food.

Prepare the turkey for cooking: remove the giblets, neck, etc. Remove any plastic or metal ties used to hold the legs in place. Rinse the turkey in tepid water and pat dry with paper towels. Apply a dry rub on the outside of the turkey. If your hands are small enough, you can also work the rub in between the skin and the meat on the breast and leg/thigh area. Lightly spray or brush oil on outside of turkey. Truss the legs and place the turkey legs down in the cooking basket.

HOT tip! To help prevent sticking, oil the wire in the cooking basket before placing the turkey in it. Insert a meat thermometer in the breast so that the tip does not touch bone and the dial is easily read when the basket is in the cooker.

Light the burner according to instructions in the manual—no pre-heating required. Plan to cook the turkey for approximately 10 minutes per pound, and monitor the temperature closely as the last "planned" 20 minutes begin.

When the thermometer registers about 3°F below the target temperature of 165°F, turn off the cooker and remove the cooking basket with the turkey in it. Place the basket on a shallow sheet pan and allow to rest for about 15 minutes while the turkey continues to cook from internal heat. Remove the turkey from the cooking basket. After the turkey rests for about 20–30 minutes total, it will be ready to carve.

HOT tip! You can use your hands to make sure the turkey doesn't get hung up while trying to remove...and invert the basket and allow the turkey to gently "fall" out.

Food is maybe the only universal thing that really has the power to bring everyone together. No matter what culture, everywhere around the world, people get together to eat.

–Guy Fieri

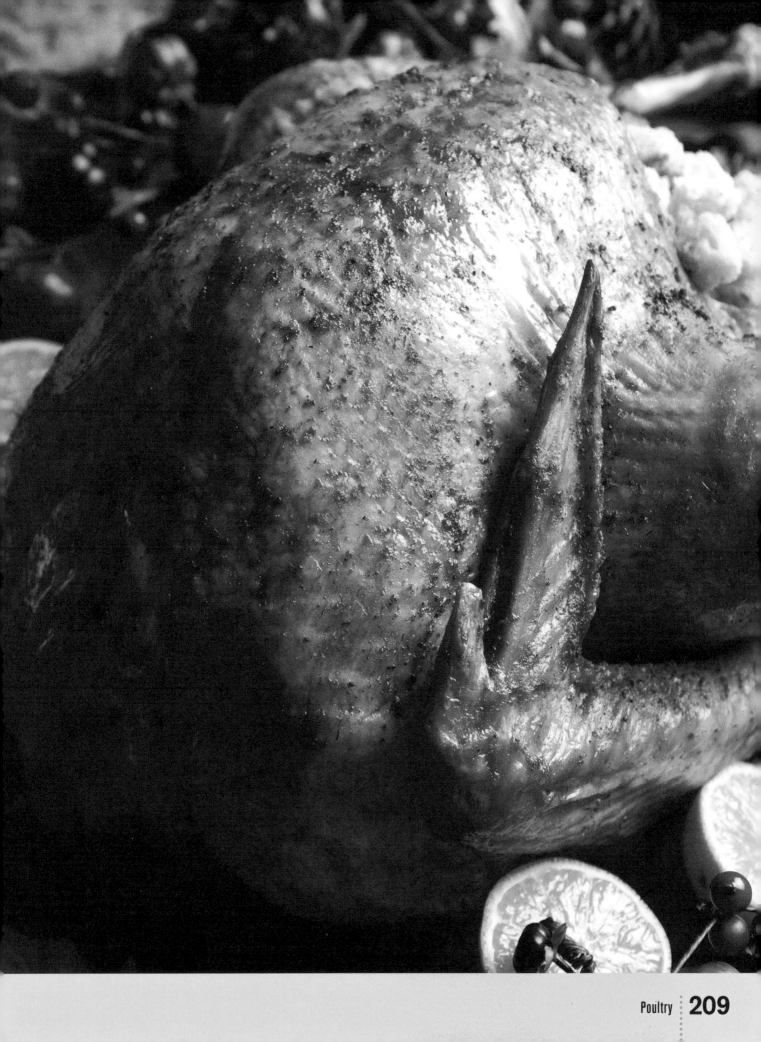

THE BIG EASY®
FRIED THANKSGIVING TURKEY

10–12 SERVINGS • PREP: 15 MIN. • SEE HOT TIP FOR COOK TIME

TURKEY

1 10–16-pound turkey
2 tablespoons of canola oil

MARINADE

½ cup melted butter
½ cup chicken stock
1 splash bourbon

DRY RUB

2 tablespoons paprika
1 tablespoon ancho chile powder
1 tablespoon cayenne
    pepper flakes
1 tablespoon onion powder
1 tablespoon garlic powder
1 tablespoon dried thyme
1 teaspoon ground bay leaves
1 tablespoon salt
1 tablespoon ground
    black pepper

HOT tip! Use the drippings from the drip tray for gravy.

Remove turkey giblets and the neck from the turkey. Rinse the bird thoroughly, and pat the turkey dry using paper towels. Brush the skin of the turkey with canola oil. Mix the melted butter, chicken stock and bourbon together. Inject the marinade into each breast and leg of the bird using a marinade injector.

Place the bird breast side up inside the cooking basket. Then, place the basket into The Big Easy® Oil-less Turkey Fryer. Turn on the cooker to medium-high, cooking to an internal temperature of 165°F in the deepest section of the breast. Remove the basket from The Big Easy® Oil-less Turkey Fryer, and let the bird rest for 10 to 15 minutes before taking it out from the basket.

HOT tip! Cook times in The Big Easy® Oil-less Turkey Fryer will vary depending on outdoor weather conditions and the weight of your turkey. In general, you can expect roughly 10 minutes of cook time per pound.

APPLEWOOD SMOKED TURKEY BREAST

2–3 SERVINGS • PREP: 20 MIN. • COOK: 3 HR.

TURKEY
1 turkey breast, split

MARINADE
1 teaspoon barbecue rub
4 tablespoons melted butter

ADDITIONAL SEASONING
Salt & pepper to taste

JUST THE FACTS . . . ABOUT TURKEY BREAST

Smoking a turkey doesn't have to be a daunting task. Using a turkey breast is more manageable than a whole turkey and takes a fraction of the time.

You can easily double this recipe by adding another turkey breast and doubling the amount of barbecue rub and melted butter.

Combine the 1 teaspoon of barbecue rub and 4 tablespoons of melted butter. Allow the combination cool to room temperature. While the combination cools, let the split turkey breast come to room temperature as well. Using a marinade injector, inject the cooled rub and butter into the turkey breast at regular intervals. If you don't own an injector, use a fork to poke holes into the meat, and massage the cooled butter and rub into the turkey breast.

Prepare your smoker according to directions. If using your grill, heat one half of the grill to medium low (300°F–325°F). Make sure to leave the other half of the grill off. This will create two separate cooking zones: one with direct heat and the other with indirect. Add applewood chips to your smoker. If using your grill, add a handful of applewood chips to an aluminum foil pouch or cast-iron smoker box. Let the pouch or smoker box heat on the direct-heat side of the grill until smoke appears.

HOT tip! If using a foil pouch, make sure to seal the foil pouch tightly. Poke a small hole in the top.

With smoke appearing, salt and pepper the turkey skin. Place the breast into the smoker or in an aluminum pan on the indirect side if using the grill. Smoking times will vary based on your smoker or grill type, weather conditions, etc. Cooking to the internal temperature is the best way to ensure that the turkey is safely prepared, but not over cooked. Use a thermometer to verify that your turkey has reached an internal temperature of 160°F in the breast meat. Check the temperature of the turkey after about 3 hours of cooking.

GRILLED SAGE & APPLE TURKEY

GRILL: 3 HR. OR UNTIL INTERNAL TEMP. REACHES 160–165°F IN BREASTS
AND 175–180°F IN THIGHS • REST: 10–15 MIN.

1 12–14-pound turkey, thawed
and spatchcocked

INJECTION
⅓ cup chicken stock
½ cup unsalted butter
¼ cup honey
¼ ounce dried apple
4 whole sage leaves

COMPOUND BUTTER
1½ sticks butter
¼ teaspoon dried lemon peel, in
addition to the apple and sage
from the injection mix

POULTRY RUB
1 tablespoon kosher salt
2 teaspoons ground black pepper
1½ teaspoons granulated garlic
½ teaspoon lemon peel
½ teaspoon dried parsley

Combine the stock, butter and honey in a saucepan over low heat. Add the apple and sage, bring to a simmer and then shut off the burner. Let the mixture steep for 5 minutes. Combine the butter and lemon peel. Remove the sage and apple from the injection mix and finely mince them. Stir into the butter and lemon peel. Set aside.

Combine the salt, black pepper, garlic, dried lemon peel, and parsley together in a small bowl. Set up the grill for raised direct cooking and preheat to medium low heat (325°F). Inject the turkey. Flip the turkey skin side down. Fill a meat syringe with the injection and inject the mixture from the back side of the breasts and thighs, refilling the syringe as needed. Inject the legs in two or three places from the front side.

HOT tip! Injecting the bird from the backside avoids tearing the skin on the front side. Inject slowly as you pull the needle back out.

Stuff the compound butter under the skin of the turkey. Whatever is left in the bowl can be melted and drizzled over the top of the turkey to help the rub stick to the bird.

HOT tip! Once under the skin, you can massage the butter into place from above. Season the turkey on front and back with the rub.

Place the turkey skin side up on the elevated grill grate, close the lid and cook over medium-low heat until the internal temperature of the breasts are 160°F–165°F and the thighs are 175°F–180°F. With this set up and heat, that should take about 15 minutes per pound or three hours total. Remove the turkey from the grill and allow to rest for 10–15 minutes before serving.

HOT tip! Always use a quality digital thermometer to verify that the breasts are 160°F–165°F and the thighs are 175°F–180°F.

I think people are intimidated by grilling . . . but I think that grilling is actually the easiest technique in cooking.
–Bobby Flay

BBQ SMOKED TURKEY WINGS

MARINATE: 2–24 HR. • SMOKE: UNTIL INTERNAL TEMP. REACHES 165°F

6 turkey wings
Favorite BBQ sauce
Cherry wood chips

Segment the turkey wings by cutting at the joints. Discard the wing tips. Marinate the wings in your favorite BBQ sauce from anywhere between 2–24 hours. If using a grill, set up heat for indirect grilling and place a smoker box with wood chips. Add the turkey wings to the other side of the grill. Let smoke until internal temperature reaches 165°F. Use your digital meat thermometer to be sure.

JUST THE FACTS . . . ABOUT TURKEY WINGS

Ditch the chicken and try smoking turkey wings instead. Just like chicken wings, turkey wings can be rubbed, coated, or slathered in any variety of delicious flavors. Even better, turkey wings are naturally larger, meaning there's more juicy meat to enjoy than what you get with just an average chicken wing. In this recipe for BBQ smoked turkey wings, we keep things simple by using any favorite BBQ sauce to flavor the smoked turkey. Feel free to switch things up to create BBQ turkey wings of your own liking. Prefer a rub? Maybe a fruity BBQ marinade? The possibilities are endless and all BBQ flavor combinations will be delicious with the added flavor of smoke.

CB'S GRILLED DUCK BREASTS WITH SWEET POTATO FRIES

2 SERVINGS • PREP: 20 MIN. • SAUTÉ AND GRILL: 10–15 MIN.

1 teaspoon garlic powder

1 teaspoon dried cumin

1 teaspoon Chinese-style
   dry mustard

1 teaspoon dry ginger

1 teaspoon curry powder

1 teaspoon kosher salt or sea salt

1 teaspoon fresh ground
   black pepper

2 medium-size duck breasts,
   approximately 6–8
   ounces each

1 tablespoon high-heat cooking
   oil (preferably canola
   or grapeseed)

1 medium-size sweet potato

4 tablespoons Parmesan cheese

2 tablespoons flat leaf
   parsley, chopped

4 tablespoons extra virgin olive oil

Combine the first seven ingredients in a bowl. Rinse duck, and pat it dry. Gently rub the spice mixture onto the duck. You may also want to pierce the skin in several places to help the fat escape. Let duck rest at room temperature for about 20 minutes. Cut the sweet potato into equal-size slices, and place in cold, salted water.

Preheat the grill to high. Preheat a cast-iron skillet to hot; add 1 teaspoon of canola oil. Gently place duck in the skillet, fat side down. Cook, without turning, for about 3 to 4 minutes. When skin is golden, turn the breasts over, and sear the meat for an additional minute; then lift and place meat side down on the grill. Reserve the duck fat in the skillet. Reduce grill heat to medium-low, and close the lid. Cook duck for 4 minutes; then remove, and cover until meat reaches 135°F for rare.

Add the remaining canola oil to duck fat in skillet, and allow to heat to smoking point. Remove potato slices from the water; pat very dry; then place about half of the slices in the skillet. Cook fries in batches until tender, but not browned. When all the fries are done, return them to the hot oil to brown; drain on paper towels. Sprinkle fries with Parmesan and parsley, and arrange them on a plate. Slice the duck meat, and arrange on plate with the fries. Drizzle with olive oil, and serve.

6

The key to good grilling is to recognize that you are setting yourself up to cook in a whole new environment. This is actually one of the main purposes of grilling—to get yourself outside.

–Barton Seaver

Seafood

GRILLED CLAMS

PREP: 30 MIN. • COOK: 10 MIN. • TOTAL TIME: 40 MIN.

3–4 pounds littleneck or
    Venus clams
1 pound ground chorizo
2 shallots, sliced
2 medium tomatoes, diced
1½ cups dry white wine
1½ teaspoons smoked paprika
3 cloves garlic, minced
1 stick unsalted butter
2 tablespoons extra-virgin olive oil
Salt and pepper, to taste
French baguette, sliced 1-inch
    thick on the diagonal

Put clams in a bowl of cold water and let stand at least 30 minutes to an hour. Remove the clams one by one, scrub free of dirt and place in a colander. Rinse one more time with cold water.

On the side burner of your Char-Broil Signature Tru-Infrared Grill, heat a small drizzle of extra-virgin olive oil over medium-high heat in a heavy-bottomed skillet. Add the chorizo and cook until cooked through, approximately 6 to 8 minutes. Using a slotted spoon, remove the chorizo and leave approximately 2 tablespoons of the chorizo fat in the pan. Add shallots and sauté for 2 minutes. Add in the white wine, tomatoes, smoked paprika, garlic, unsalted butter, salt, and pepper. Let simmer for 8 minutes.

Meanwhile, preheat the grill to 500°F. Add the clams and cook for about 6 minutes, until the shells pop open. As they open, remove from the grill grate and toss into the sauce simmering on the side burner. (Note: If a clam doesn't open up, toss it, it's no good!) When all of the clams are removed, lay the slices of baguette on the grill to warm up and get extra crispy around the edges, approximately 1 minute per side. When all of the clams are in the sauce, stir to coat. Serve with grilled bread or even on top of a plate of linguine.

MINI TEQUILA LIME SHRIMP TACOS AND PINEAPPLE SALSA

PREP: 10 MIN. • MARINATE: 30 MIN. • COOK: 2 MIN.

SHRIMP

1 pound 21/30 size shrimp, fully
    peeled and deveined
2 limes, juice from both, zest
    from 1
¼ cup tequila
2 teaspoons chili powder
1 teaspoon salt
¼ teaspoon black pepper

SALSA

1½ cups finely diced
    fresh pineapple
1 small avocado, finely diced
1 plum tomato, seeded and
    finely diced
1 tablespoon cilantro, minced
1 jalapeño, seeds and ribs
    removed, finely diced
1 lime, juiced
Salt and pepper, to taste

TACO ASSEMBLY

16–20 small soft flour tortillas
1 cup finely shredded
    green cabbage
1 cup finely shredded
    purple cabbage
½ cup sour cream
1 teaspoon chili powder

Combine the juice from 2 limes, the zest from 1 lime, tequila, 1 teaspoon chili powder, 1 teaspoon salt, and ½ teaspoon black pepper in a bowl with a lid. Add shrimp, cover, and let marinate 30 minutes. Note: Do not marinate longer than 30 minutes, as the acid will begin to cook and break down the shrimp.

For the salsa, combine pineapple, avocado, tomato, cilantro, jalapeño, juice of one lime and salt and pepper. Set aside. Combine ½ cup sour cream and 1 teaspoon chili powder. Set aside.

Using a 4-inch round cookie cutter, cut circles out of the tortillas to create "mini" soft taco shells. Preheat your Patio Bistro Electric Grill on high heat for 10 to 15 minutes. While preheating, skewer your marinated shrimp using wooden skewers that have been soaked for at least 10 minutes or, preferably, using Char-Broil's stainless steel skewers.

Place shrimp skewers on the grill and cook over medium-high for approximately 1–2 minutes per side, being careful not to overcook. Remove from grill. Add tortillas to the grill for 1 minute per side to get nice grill marks and make tortillas warm and pliable.

Begin building tacos. Add a teaspoon or so of the sour cream mixture to the center of each tortilla. Spread it evenly and top with a bit of red and green cabbage. Top cabbage with 2 shrimp and a nice spoonful of the pineapple salsa. Serve immediately.

BROWN SUGAR-BRINED SMOKED SALMON

MARINATE: 6–7 HR. • COOK: 3 HR. OR UNTIL INTERNAL TEMP. REACHES 160°F

BRINE
3 cups warm water

1 cup soy sauce

½ cup brown sugar

1 tablespoon fresh garlic, diced

1 tablespoon onion powder

½ tablespoon fresh ginger, grated

SALMON
2 pounds salmon fillets

In a large baking dish, mix water, soy sauce, brown sugar, garlic, onion powder, and ginger until well combined. Let cool completely. Add fish fillets and let rest in the fridge for 6–7 hours.

Preheat the smoker to 160°F and add alder wood chips to the smoker box. Place the salmon in the smoker and cook for about 3 hours.

Use a digital thermometer to check the internal temperature of the salmon. Remove from smoker once the fish reaches 160°F or until the fillets take on a light pink color and begin to flake apart.

An instant-read thermometer is your best bet for making sure that meat and fish are cooked to the proper temperature.
–Bobby Flay

BOURBON-MARINATED SMOKED SALMON

MARINATE: 1 ½ HR. • COOK: UNTIL INTERNAL TEMP. REACHES 150°F

MARINADE

2 tablespoons bourbon
3 tablespoons brown sugar
2 tablespoons soy sauce
1 tablespoon Dijon mustard

SOUR CREAM SAUCE

½ cup sour cream
2 tablespoons Dijon mustard
2 tablespoons finely chopped dill
1 teaspoon lemon juice
4 boneless, skinless salmon filets
Salt and pepper to taste

Combine the bourbon, brown sugar, soy sauce and mustard. Put the salmon in a gallon plastic bag, add the marinade and distribute evenly. Refrigerate for 1 ½ hours. Add a handful of cherry wood chips to the smoker box of the Char-Broil Digital Smoker. Add water to the recommended level in the water pan. Preheat the smoker for 40 minutes. Once preheated, set the temperature for 210°F.

Remove the salmon from the refrigerator and place on a foil-lined rimmed baking sheet, spacing the salmon apart so the smoke can circulate freely. Put the salmon in the smoker, attach the digital thermometer and put the probe in the thickest part of the salmon. Set the thermometer for 150°F internal temperature. Smoke the salmon until the internal temperature of 150°F is reached.

Remove the salmon and let rest while combining the sour cream, mustard, dill and lemon juice in a small bowl. Mix thoroughly. Serve the salmon with the sour cream sauce on the side.

CB'S GRILLED SALMON WITH SHALLOT & LEMON GLAZE

2 SERVINGS • PREP: 10 MIN. • GRILL: 10–15 MIN.

12- to-16-ounce salmon fillet

SAUCE
4 ounces anchovy fillets or paste
2 tablespoons finely
    chopped shallots
3 tablespoons extra-virgin olive oil
3 garlic cloves, finely chopped
½ teaspoon Worcestershire sauce
Juice from ½ lemon
3 tablespoons chopped parsley
1 tablespoon red wine vinegar
Canola oil spray

Rinse the fish under cool water, and pat dry with paper towels. Place portions in freezer to chill, but do not freeze.

Rinse and drain anchovies. Mash them in a bowl with shallots, olive oil, minced garlic, and Worcestershire sauce. Stir in lemon juice; vinegar; parsley; cover; and let stand for at least 1 hour. (If you prefer to make this ahead, chill the fish.)

Preheat grill to high. Remove fish from freezer, and spray both sides with canola oil. Place fish on grates, and sear, skin side down, about 3 to 5 minutes. Use a lightly oiled spatula to turn, and then sear the other side, about 3 to 5 minutes. Move seared fish to unheated section of grill. Brush sauce onto fish, and allow it to finish cooking. Gently insert knife into center of fillet. Fish is done when the interior is translucent and firm but not dry. Arrange fish on platter, and add more sauce if desired.

CB'S GRILLED SALMON WITH BACON & TOMATO SALSA

4 SERVINGS • PREP: 20 MIN. • GRILL: 15 MIN.
(UNTIL INTERIOR TEMP. OF THICKEST PART IS 145°F)

4 salmon steaks or fillets, approximately 6 ounces each
10 to 12 sprigs fresh thyme
2 slices thick bacon
½ cup diced red onions
1 tablespoon minced garlic
Freshly ground coarse salt and black pepper to taste
Canola, safflower, or other neutral, high-temperature oil
10 ounces (about 1 can) mild diced tomatoes with green chilies, well drained

Preheat grill to medium high. Finely chop thyme, and discard stems.

Cut bacon into ¼-inch pieces; lightly brown in a pan; and remove. Add onions to the bacon drippings, and cook until onions are sweated. Combine onions, bacon, and garlic; heat gently.

Season the salmon with salt, pepper, and thyme. Spray salmon with canola oil. Sear on both sides.

Place salmon in a foil pan on an unheated section of the grill. Close hood, and allow salmon to finish cooking until the fish is opaque in the center; the thickest part of the fish should register 145°F.

Add tomatoes to bacon mixture; simmer 4 to 5 minutes until thick. Spoon salsa over the salmon.

SUGGESTED FLAVOR COMBINATIONS

Mexican–lime, cilantro, onion, Mexican seasoning
Mediterranean–lemon, oregano, basil, Italian seasoning
Continental–lemon, dill, leeks, lemon-pepper seasoning
Cajun–lemon, onion, celery salt, Cajun seasoning

HERBED WHOLE SALMON ON THE GRILL

8 SERVINGS • PREP: 20 MIN. • GRILL: 45–60 MIN.

1 whole salmon or large salmon fillet, fresh, thawed, or frozen

4 sheets heavy-duty aluminum foil, 6 inches larger than length of salmon

1 large onion, sliced, or 2 leeks, separated into leaves

1 lemon or lime, halved

1 tablespoon preferred seasoning mix

1½ cups coarsely chopped fresh herbs (See suggested combinations of seasonings and herbs, above.)

Rinse any ice glaze from frozen salmon under cold water, and pat dry with paper towels. Lay out two sheets of aluminum foil, double thickness, on a large tray. Spray top layer with cooking spray.

Lay half of the onions or leeks lengthwise in center of the foil. Place salmon on top of onions; then squeeze lemon or lime on both sides of fish. Sprinkle dry seasoning on both sides of salmon. Place fresh herbs over, under, and–if fish is not frozen–inside the belly cavity of the fish.

Lay out remaining two sheets of foil, double thickness. Spray top sheet with oil; then place, coated side down, over salmon. Roll up, crimp, and seal all sides of foil to form a packet.

Cook salmon over medium-hot grill, 5 to 6 inches from heat, for 50 to 60 minutes if frozen; 45 to 55 minutes if fresh or thawed, turning packet every 15 minutes. Cook just until fish is opaque throughout.

ASIAN SALMON BURGERS

4 SERVINGS • PREP: 30 MIN. • GRILL: 10 MIN.

1 pound salmon fillet, skin and pinbones removed, cut into 1-inch pieces
1 tablespoon minced ginger
1 tablespoon minced garlic
2 green onions, including 2 inches of green tops, very thinly sliced
½ tablespoon chopped fresh cilantro
1 teaspoon kosher or sea salt
1 tablespoon fresh lemon juice
½ tablespoon soy sauce
½ cup cracker meal
2 large eggs, lightly beaten

In a food processor fitted with a metal blade, pulse salmon just until coarsely ground, scraping down sides of work bowl once or twice. (Be careful; it's easy to go from chopped to mashed paste in seconds!)

Transfer salmon to a medium bowl. Add ginger, garlic, green onions, cilantro, salt, lemon juice, and soy sauce. Using a rubber spatula, mix to combine. Mix in cracker meal; add eggs. Dividing salmon mixture evenly; form into four 1-inch-thick patties. Refrigerate for at least 20 minutes before cooking. Patties can be prepared and refrigerated up to 8 hours ahead.

Preheat grill to medium. Place salmon burgers on grill, and cook for 4 to 5 minutes. Turn, and cook for an additional 4 to 5 minutes.

**Food is not just eating energy. It's an experience.
–Guy Fieri**

CHARRED SUGAR-CRUSTED SALMON

4 SERVINGS • PREP: 10 MIN. • GRILL: 10 MIN.

4 to 6 skinless salmon fillets (4 to 6 ounces each)
2 tablespoons canola oil
¼ to ⅓ cup hot Chinese-style or Dijon-style mustard, if desired

DRY SUGAR RUB

2 tablespoons sugar
1 tablespoon chili powder
1 teaspoon black pepper
½ tablespoon ground cumin
½ tablespoon paprika
½ tablespoon salt
¼ teaspoon dry mustard
Dash of cinnamon

Oil a cast-iron griddle, and preheat over grill or outdoor stovetop over medium-high heat. Blend all ingredients for dry sugar rub. Generously coat one side of each salmon fillet with rub.

Carefully place salmon fillets on griddle, seasoned side down. Cook about 2 minutes to sear; turn fillets over. Reduce heat to medium, and continue cooking 6 to 8 minutes. Cook just until fish is opaque throughout.

Serve salmon over rice with mustard if desired.

LEMON & GINGER GRILLED ALASKAN SALMON STRIPS

4 SERVINGS • PREP: 25 MIN. • MARINATE: 30 MIN. • GRILL: 7–10 MIN.

1 ½ pound Alaskan salmon fillet, skin on
¼ cup canola oil
¼ cup lemon juice
2 tablespoons soy sauce
2 tablespoons honey
½ teaspoon ground ginger
¼ cup chopped green onion
1 teaspoon lemon peel

Cut salmon fillet into 1 ¼-inch strips. Mix canola oil, lemon juice, soy sauce, honey, ginger, green onion, and lemon peel together in a large, shallow glass dish. Add salmon strips, and coat well. Marinate 30 minutes, turning several times. Preheat grill to medium high. Remove salmon strips from marinade; discard the liquid.

Place salmon, skin side up, on grill for 3 minutes. Turn carefully, and continue to cook, skin side down, for an additional 3 to 4 minutes, or until just done and center flakes with fork. To remove strips from grill, run spatula between skin and salmon. This will provide a plate-ready, skinless strip. Garnish dish with chopped green onion, lemon peel, and lemon slices.

NORTH AFRICAN-STYLE GRILLED SALMON

4 SERVINGS • PREP: 30 MIN. • GRILL: 10 MIN.

4 salmon steaks or fillets (4 to 6 ounces each), fresh, thawed, or frozen

1 4-ounce jar green olives, drained and sliced

¾ cup low-fat plain yogurt

½ cup chopped parsley

¼ cup chopped cilantro

3 tablespoons lemon juice

2 tablespoons olive oil

1 tablespoon minced garlic

2 teaspoons paprika

1 teaspoon ground cumin

1 teaspoon turmeric

½ teaspoon salt

¼ teaspoon red pepper flakes

1½ tablespoons olive or canola oil

1 teaspoon lemon-pepper seasoning

2 tablespoons slivered red onion

Reserve 2 tablespoons of the olives. Blend remaining olives, yogurt, parsley, cilantro, lemon juice, olive oil, garlic, paprika, cumin, turmeric, salt, and pepper flakes; set aside. Rinse any ice glaze from frozen salmon under cold water, and pat dry with a paper towel. Preheat grill to medium-high.

Coat a heavy skillet with oil, and place on grill to preheat. Brush both sides of salmon with oil. Place salmon in heated skillet, and cook, uncovered, about 3 to 4 minutes, until browned. Turn salmon over, and sprinkle with lemon pepper. Cover pan tightly, and reduce heat to medium. Cook an additional 6 to 8 minutes for frozen salmon; 3 to 4 minutes for fresh or thawed fish. To serve, spoon sauce over each salmon portion, and sprinkle with reserved olives and slivered onion.

SALMON TARRAGON

4 SERVINGS • PREP: 30 MIN. • GRILL: 10 MIN.

4 salmon fillets (6–8 ounces each)
Salt and pepper
1 medium onion, diced
2 teaspoons dried tarragon
2 tablespoons chopped shallots
½ cup white wine
2 tablespoons Dijon mustard
¼ cup chicken stock
¼ cup light cream

Preheat grill to medium-high. Sprinkle salmon fillets with salt and pepper; let stand for 5 to 10 minutes.

Add remaining ingredients to medium saucepan; bring to a slow boil.

Grill salmon over medium-high heat until flesh is just opaque throughout. Drizzle with sauce, and serve.

GRILLED TILAPIA WITH SUN-DRIED TOMATOES

2 SERVINGS • PREP: 20 MIN. • GRILL: 10 MIN.

2 tilapia fillets (8 to 10
    ounces each)
1 teaspoon lemon juice
Salt and pepper to taste
1 teaspoon chopped
    fresh cilantro
2 sun-dried tomatoes, julienned
1 medium tomato, diced
½ cup white wine
¼ red onion, diced
1 teaspoon chopped fresh parsley
¼ cup light cream

Preheat grill to medium low. Mix together lemon juice, salt, pepper, and cilantro. Pour over fish in a flat dish. In a medium saucepan, mix together all remaining ingredients except for cream. Bring to a boil; then add cream. Remove from heat. Grill tilapia 8 to 10 minutes, turning once. Place on plate; cover with sauce; and serve.

Wrap fish fillets, sliced veggies, and other quick-cooking items inside foil packets with bundles of fresh herbs and throw them directly on the grill; the steam will release the herb's perfume and flavor anything contained inside the pouch.

–Emeril Lagasse

CB'S SNAPPER GRILLED ON A BED OF LIMES

2 SERVINGS • PREP: 10 MIN. • GRILL: 10–15 MIN.

2 snapper fillets or other delicate fish

3 large limes, very thinly sliced

2 teaspoons melted butter per fillet

Smoked paprika for seasoning and color

Canola oil spray

Preheat the grill to medium high. Carefully rinse the fish, and pat dry with paper towels. Spray one side of the lime slices with canola oil, and arrange them in the center of the grill to form a "bed" for each fillet.

Lay the fish atop the lime slices, and baste with melted butter and a generous pinch of smoked paprika. Lightly tent the fish fillets with heavy-duty aluminum foil, or cover each with a small foil pan. Reduce the heat to medium, and allow the limes to char and release their juices to flavor the fish.

Check the fish after about 10 to 15 minutes. When fish is opaque and firm to the touch, slip a lightly oiled spatula beneath the limes and lift the fish off the grill. Serve fish on individual plates, and garnish with parsley if desired.

This is an easy, flavorful method for grilling snapper, sole, or any thin fish fillets, which tend to fall apart on a hot grill.–CB

CAJUN GRILLED MAHI-MAHI WITH AVOCADO SALAD

4 SERVINGS • PREP: 20 MIN. • GRILL: 8–10 MIN.

4 fillets of mahi-mahi, 4 ounces each
1 tablespoon canola oil
1 tablespoon Cajun seasoning
2 large, ripe avocados, peeled and diced
1 cup corn kernels, cooked

1 16-ounce can black beans, drained and rinsed
¼ cup red onion, diced
1 medium tomato, diced
1 medium green bell pepper, diced
2 tablespoons fresh cilantro, chopped

1 tablespoon jalapeño, minced (optional) 2 tablespoons lime juice
¼ cup olive oil
½ teaspoon cumin
Salt and pepper to taste

Preheat grill to medium high. Brush the fillets with the oil, and sprinkle both sides with Cajun seasoning. Grill for about 4 to 5 minutes on each side, until the fish is cooked to your desired doneness and nicely browned.

Meanwhile, combine in a bowl the avocado, corn, black beans, red onion, tomato, bell pepper, cilantro, and jalapeño. Stir together olive oil, lime juice, and cumin, and add to salad. Season to taste with salt and pepper, and toss.

Top each fillet with some of the avocado salad, and serve immediately.

CB'S RAINBOW TROUT STUFFED WITH LEMON, SHALLOTS & HERBS

2 SERVINGS • PREP: 10–15 MIN. • GRILL: 15–20 MIN.

2 12- to 14-inch rainbow trout, cleaned (head and tail removed if desired)
Salt and freshly ground pepper

2 tablespoons shallots, minced
2 small lemons, sliced very thin
1 bunch dill, divided
1 bunch tarragon, divided

Canola oil spray
Seasoned wood chips if desired

Preheat grill to high. Season the cavity of each fish with salt and pepper; add 1 tablespoon of shallots to each; and rub all ingredients into the fish. Add lemon slices, dill, and tarragon. Secure stuffing by wrapping fish with kitchen twine or sealing with toothpicks if necessary.

Spray skin of each fish with canola oil. Place fish in grill basket and close.

Reduce heat of grill to medium. Place fish basket on the grill, and cover with a piece of aluminum foil to retain heat and moisture. Close hood, and cook for approximately 5 to 7 minutes. Lift basket off grill to check for grill marks; turn basket; and grill on other side, about 5 to 7 minutes.

Remove basket, and place it in a pan to allow the fish to rest for a few minutes. Using two spatulas to support the fish on each end, remove from the basket, and place on a plate.

To debone fish, insert the tip of a sharp boning knife into the top of the fish and "feel" your way to the spine. Run the knife gently along the spine toward the tail. Use two forks to lift off this half of the fish; then pinch the top end of the spine with two fingers, and peel it away from the bottom half of the fish. Replace the top half.

For a quick sauce, briefly sauté thin lemon slices with pinches of the tarragon and dill in a touch of butter and olive oil until the lemon releases its aroma. Drizzle over each fish serving, and place a lemon slice on top.

Trout is available nearly year-round in just about every market. This recipe is easy because I use a fish basket to hold the stuffed fillets—it makes turning a breeze.—CB

FAST & SPICY HALIBUT

4 SERVINGS • PREP: 15 MIN. • GRILL: ABOUT 15 MIN.

4 halibut steaks or fillets (4 to 6 ounces each), fresh, thawed, or frozen

1 tablespoon paprika

1½ teaspoons each dried oregano and dried thyme

1 teaspoon each onion powder and garlic powder

1 teaspoon each black pepper and salt

½ teaspoon cayenne pepper, or to taste

1½ tablespoons butter, melted

Preheat grill to medium high. Mix together all dry-seasoning ingredients until well combined. Rinse any ice glaze from frozen halibut under cold water; pat dry with paper towel. Place fish on a spray-coated or foil-lined baking sheet. Brush butter onto top surfaces of halibut, and sprinkle with ½ teaspoon seasoning mixture.

Grill halibut 5 to 7 inches from heat for 13 to 15 minutes for frozen halibut or 8 minutes for fresh fish. Note: For best results with frozen fish, cook halibut 4 minutes before adding butter and spices. Cook just until fish is opaque throughout.

GRILLED HALIBUT WITH A GREEN-CHILI BLANKET

4 SERVINGS • PREP: 10 MIN. • GRILL: 10–20 MIN.

Recipe by Toni Bocci of Cordova, Arkansas

4 halibut steaks or fillets, fresh or frozen (4 to 6 ounces each)
½ cup mayonnaise or plain, low-fat yogurt
1 4-ounce can mild green chilies, diced
1 tablespoon fresh lime juice
1 12 x 18-inch sheet aluminum foil
1 tablespoon chopped fresh cilantro or chives

Preheat grill to medium-high. Combine mayonnaise, green chilies, and lime juice; set aside.

Rinse any ice glaze from frozen halibut under cold water; pat dry with a paper towel. Place halibut on spray-coated foil sheet on grill. Cook 9 minutes for frozen halibut; 5 minutes for fresh or thawed fish.

Turn halibut over, and liberally spoon mayonnaise mixture onto cooked side of each portion. Sprinkle with cilantro, and cook an additional 5 to 10 minutes until fish is just opaque throughout.

THAI-STYLE HALIBUT SKEWERS

6 SERVINGS • PREP: 30 MIN. • GRILL: 10 MIN.

1½ pounds boneless, skinless halibut steaks or fillets, cut into 1½ inch pieces
2 tablespoons vegetable oil
1 tablespoon Thai green curry paste
1 tablespoon freshly grated ginger
1 tablespoon rice wine vinegar
1 teaspoon nam pla (Thai fish sauce)
1 teaspoon toasted sesame oil
12 wood skewers, soaked for 30 minutes

Thoroughly blend oil, curry paste, ginger, vinegar, fish sauce, and sesame oil. Brush mixture on fish; cover; and refrigerate for 30 minutes.

Preheat grill to medium high. Thread halibut onto skewers, two to three pieces per skewer. Place skewers on well-oiled grill. Grill halibut directly above heat source for 4 to 5 minutes per side, turning once during cooking. Cook just until fish is opaque throughout.

GRILLED HALIBUT WITH LEMON-CAPER BUTTER

2 SERVINGS • PREP: 5 MIN. • GRILL: 7–10 MIN.

Courtesy of Jess Thomson at jessthomson.wordpress.com

2 halibut fillets
   (about ¾ pound total)
Olive oil
Salt and pepper
3 tablespoons butter
2 tablespoons capers
2 tablespoons freshly squeezed
   lemon juice

Preheat grill to medium high. Pat the fish dry. Brush with olive oil, and season with salt and pepper on both sides. Grill halibut 5 minutes on the first side and 2 to 5 minutes on the other side, depending on the thickness of the fish.

Meanwhile, melt the butter over low heat in a small saucepan. When melted, stir in the capers and lemon juice, and season with salt and pepper. Spoon the sauce over the fish right after it comes off the grill.

Here's a quick sauce for grilled fish that delivers a huge citrus punch. It's less like a lemon-caper butter than caper- and butter-flavored lemon juice.

Our smoky seared tuna loin is a terrific summer entrée for an intimate dinner party. We start with the freshest and best tuna "tenderloin" we can buy, and then we do our best to leave it alone. Just add a simple marinade, some heat, some smoke, and WOW!–"Girls on a Grill," *girlsonagrill.com*

SMOKY SEARED TUNA LOIN

6 SERVINGS • PREP: 6 HR. • MARINATE: 2–6 HR. • GRILL: 6–10 MIN.

1 fresh sashimi-grade tuna loin, about 3 pounds
¼ cup soy sauce
2 tablespoons honey
Juice and zest of one lime
1 teaspoon sesame oil
1 teaspoon hot sauce
½ teaspoon ground ginger
½ teaspoon garlic powder
2 tablespoons fresh cilantro, stems and leaves, chopped
2 limes, quartered
Wood chips

Mix all of the ingredients, except the tuna, in a bowl; pour ¾ of it into a sealable plastic bag. Reserve remaining portion for sauce. Place tuna loin in bag; seal; and allow to rest in the refrigerator between 2 and 6 hours.

About 30 minutes before grilling, remove tuna from bag; wipe off excess marinade using paper towels; and discard marinade. Return tuna to the refrigerator to air-dry, and keep chilled. (You can also place in the freezer for up to 10 minutes.)

Preheat the grill to medium high, at least 450°F, and prepare smoker box or scatter wood chips. Remove tuna from the refrigerator, and spray all sides with canola oil.

Put the tuna on the grill, and don't touch until good sear marks appear. (You can actually watch the tuna cooking by checking the sides: the meat will turn opaque and brown-beige as it cooks.) You only want to cook about ¼ inch in for rare; ½ inch in for medium. Use tongs to turn the tuna, and sear the other side.

Remove tuna to a platter, and squeeze lime juice over it. Let it rest for a couple of minutes before slicing and dressing with sauce.

GRILLED TUNA WITH ROASTED CIPOLLINI ONIONS

6 SERVINGS • PREP: 20 MIN. • GRILL: 6–8 MIN. + 1 HR. FOR ONIONS

Courtesy of christopherranch.com

6 (6-ounce) tuna steaks, about
    1 inch thick
2 pounds cipollini onions
⅔ cup balsamic vinegar
1 tablespoon plus ⅓ cup extra-
    virgin olive oil
1 teaspoon salt, plus more
    for seasoning
¼ teaspoon freshly ground
    black pepper, plus more
    for seasoning
3 tablespoons fresh lemon juice
2 teaspoons fresh thyme
    leaves, chopped

Bring a large pot of water to boil. Add the onions, and cook for 2 minutes. Drain and cool. Peel the onions, and cut off the root ends.

HOT tip! If you can't find cipollini (pronounced chip-oh-LEE-nee) onions in the supermarket, you can substitute pearl onions.

Preheat one side of the grill to high. Toss the onions, vinegar, 1 tablespoon oil, ½ teaspoon of salt, and ¼ teaspoon of pepper in a baking dish. Close cover, and roast over indirect heat until the onions are tender and golden, about 1 hour.

Marinate tuna in the oil, lemon juice, thyme, rest of salt, and dash of pepper, 5 minutes on each side.

Grill the steaks over direct heat to desired doneness, about 3 minutes per side for medium. Spoon the onion mixture around the tuna and serve.

CB'S GRILLED GROUPER
WITH GARLIC BUTTER

6 SERVINGS • PREP: 10–15 MIN. • GRILL: 15 MIN.

2 pounds grouper (or black sea bass, monkfish) 6- to 8-ounce portions, about 1 inch thick

3 tablespoons butter

1½ tablespoons extra-virgin olive oil

1 tablespoon fresh cilantro, finely chopped

2 cloves garlic, minced

¼ teaspoon smoked paprika

¼ teaspoon ground ginger

Juice from ½ lemon

1 tablespoon lemon zest

Rinse fish in cold water; pat dry. Place fish in freezer until chilled but not frozen, about 10 to 15 minutes.

Preheat grill to high. Remove fish from freezer, and spray both sides with canola oil. Sear on both sides, about 4 to 5 minutes each. Use a lightly oiled spatula to turn.

Place seared fish in a holding pan away from direct heat to finish. Fish is done when flaky and opaque.

Combine butter, garlic, paprika, ginger, and lemon zest in saucepan over medium heat until the aromas are released; do not brown the garlic. Reduce heat, and add cilantro, lemon juice, and olive oil; then remove from heat. Spoon the garlic butter sauce over the fish.

An alternative method is to baste the fish while cooking to add a tasty glaze. However, if you are not experienced with grilling fish, the original method works well.

HAWAIIAN-STYLE MARLIN WITH POKE SAUCE

4 SERVINGS • PREP: 20 MIN. • MARINATE: 1 HR. • GRILL: 6 MIN.

16 ounces fresh marlin cut into 4
    portions, about 1 inch thick
2 teaspoons fresh ginger,
    finely minced
1½ cups soy sauce
1 tablespoon brown sugar
½ teaspoon sesame oil
2 tablespoons chili oil
Shredded Napa cabbage
    (garnish)
Cooked white rice

POKE SAUCE

¼ cup fresh ginger, minced
½ cup cilantro
¼ cup scallions, minced
3 cloves garlic, minced
½ cup peanut oil
½ teaspoon Tabasco sauce

Combine ginger, soy sauce, brown sugar, sesame oil, and chili oil in a small bowl. Place the fish in a resealable plastic bag; pour in the marinade; seal bag; and let rest in refrigerator for up to 1 hour.

Mix poke sauce ingredients in a blender or by hand until emulsified. Refrigerate until ready to use.

Preheat grill to high. Remove fish from bag, and discard the marinade. Place fish on the grill, and sear one side, about 2 to 3 minutes. Use a lightly oiled spatula to turn and sear the other side, about 2 to 3 minutes. Remove, and plate.

The marlin will be seared on the surface and very rare in the middle. Serve garnished with chopped Napa cabbage, white rice, and ramekin of poke sauce.

CB'S THAI-GLAZED SWORDFISH

2–4 SERVINGS • PREP: 15 MIN. • GRILL: 10 MIN. (UNTIL INTERNAL TEMP. IS 145°F)

2 swordfish steaks (about 6 to 8 ounces each) or other firm, white fish, such as halibut or mahi-mahi
Canola oil spray

THAI GLAZE
½ cup honey
2 tablespoons soy sauce
1 tablespoon freshly grated ginger
1 teaspoon grated lime peel
1 teaspoon minced garlic
Red pepper flakes (optional)
2 tablespoons chopped basil leaves
Juice from 1 lime

Mix first six glaze ingredients in a nonreactive bowl.

Preheat one side of the grill to medium high. Lightly spray fish steaks with canola oil, and place on hot grates. Sear for about 2 to 3 minutes or until sear marks appear. Lightly spray a flat, thin spatula with canola oil. Quickly slip the spatula under the fish, and turn over to a clean section of the grates to sear the other side, about 2 to 3 minutes.

When both sides are seared but fish is not quite cooked through, remove it to a holding tray away from direct heat, and brush on the glaze. Turn, and repeat on other side of fish. Fish is done when center is opaque and approximately 145°F. Place fish steaks on platter, and top with lime juice and chopped basil.

GRILLED SWORDFISH WITH CITRUS SALSA

4 SERVINGS • PREP: 15 MIN. • MARINATE: 2 HR. • GRILL: 10–15 MIN.

4 5-ounce swordfish steaks
1 tablespoon corn oil
Salt and pepper to taste

CITRUS SALSA
1 ruby red grapefruit
½ orange, peeled
½ lime, peeled
1 lemon, peeled
1 medium red onion
1 cup diced red, green, and
    yellow bell pepper
1 tablespoon chopped cilantro
1 tablespoon chopped mint
1 ounce tequila

Prepare the citrus salsa—mix all ingredients except swordfish, corn oil, salt, and pepper, and let marinate for a couple of hours.

Season the swordfish steaks with salt and pepper to personal taste. Brush lightly with one tablespoon corn oil. Grill for about 5 minutes per side until fish is firm and slightly opaque. (Use a knife to check.)

Spoon the salsa over the charbroiled swordfish steaks. Garnish with mint sprigs. Great served with saffron rice, fresh asparagus, and baby carrots.

For the salsa: Section and remove white membrane from grapefruit, orange, lime, and lemon; then cut each fruit into bite-size pieces. Finely dice onion. Mix together fruit, onion, peppers, cilantro, mint, and tequila. Let salsa marinate for 1 to 2 hours before serving.

CB'S BAJA-STYLE GRILLED SEA BASS

2 SERVINGS • PREP: 15 MIN. • CHILL: 2 HR. • GRILL: 10 MIN.

1 whole sea bass (or other firm-flesh fish, such as snapper or trout) about 2 pounds, head and fins removed

½ cup achiote paste (usually found in the Mexican food section of the supermarket)

½ cup orange juice

3 tablespoons lemon juice

3 tablespoons lime juice

Salsa to garnish

Ask your fishmonger to dress and butterfly the fish. Rinse the fish, and pat it dry. Use a sharp knife to score the skin lightly. Spread a mixture of achiote paste and citrus juices over the inside of the fish, avoiding the skin. Refrigerate for at least 2 hours.

Preheat the grill to medium. Spritz the skin of the fish with canola oil; place it, skin side down, on the grill. Tent the fish with heavy-duty aluminum foil, shiny side facing the fish, taking care not to let the foil touch the fish, or cover with a disposable aluminum tray.

Cook the fish until the fish juices and seasonings begin to steam and the flesh of the fish is firming up to your desired taste. Serve with a lightly sweet salsa.

Creamy Zucchini & Garlic, page 278

MARY'S "CAPE" COD WITH BACON & LEEKS

4 SERVINGS • PREP: 20 MIN. • GRILL: 15–20 MIN.

16 ounces cod in 4 equal portions, skin removed

6 strips thin-cut bacon, cut into thirds

2 leeks, trimmed and sliced lengthwise

2 tablespoons minced fresh ginger

2 tablespoons minced fresh garlic

¼ cup chopped parsley

Coarse salt and ground black pepper to taste

Canola oil spray

Rinse fish under cool water, and pat dry with paper towels. Place fish in freezer to chill, but do not freeze.

In a heavy skillet, slow-fry the bacon until almost crisp; remove to drain on paper towel. When cooled, chop into large bits.

Add leeks to the pan, and sauté in the bacon fat until browned. Remove the leeks; place in bowl with ginger, garlic, bacon, and parsley; and toss to combine.

Preheat one side of the grill to high. Remove fish from freezer, and spray each side with canola oil. Place fish over hot part of grill to sear, about 3 to 5 minutes on each side. Remove fish to a holding pan on unheated side of the grill to finish cooking. Fish is cooked when the interior is flaky but not dry. Place fish on platter, and top each portion with the leek-and-bacon mixture.

MARGARITA GRILLED SHRIMP

4–6 SERVINGS • PREP: 20 MIN. • MARINATE: 30 MIN. • GRILL: 6–8 MIN.

1½ pounds shrimp, peeled and deveined
¼ cup vegetable oil
3 tablespoons fresh lime juice
3 tablespoons tequila
2 tablespoons triple sec
1 large jalapeño chili, seeded and minced
1½ teaspoons grated lime zest
1 teaspoon chili powder
½ teaspoon coarse salt
1 teaspoon sugar

Whisk all ingredients together, except shrimp, in a medium-size bowl. Allow the mixture to rest for at least 20 minutes. This marinade can be prepared 1 day in advance. Simply cover and refrigerate for up to 24 hours.

Pour about ¼ cup of the marinade mixture into a container, and reserve. Place shrimp in a large baking dish or sealable plastic bag, and cover with remaining marinade. Cover dish with plastic wrap, or seal bag and refrigerate shrimp for 30 minutes.

Remove shrimp from container, and discard marinade. Grill shrimp on indirect heat for 3 to 4 minutes per side, basting with the reserved marinade. Serve over rice.

CHIPOTLE SHRIMP

6 SERVINGS • PREP: 20 MIN. • MARINATE: 2 HR. • GRILL: 10–15 MIN. COMBINED

1½ pounds uncooked jumbo
   shrimp, peeled and deveined
2 teaspoons olive oil
1 cup finely chopped onion
4 garlic cloves, minced
2 teaspoons ground cumin
1 teaspoon dried oregano
1 cup water
¼ cup apple cider vinegar
2 teaspoons chopped canned
   chipotle chilies
¼ cup orange juice
2 teaspoons light brown sugar

Heat oil in heavy skillet over medium heat. Add onion; sauté for about 10 minutes or until golden brown. Add garlic, cumin, and oregano; stir 1 minute. Transfer mixture to blender. Add water, vinegar, and chipotles to blender; puree until smooth. Transfer half of puree to medium bowl; cool. Add shrimp to bowl, and toss to coat. Cover; chill 2 hours.

Pour remaining puree into heavy medium saucepan. Add orange juice and brown sugar; bring to a boil. Reduce heat; simmer for about 10 minutes or until glaze is slightly thickened and reduced to ½ cup. Remove from heat, and cool.

Preheat grill to medium high. Remove shrimp from marinade; pat dry using paper towels. Lightly brush shrimp with orange juice glaze. Grill shrimp, brushing once more with marinade, until shrimp are opaque in center, about 2 minutes per side. Transfer to platter.

GRILLED SHRIMP & VEGETABLE KEBABS

2–4 SERVINGS • PREP: 20 MIN. • MARINATE: 1 HR. • GRILL: 4–6 MIN.

Courtesy of www.cookthink.com

2 pounds shrimp, peeled
   and deveined
4 to 6 wooden skewers
2 medium zucchini, cut into ½-
   inch half-rounds
2 medium yellow squash, cut into
   ½-inch half-rounds
1 medium onion, cut into ½-
   inch pieces

MARINADE
2 garlic cloves, minced
1 tablespoon chopped
   fresh oregano
2 teaspoons lemon juice
1 teaspoon lemon zest
¼ cup olive oil

Soak the skewers in water for 20 minutes. For the marinade, whisk together the garlic, oregano, lemon juice, zest, and oil.

Thread each skewer with alternating shrimp and vegetables. Place the skewers in a large baking dish, and pour the marinade over them. Turn the skewers to coat with the marinade, and refrigerate up to 1 hour.

Preheat one side of the grill to high. Lightly spray the hot side of grill with vegetable oil.

Shake any excess marinade off the skewers, and place them on the hot side of the grill. Leave them alone to brown on the one side, a minute or so. Turn skewers, and brown the vegetables on all sides until the shrimp is cooked, about 4 to 6 minutes.

HOT tip! These shrimp kebabs are a tasty main dish when paired with rice or another grain. At a casual gathering, guests can even assemble and grill their own kebabs.

CB'S GRILLED LOBSTER TAIL WITH BOURBON-HERB SAUCE

2 SERVINGS • PREP: 15 MIN. • GRILL: 15 MIN.

2 lobster tails removed from shell,
    about 6 ounces each
Canola oil

SAUCE
5 tablespoons butter, melted
1 tablespoon olive oil
¼ cup finely diced shallots
1 garlic clove, finely minced
Coarse salt and freshly ground
    black pepper to taste
¼ cup Kentucky bourbon
1 tablespoon finely
    chopped chives
1 tablespoon finely
    chopped tarragon
2 tablespoons dry white vermouth

Melt butter in a heavy saucepan over medium heat. Add olive oil and shallots, and cook until translucent; stir in garlic, and heat until aroma is released. Add salt and pepper to taste. Add bourbon; allow alcohol to vaporize; remove from heat; and set aside, covered.

Preheat grill to medium high. Dry lobster with paper towel, and then lightly spray with canola oil. Place lobster tails on hot grill to sear, using tongs to turn. When seared, remove to an aluminum pan away from direct heat, and continue to cook until lobster is firm but not rubbery, about 15 minutes.

Prior to serving, add the chives, tarragon, and vermouth to the sauce; re-warm to release the flavors. Serve on plates with sauce drizzled over the lobster or as a dipping sauce.

CB'S GRILLED SCALLOPS WITH ASPARAGUS & TOASTED WALNUTS

6 SERVINGS • PREP: 10 MIN. • GRILL: 5–10 MIN.

1 dozen sea scallops, cleaned
   and dried with a paper towel
3 large walnut halves or 6 large
   hazelnuts, chopped
1 pound asparagus, woody
   ends removed
Salt and pepper to taste
Juice from ½ lemon
Soy sauce

To toast nuts, place them in a dry skillet over medium-low heat, shaking pan to prevent burning, for about 2 to 3 minutes until aroma is released. When cool, chop nuts, and set aside.

Preheat the grill to medium. Spray the scallops and asparagus with canola oil, and season with salt and pepper to taste. Place asparagus on the grill, and use tongs to turn until all sides are charred and spears are tender, about 4 to 5 minutes. Remove to serving plate, and lightly cover with foil. Use tongs to place the scallops on a clean section of the grill. Leave in one place until seared; use tongs to turn the scallops; and sear the other sides. Remove, and place atop seared asparagus. Serve with a mixture of equal parts fresh lemon juice and soy sauce. Garnish with lemon zest and chopped nuts.

CB'S GRILLED SOFT-SHELL CRABS

4 SERVINGS • PREP: 15 MIN. • GRILL: 6–15 MIN.

8 soft-shell crabs, cleaned
Coarse salt and pepper to taste
Canola oil spray
1 lime cut into quarters

SAUCE

2 cloves minced garlic
1 tablespoon minced ginger
1 chipotle pepper, finely diced
3 tablespoons canola oil
1 teaspoon anchovy paste
1 cup finely chopped
    fresh cilantro
1 cup finely chopped Thai basil
Combine all sauce ingredients,
and set aside.

Preheat the grill to high. Season the crabs with salt and pepper to taste; spritz with canola oil; place on clean grates; and sear on both sides–about 3 minutes per side–using tongs to turn.

Remove crabs, and place them on a platter where the sauce is spread as a base. Squeeze limes over grilled crabs; then spoon sauce over the crabs, and serve.

SMOKY GRILLED KING CRAB

4–6 SERVINGS • PREP: 10 MIN. • GRILL: 8–10 MIN.
(UNTIL TEMP. INSIDE SHOULDER IS 145°F)

2 to 3 pounds Alaska King Crab legs, frozen

Wood chips (alder, cedar, apple, etc.)

2 to 3 tablespoons olive oil

2 to 3 teaspoons favorite seafood spice blend

1 large-size foil cooking bag or 2 sheets (15-inch) heavy-duty aluminum foil

Soak wood chips in water for 30 minutes; drain. Preheat grill to medium high. Add chips to grill or smoker box.

Rinse crab legs under cold water to remove any ice glaze; pat dry with paper towels. For each pound of crab, use 1 tablespoon olive oil and 1 teaspoon of seafood spice. Blend olive oil and seasoning. Place foil bag in a 1-inch-deep baking pan. Place crab legs in bag. Pour or brush oil blend onto legs; seal the bag tightly. If using foil sheets, place crab legs on the foil, and pour or brush oil blend onto legs. Lay second foil sheet over crab, and tightly crimp edges to seal foil, leaving room for heat circulation inside.

To cook, slide bag onto grill, and cook for 8 to 10 minutes, until the internal temperature of the crab reaches 145°F. (Use an instant-read thermometer, and test crab in shoulder section.)

GRILLED ALASKA CRAB WITH TRINIDAD SALAD

4–6 SERVINGS • PREP: 15 MIN. • GRILL: 4–5 MIN.

3 to 4 pounds Alaska crab legs (King, Snow, or Dungeness), split open to expose meat

⅓ cup butter, melted

¼ to ½ teaspoon chili oil

⅛ teaspoon cayenne pepper

TRINIDAD SALAD

½ cup extra-virgin olive oil

1 lime, juiced and divided

¼ cup dry white wine

2 tablespoons whole-grain mustard

1 can (14 to 15 ounces) palm hearts, drained and sliced crosswise

1 large, firm ripe papaya, skinned and chunked

1 cup celery, thinly sliced

½ fresh small red chili pepper, sliced and minced

¼ small sweet onion, thinly sliced then quartered

2 large, firm ripe avocados, pitted and diced in large chunks

Whisk together olive oil, one-half of the lime juice, wine, and mustard for salad dressing. In large bowl, add salad ingredients, topping with avocado. Pour dressing over avocado; cover; and refrigerate.

Preheat grill to medium high. Blend butter, chili oil, cayenne, and remaining lime juice. Brush butter mixture onto exposed crabmeat; place crab legs on grill; and cook 4 to 5 minutes, until heated. Save the unused sauce so that you can drizzle some over the crab legs at the table. Gently stir salad mixture to coat evenly; serve the dressed salad with the crab legs.

7

Most of the time, I grill over high heat. I like things to move fast. I like the sound and smell of a very hot fire. I gravitate towards dishes that you can get on and off the grill as quickly as possible. After a while, you'll know without thinking about it how hot the fire is.

–Bobby Flay

Vegetables, Sides & Salads

CHARRED SHISHITO PEPPERS WITH SRIRACHA LIME HONEY DRIZZLE

PREP: 10 MIN. • COOK: 8 MIN.

10 ounces shishito peppers
12 slices prosciutto
¼ cup honey
1 lime, juiced
1 teaspoon sriracha
1 tablespoon extra-virgin olive oil
½ teaspoon salt
½ teaspoon pepper
Toothpicks for securing prosciutto

Preheat your Char-Broil Signature Tru-Infrared Grill over high heat for 10 minutes. Meanwhile, toss the shishito peppers, extra-virgin olive oil, salt and pepper in a large bowl to coat. Set aside.

Carefully quarter each piece of prosciutto by slicing in half both lengthwise and crosswise. Wrap each shishito pepper with a piece of prosciutto and secure with a toothpick.

Grease the grill grates with vegetable oil or a nonstick spray. Carefully place the wrapped peppers on the grill, and cook for 3 to 4 minutes per side or until charred. Remove from grill and let cool slightly before removing toothpicks.

In a small bowl, combine honey, lime juice and sriracha. Stir. To serve, spread peppers onto a platter and drizzle with sriracha lime honey.

BRUSSELS SPROUTS WITH BALSAMIC VINAIGRETTE

4–6 SERVINGS • PREP: 15 MIN. • COOK: 10 MIN.

BRUSSELS SPROUTS

1 pound Brussels sprouts
1 tablespoon olive oil
Salt & pepper to taste

BALSAMIC VINAIGRETTE

¼ cup balsamic vinaigrette
1 small clove garlic, minced
1 teaspoon Dijon mustard
1 teaspoon honey
⅔ cup extra virgin olive oil
Salt & pepper to taste
Grated Parmesan cheese

Preheat your grill to medium high. Trim the tough ends off the sprouts and remove any discolored outer leaves. Cut in half through the stem. Toss the sprouts with olive oil, and season with salt and pepper. Put the sprouts in a grill basket, cut side down. Grill for 5–6 minutes or until the sprouts have nice char marks. Turn the sprouts over and continue to grill for another 4–5 minutes.

Put the sprouts in a bowl and cover with aluminum foil. This will allow them to steam for a few minutes. While the sprouts steam, make the vinaigrette. Combine the vinegar, garlic, mustard and honey in a small bowl. Whisk to combine thoroughly. Slowly whisk in the olive oil to create an emulsion. Season with salt and pepper to taste. Arrange the sprouts in a bowl. Drizzle with the vinaigrette and scatter with grated Parmesan cheese.

TIPS

- This recipe calls for cutting the sprouts in half before grilling. If you have sprouts of varying sizes, you may need to cut some of them into quarters. This will allow them grill a little more evenly.
- This vinaigrette will pair nicely with other veggies or even salad.

GRILLED STUFFED TOMATOES CAPRESE

6 SERVINGS • PREP: 15–20 MIN. • GRILL: 10 MIN.

Thanks to www.girlsonagrill.com for their contribution as guest chefs and writers.

6 plum tomatoes, stemmed, tops
   cut off, and insides scooped out
Small bocconcini or other fresh
   mozzarella, cut into 6
   1-inch cubes

DRY INGREDIENTS

½ cup Italian bread crumbs
⅓ cup freshly grated Parmesan
   or Romano cheese, plus extra
   for topping
8 fresh basil leaves, chopped, with
   6 additional leaves for garnish

WET INGREDIENTS

1 tablespoon balsamic vinegar
2 tablespoons extra-virgin olive oil
1 teaspoon sugar
Dash hot sauce

Clean and scoop out the plum tomatoes; then insert 1 bocconcini or piece of mozzarella into each.

Separately combine the dry and wet ingredients, and then mix them together well. Stuff the tomatoes with the mixture, mounding it slightly. Top each tomato with extra grated Parmesan, and place them into a greased muffin pan.

Preheat your grill for indirect cooking, with one side hot and one side warm. Grill the tomatoes over the hot side for about 4 minutes, turning them often. Then move them to the warm side; close the grill lid; and let them cook an additional 5 minutes, turning pan occasionally, until all the cheese is melted.

Top each tomato with a small basil stem and leaf, and serve hot as a side dish or appetizer.

CB'S FIRE-CHARRED GREEN BEANS WITH VINAIGRETTE

4–6 SERVINGS • PREP: 20 MIN. • GRILL: 10–20 MIN.

1 to 2 pounds fresh green beans,
　　washed, trimmed, and dried
Canola oil
Parmesan cheese, shaved
　　(optional)

VINAIGRETTE

1 teaspoon anchovy paste
1 to 2 mashed garlic cloves
1 tablespoon Dijon mustard
½ teaspoon Tabasco sauce
1 teaspoon Worcestershire sauce
2 to 3 tablespoons red
　　wine vinegar
2 tablespoons freshly squeezed
　　lemon juice
Extra-virgin olive oil, as needed
Freshly ground coarse salt and
　　black pepper to taste
Shavings of Parmesan cheese
　　if desired

Place beans in a bowl, and coat lightly and evenly with canola oil. In a nonreactive bowl, mix together anchovy paste, garlic cloves, Dijon-style mustard, Tabasco sauce, Worcestershire sauce, red wine vinegar, and lemon juice, using a whisk or fork.

Gently add olive oil as you continue to stir until all of the ingredients emulsify. Add the salt and pepper as desired. Keep covered and cold until just before serving.

Preheat grill to high. Place the beans at a 90-degree angle to the grates. (Use a grill basket to keep the beans from falling through the grates.) The beans will brown quickly, and the oil can cause flare-ups, so use tongs to move beans often as they cook. When beans are lightly charred, remove to platter, and drizzle with vinaigrette immediately before serving. You can top this dish with shavings of Parmesan cheese after drizzling the dressing on the veggies.

HOT tip! This recipe also works well with sliced zucchini, asparagus, broccoli spears, or steamed artichoke quarters.

GARLIC-GRILLED PORTOBELLOS

4 SERVINGS • PREP: 30 MIN. • GRILL: 6–8 MIN.

4 portobello mushrooms, about
   1 pound
⅓ cup extra-virgin olive oil
3 tablespoons lemon juice
2 cloves garlic, peeled
   and minced
Salt and pepper to taste
2 tablespoons minced
   fresh parsley

Preheat the grill to medium-high. Brush any dirt or grit off the mushrooms with a damp paper towel. Remove the stems. Combine the oil, lemon juice, and garlic in a bowl. Brush the caps on both sides with the garlic oil; sprinkle salt and pepper on both sides, and let them stand for 15 minutes, stem side up. Place the caps on a well-oiled grill, stem side up; grill them for 3 to 4 minutes. Turn the caps over, and grill them for another 3 to 4 minutes or until easily pierced with a knife. Do not burn or overcook them; the centers should be tender and moist. Transfer the caps to a platter, and cut them into thick slices. Garnish with parsley before serving.

One of the very nicest things about life is the way we must regularly stop whatever it is we are doing and devote our attention to eating.

–Luciano Pavarotti

HONEY-GRILLED CAULIFLOWER

6 SERVINGS • PREP: 5 MIN. • COOK: 5 MIN. • GRILL: 5 MIN.

Courtesy of www.oceanmist.com

1 cauliflower head, rinsed and cut
    into florets
1 cup honey
Salt and pepper
Nonstick cooking spray
6 wooden skewers (soaked
    in water)

Preheat grill to medium. In a microwavable bowl filled with 1 inch of water, microwave cauliflower on high for 5 minutes or until the florets are crisp on the outside and tender on the inside.

Arrange four florets on each wooden skewer, and spritz with cooking spray. Place skewers over direct heat; turn until there is an even, light charring on each floret. Remove skewers from the grill.

Brush honey onto the cauliflower; then add salt and pepper to taste. Put back on the grill for another minute or until the honey melts into cauliflower. Remove, and serve immediately.

ROASTED ASPARAGUS WITH CHERRY TOMATOES, GARLIC & OLIVE OIL

4 SERVINGS • PREP: 10 MIN. • GRILL: 20–25 MIN.

2 pounds pencil asparagus, woody ends trimmed

2 cups washed and stemmed cherry tomatoes

12 garlic cloves, peeled and smashed

¼ cup extra-virgin olive oil

1 teaspoon coarse salt

½ teaspoon freshly ground black pepper

¼ cup fresh lemon juice, reserve lemon halves

Preheat the grill to medium high. In a large bowl, combine the asparagus, tomatoes, and garlic. Drizzle with the olive oil, and season with the coarse salt and pepper. Toss to coat; then transfer to a large aluminum baking sheet. Drizzle the lemon juice over the asparagus; add the lemon halves to the pan; and place on the grill. Roast until the asparagus stalks are tender and the tomatoes begin to caramelize, about 20 to 25 minutes. Remove from the grill, and serve hot or at room temperature.

It's difficult to think anything but pleasant thoughts while eating a homegrown tomato.

–Lewis Grizzard

GRILLED CORN WITH SUN-DRIED TOMATO PESTO

4 SERVINGS • PREP: 45–60 MIN. • GRILL: 8–10 MIN.

4 ears of corn in husks
½ cup sun-dried tomatoes
2 tablespoons whole pine nuts
¼ cup olive oil
1 teaspoon chopped garlic
Salt and pepper to taste

Soak the corn in water for 45 minutes to 1 hour. Place the remaining ingredients in a blender; puree until smooth.

Preheat grill to medium. Remove the corn from the water. Peel back the husks, leaving them attached at the stem. Grill the corn for 8 to 10 minutes, turning often. Remove from the grill, and spread the corn with the sun-dried pesto. Serve immediately.

Serve these hearty potatoes as a main dish with salad or as a side dish.

DOUBLE-GRILLED STUFFED POTATOES

6 SERVINGS • PREP: 30 MIN. • GRILL: 45–60 MIN.

6 large baking potatoes

STUFFING MIXTURE

1 16-ounce carton sour cream
1½ cups shredded cheddar
    cheese, divided
1 stick butter, softened
2 teaspoons salt
Pepper to taste
1 pound barbecue pork butt,
    finely chopped
1 each large red, yellow, and
    green bell pepper, finely diced

Place the hot potatoes in a large mixing bowl. Add the sour cream, ¾ cup of cheese, and butter, blending well. Stir in the salt, pepper, and finely chopped pork.

Preheat the grill to high. Wash the potatoes; pierce them with a fork; and wrap them in aluminum foil. Grill for 45 minutes or until the potatoes test done. Allow them to cool slightly.

Unwrap the potatoes. Cut each in half lengthwise. Carefully scoop the potato out of each half to within ¼ inch of skin, reserving the skins. Add potatoes to stuffing mixture. Spoon the mixture into the reserved potato skins. Sprinkle the remaining cheese and finely diced bell peppers over the potatoes. Return them to the grill, and cook them over medium heat until the cheese melts.

Note: Potatoes can be prepared ahead of time and returned to the grill or oven just before serving.

SPICY GRILLED FRIES

4–6 SERVINGS • PREP: 15 MIN. • GRILL: 30–35 MIN.

1 tablespoon paprika

1 teaspoon freshly ground black pepper

1 teaspoon kosher salt

½ teaspoon chili powder

Pinch of cayenne (optional)

4 large russet or baking potatoes, scrubbed but not peeled

Olive oil

Preheat the grill to medium low. Combine the first five ingredients in a small bowl. Cut the potatoes in half lengthwise; then slice each half into long wedges that are about ½ inch thick in the middle. Place the potatoes in a large plastic storage bag, and pour the oil on top. Shake well to coat; then sprinkle the potatoes generously with the spice mixture, and shake again until they are well coated. Place the potatoes directly on the grate, and grill for 30 to 35 minutes, turning every 5 to 7 minutes. Dab them lightly with additional oil as needed. The potatoes are ready when crisp and golden brown outside and soft in the middle.

This version of slaw was something my Aunt Sylvia would make for summer backyard cookouts. It's great as a side to grilled meat and a tasty topping over a pulled-pork sandwich!–CB

AUNT SYLVIA'S BUTTERMILK COLE SLAW

8 SERVINGS • PREP: 1 HR. • REFRIGERATE: 1–2 HR.

5 to 6 cups Savoy or other cabbage, tightly packed

1 large carrot, julienned or grated

1 cup jicama or Granny Smith apple, julienned

1 cup sweet onion, diced or thinly sliced

Coarse salt

2 garlic cloves, mashed

⅓ cup buttermilk

¼ cup extra-virgin olive oil

2 tablespoons fresh lemon juice

¼ teaspoon celery seeds

Black pepper, freshly ground

Combine the cabbage, carrot, jicama, and onion in a colander, and lightly season with salt. Put the colander in a large bowl; set a plate on top of the vegetables; and place a can of soup or beans on top of the plate for extra weight. Allow the vegetables to drain for 1 to 2 hours in the refrigerator. Then turn the mixture onto a sheet pan lined with paper towels; pat dry; and transfer to a dry bowl.

In a small bowl, mix the mashed garlic, buttermilk, olive oil, lemon juice, celery seeds, and pepper. Toss the slaw with the dressing, and season with salt, pepper, and lemon juice to taste. May be kept in the refrigerator for up to a day before serving.

PEG'S MAGIC BEANS

7–10 SERVINGS • PREP: 20 MIN. • REFRIGERATE: OVERNIGHT • COOK: 4–5 HR.

1 pound maple-cured bacon

1 large white onion, finely chopped

1 pound 80% lean ground beef

1 can (15½ ounces) dark-red kidney beans

1 can (15½ ounces) white cannellini beans or great northern beans

1 can (15½ ounces) black-eyed peas or navy beans

1 can (8 ounces) baked beans

1 can (15½ ounces) medium to hot chili beans

1 bottle (12 ounces) chili sauce

1 cup brown sugar

6 ounces apple cider vinegar

1 tablespoon garlic powder

1 tablespoon chili powder

½ tablespoon paprika

Hot sauce to taste

The night before cooking beans, fry one pound of maple-cured bacon in a large skillet or frying pan until crisp. Remove the bacon; crumble when cool. Drain fat from skillet, reserving about 1 teaspoon. Cook onion and ground beef in the skillet with the reserved bacon fat until meat is browned. Drain off the fat, and transfer the onions, cooked ground beef, and bacon to the cooking sleeve of a 5-quart slow cooker.

Drain and rinse all of the beans except the chili and baked beans. Then add all of the beans, chili sauce, brown sugar, vinegar, and spices to the rest of the ingredients. Stir well. Cover with plastic wrap, and store in the refrigerator overnight.

The next day, transfer the cooking sleeve with the beans and meat to the slow cooker, set on low, for a minimum of 4 cooking hours. Serve warm.

From "Sizzle on the Grill." I can testify to the great taste of these beans!–CB

GREEK POTATO SALAD WITH SUN-DRIED TOMATOES

6 SERVINGS • PREP: 35 MIN. • COOK: 12 MIN.

1 pound (3 medium) potatoes, cut into ¼-inch slices

1 cup (1½ ounces) sun-dried tomatoes, halved lengthwise

1 cup seedless cucumber, sliced

½ cup red onion, sliced

1 cup feta cheese, crumbled

½ cup Greek olives or pitted black olives

LEMON DRESSING

¼ cup olive oil

¼ cup water

2½ tablespoons lemon juice

1 large garlic clove, pressed

1 tablespoon oregano, freshly chopped, or 1 teaspoon dried oregano leaves

1 teaspoon salt

½ teaspoon pepper

In 2-quart saucepan over medium heat, cover potatoes with 2 inches of water. Bring to a boil; reduce heat; and cook until tender, about 12 minutes. Drain, and set aside. Meanwhile, put the sliced sun-dried tomatoes in a small bowl, and pour boiling water over them; set aside 10 minutes.

Whisk together all of the dressing ingredients in a large bowl. Thoroughly drain tomatoes, and pat dry with paper towels. Add potatoes, tomatoes, and cucumbers to the bowl, and toss with the dressing. Transfer the potato salad to a serving plate. Garnish with onion, cheese, and olives.

SAVORY CORN PUDDING

6 SERVINGS • PREP: 15 MIN. • COOK: 12–15 MIN.

Courtesy of cookbook author and food blogger Cathy Erway

2 tablespoons butter, melted

4 medium shallots, finely chopped

1 small cubano or jalapeño pepper, seeded and finely chopped

1 ripe tomato, chopped

8 ears fresh corn

¾ cup whole milk

½ cup heavy cream or milk

Salt and pepper to taste

1 to 2 teaspoons red pepper flakes (optional)

2 tablespoons fine yellow cornmeal (optional)

2 to 3 tablespoons fresh lime juice

1 cup fresh basil, slivered

1 tablespoon olive oil

1 tablespoon fresh chives (optional)

1 to 2 teaspoons fresh oregano, finely chopped (optional)

In 3-quart saucepan over medium-low heat, sauté shallots in butter 6 minutes or until translucent. Add pepper and tomato; cook another 2 to 3 minutes.

Using a sharp paring knife, scrape kernels from the corncobs over a bowl; transfer corn and juices to the saucepan, and stir another 2 to 3 minutes. Add milk, ¼ cup at a time, stirring until absorbed; then pour in the cream, and season with salt, pepper, and pepper flakes if desired. If necessary, thicken mixture with cornmeal, 1 tablespoon at a time, until it is puddinglike. Add the lime juice, basil, olive oil, and optional herbs.

BLACK-EYED-PEA SALAD

6–8 SERVINGS • PREP: 5 MIN. • COOK: 35 MIN. +

BEANS

1 tablespoon extra-virgin olive oil

1 medium onion, chopped

3 or 4 garlic cloves, minced

1 pound black-eyed peas, rinsed
    and drained

6 cups water

1 bay leaf

Salt to taste

DRESSING AND SALAD

¼ cup red wine vinegar or
    sherry vinegar

1 garlic clove, minced

Salt and pepper, freshly ground,
    to taste

1 to 2 teaspoons cumin, lightly
    toasted and ground

1 teaspoon Dijon mustard

½ cup broth from the beans

⅓ cup extra-virgin olive oil

1 large red bell pepper, diced

½ cup cilantro, chopped

Heat 1 tablespoon olive oil in a large, heavy soup pot over medium heat; add onion; and cook until tender, about 5 minutes. Add half the garlic. Once it is fragrant, about 30 seconds to 1 minute, add the black-eyed peas and the water. Simmer, skimming off any foam from the surface. Add the bay leaf and salt, to taste (1 to 2 teaspoons). Reduce the heat; cover; and simmer 30 minutes. Taste and adjust salt, if needed. Add the remaining garlic; cover; and simmer until the beans are tender but intact. Remove from the heat; drain over a bowl. Transfer the beans to a large salad bowl.

In a small bowl, whisk together vinegar, garlic, salt, pepper, cumin, and mustard; add ½ cup of the bean broth and the olive oil; blend with the whisk. Taste and adjust seasonings. Toss dressing with the warm beans. Stir in the red pepper and cilantro. Serve warm or at room temperature.

CARROTS & RAISINS REVISITED

6 SERVINGS • PREP: 10 MIN. (1 ½ HR. TO DRAIN YOGURT) • CHILL: 20–30 MIN.

2 cups plain non- or low-fat yogurt
1 tablespoon packed brown sugar
¼ teaspoon orange peel, grated
2 tablespoons orange juice
¼ teaspoon nutmeg or
   cardamom, ground
¼ teaspoon Tabasco sauce
6 to 7 medium carrots, peeled
   and shredded coarsely
3 cups dark raisins
3 tablespoons cashews, almonds,
   or pecans, chopped

Line a medium-size strainer with a double layer of rinsed cheesecloth or a triple layer of white paper towels. Place the strainer over a large bowl, and spoon yogurt into it. Let yogurt drain for 1½ hours; then scrape it into a medium-size bowl. Discard strained liquid.

Stir brown sugar, orange peel and juice, nutmeg, and Tabasco sauce into the yogurt until smooth. Mix in carrots and raisins, and toss to coat. Cover, and chill 20 to 30 minutes. Just before serving, sprinkle with chopped nuts.

CB'S CUCUMBER SALAD

6–8 SERVINGS • PREP: 30 MIN.

2 to 4 medium-size cucumbers (7 to 10 inches each), thoroughly washed and dried
Salt

GINGER DRESSING

3 tablespoons Japanese rice vinegar or apple cider vinegar
1 tablespoon coarse salt
1 tablespoon lemon juice, freshly squeezed
1 tablespoon sugar
1 tablespoon ginger, peeled and finely grated
¼ teaspoon lemon rind, grated

Score the skin of the cucumbers with a fork, or peel off skin in strips. Slice cucumbers into very thin rounds; place sliced cucumbers in a colander; sprinkle with salt; and toss to mix thoroughly. Let cucumbers rest for 15 to 20 minutes. Meanwhile, make the dressing by mixing together the vinegar, salt, lemon juice, sugar, ginger, and lemon rind in a nonmetallic bowl. Set aside.

Once the salted cucumbers have drained, remove them from the colander, and place them into a large, clean dishtowel or cheesecloth; gently blot excess moisture. Then add cucumbers to the bowl, and toss with the dressing. Chill before serving.

CB'S SMOKY, CHEESY CORNBREAD

8–10 SERVINGS • PREP: 10 MIN. • GRILL: 30–35 MIN.

1½ cups cornmeal
1 cup all-purpose flour
1 teaspoon baking soda
½ teaspoon salt
3 tablespoons sugar
¼ cup vegetable oil
2 large eggs
1 cup buttermilk
4 ounces smoked cheese, such
  as smoked Gouda or smoked
  bleu cheese

Preheat grill to medium. Lightly grease a small cast-iron skillet or a 9 x 5 baking pan.

Whisk together first five ingredients; then add oil, eggs, and buttermilk; use spatula to mix until just combined. Ladle batter evenly into pan. Crumble cheese on top, and let rest for 15 minutes; then bake in grill over indirect heat for 30 to 35 minutes. (Check doneness by inserting a toothpick in the center; it should come out clean.) Remove, and cool for a few minutes. Run a butter knife around the edge; place cooling rack on top of skillet or pan; and flip. Cool for 30 minutes before slicing.

CB'S GRILLED FENNEL

2 SERVINGS • PREP: 5 MIN. • MARINATE: 15–20 MIN. • GRILL: 15 MIN.

2 large fennel bulbs
2 tablespoons brown sugar
1 teaspoon Worcestershire sauce
2 tablespoons peanut oil or
    clarified butter
Coarse salt

Remove the green top and fronds from the fennel, and reserve. Quarter each bulb, leaving the root bottoms in place to hold the leaves together during roasting. Whisk together the brown sugar, Worcestershire sauce, and oil. Marinate the pieces in the mixture for 15 to 20 minutes.

Preheat the grill to medium. Using tongs, arrange fennel slices on grates; turn to sear and caramelize all sides, about 3 to 5 minutes. As the edges begin to crisp and char just a bit, remove to a holding pan to finish over indirect heat with the hood closed. The fennel bulbs are cooked when they are fork-tender but not too soft. Serve on a platter with freshly ground salt and a teaspoon or two of finely minced fennel tops.

This recipe will drive you crazy-go-nuts because it pairs deliciously with just about any grilled meat or fish.–CB

CB'S GRILLED POTATOES WITH BACON, CHEESE & ROASTED JALAPEÑO

4 SERVINGS • PREP: 15 MIN. • GRILL: 1 HR.

2 large russet potatoes, scrubbed and dried

Olive oil

3 strips cooked center-cut bacon, crumbled

4 jalapeño peppers, roasted and diced

¼ cup smoked Gouda cheese, shredded

¼ cup Parmesan cheese, shredded

¼ cup sour cream

2 tablespoons green onions, minced

Coarse salt and black pepper, freshly ground

½ cup prepared adobo sauce

Preheat grill to high. Rub potatoes with the oil. Poke small holes in each end to allow steam to escape; then grill over high heat for about 1 hour, turning every 15 minutes. (Or roast on warming rack without turning.)

Slice cooked potatoes in half lengthwise. Scoop all but ¼ inch of the potato into a bowl. Leave the rest inside the skin.

Add the remaining ingredients to the bowl; mix; then spoon into the skins. Top with additional Gouda, and melt over indirect heat with the hood closed. Drizzle with the adobo sauce when you serve.

Note: The potatoes can be roasted a day in advance.

CRANBERRY-PECAN RICE PILAF

4 SERVINGS • PREP: 10 MIN. • COOK: 18–20 MIN.

2 tablespoons butter or margarine

1 cup uncooked rice

1 can (14½ ounces)
    chicken broth

1 cup Parmesan cheese, grated

½ cup dried cranberries

½ cup pecans, chopped
    and toasted*

¼ cup green onions, sliced

Salt and black pepper, ground,
    to taste

*To toast pecans, spread nuts on
small baking sheet. Bake 5 to
8 minutes at 350°F, or until golden
brown, stirring frequently.

Melt butter in 2-quart saucepan over medium heat. Add rice; cook, stirring, 2 to 3 minutes. Add broth, and heat to boiling, stirring once or twice. Reduce heat; cover; and simmer 15 minutes or until liquid is absorbed.

Remove from heat. Stir in cheese, cranberries, pecans, and onions. Season to taste with salt and pepper.

LIVEFIRE'S HOLIDAY POTATO TORTE

6 SERVINGS • PREP: 20 MIN. • GRILL: 35–40 MIN.

3 to 4 russet potatoes, scrubbed
 but not skinned
Olive oil
Salt and black pepper to taste
2 tablespoons fresh
 rosemary, chopped

Preheat grill to medium high. Generously butter a well-seasoned 10-inch cast-iron or other heavy skillet. Using a V-slicer or mandolin, thinly slice each potato, placing slices in the skillet as you go to prevent oxidation.

Because you will invert the torte after it is cooked, the bottom layer of potatoes will be the top of the torte, so make sure to arrange the slices in an attractive pattern. As you add each layer, brush it with olive oil, and sprinkle with salt and pepper and about ½ teaspoon of rosemary. When you're finished, you should have about 7 layers of potatoes.

Place skillet on the grill, and cook until the potatoes are sizzling nicely, about 12 to 15 minutes. Using heat-resistant gloves or potholders, remove skillet from the grill, and drain off excess oil. Carefully invert the torte onto a clean plate, and then slide the potatoes, bottom side up, back into the skillet. Return to the grill, and cook, with lid closed, for about 20 to 25 minutes or until potatoes are browned and crispy and inner layers are tender.

CREAMY ZUCCHINI & GARLIC

3–4 SERVINGS • PREP: 5 MIN. • COOK: 5–10 MIN.

Courtesy of christopherranch.com

2½ tablespoons butter
6 garlic cloves, minced
6 medium zucchini, grated
2½ tablespoons garlic powder
1 teaspoon thyme, chopped
2½ tablespoons sour cream
Fresh pepper

Melt the butter in a heavy-bottom skillet over medium heat. Lower the heat; add the minced garlic; and sauté for about 1 to 2 minutes. (Do not let the garlic burn.) Add the grated zucchini, garlic powder, and thyme.

Cook, stirring frequently until the zucchini is tender. Remove from the heat, and stir in the sour cream. Season with fresh pepper. Serve immediately.

GARLIC-ROASTED SWEET POTATOES WITH ARUGULA

6 SERVINGS • PREP: 15 MIN. • GRILL: 40–45 MIN.

Courtesy of christopherranch.com

2 pounds sweet potatoes, peeled
　　and cut into 2-inch pieces
4 garlic cloves, peeled and sliced
2 tablespoons extra-virgin olive oil
½ teaspoon salt
½ teaspoon black pepper, ground
2 Bartlett pears, cored and cut
　　into 2-inch pieces
1 5-ounce package arugula
½ teaspoon lemon peel, grated

Preheat grill or oven to medium high. In large roasting pan, combine potatoes, garlic, oil, salt, and pepper, and toss to coat well. Roast for 30 minutes, tossing occasionally, until tender and browned. Add pears, and roast another 10 minutes.

Place the arugula in a large bowl. Add the cooked potatoes and pears, and toss until the arugula wilts. Sprinkle with the lemon peel.

BETTER-THAN-MOM'S MAC & CHEESE

8 SERVINGS • PREP: 20 MIN. • BAKE: 20 MIN.

1 box (16 ounces) corkscrew or
  mini penne pasta
¼ cup butter or margarine
¼ cup all-purpose flour
4 cups milk
¾ teaspoon salt
1½ teaspoons Tabasco sauce
1 cup Gruyère cheese, shredded
1 cup sharp cheddar
  cheese, shredded

BREAD-CRUMB TOPPING

⅓ cup butter or margarine
½ cup dried seasoned
  bread crumbs
½ teaspoon Tabasco sauce

Prepare pasta as directed on box. Drain; set aside.

Meanwhile, melt butter in 3-quart saucepan over medium heat. Stir in flour until blended and smooth. Gradually whisk in milk, salt, and Tabasco sauce. Cook until thickened and smooth, stirring often. Add cheese to sauce, and stir until melted. In large bowl, toss sauce with cooked pasta. Spoon mixture into an ungreased 2-quart baking dish.

Preheat oven to 375°F. To prepare bread-crumb topping, melt butter or margarine in a small skillet over medium heat. Stir in bread crumbs and Tabasco sauce; blend well. Top pasta mixture with prepared bread crumbs and cheese. Bake 20 minutes until crumbs are toasted and casserole is completely heated.

COOKOUT POTATOES

4–6 SERVINGS • PREP: 15 MIN. • GRILL: 1 HR.

Nonstick cooking spray
1 medium onion, halved and
　thinly sliced
1½ pounds Yukon Gold potatoes,
　very thinly sliced
1⅓ cups low-fat sharp cheddar
　cheese, shredded
⅓ cup real bacon bits
⅓ cup bell pepper, chopped
½ teaspoon garlic salt

Spray a 9 x 9 x 2-inch foil pan liberally with nonstick cooking spray. Layer half the onions, potatoes, cheese, bacon bits, bell pepper, and garlic salt in pan; then layer the other half over the first. Cover the top tightly with foil, and grill over medium heat for 1 hour, rotating pan occasionally to avoid hot spots.

One thing you don't want to do as a host is be running around all evening. Do as much as you can ahead of time, so all you have to do is grill the main ingredients.

–Bobby Flay

GRILLED EGGPLANT WITH CHEESE

4–6 SERVINGS • PREP: 5 MIN. • GRILL: 2–3 MIN.

4 small eggplants
Olive oil
Salt and pepper
½ pound soft goat cheese or
    feta, crumbled
2 teaspoons garlic, minced
1 teaspoon red pepper flakes
1 tablespoon fresh basil,
    finely chopped

Cut eggplants in half lengthwise. Brush cut edges with olive oil, and season with salt and pepper. In a small bowl, combine cheese, garlic, red pepper flakes, and basil with a pinch of salt, and then refrigerate until ready to use. Preheat the grill to medium. Place eggplant halves on grill over direct heat, skinless side down. Roast until almost soft (2 to 3 minutes). Remove from grill, and cool slightly. Then spread or sprinkle the cheese mixture on the warm eggplant, and serve immediately.

HARVEST SLAW WITH SWEET POTATOES

8 SERVINGS • PREP: 10 MIN. • COOK: 3½ MIN. • CHILL: UP TO 8 HR.

12 ounces sweet potatoes, cubed

12 ounces packaged broccoli slaw

½ cup dried cranberries or raisins

1 green apple, diced

½ cup almonds, sliced

1 teaspoon cinnamon, ground

¼ teaspoon garlic salt

¼ teaspoon black pepper

½ cup ranch dressing

Place sweet potatoes in a microwave-safe dish or plastic food bag. Microwave for 3½ minutes; let cool for 5 minutes. In a large bowl, combine the potatoes with the rest of the ingredients. Toss with ranch dressing. Chill up to 8 hours before serving.

GRILLED CHICKEN SKEWERS WITH GRILLED CAESAR SALAD

2 SERVINGS • PREP: 25 MIN. • MARINATE: 1 HR.–OVERNIGHT
GRILL: 8–10 MIN. COMBINED

Provided by Erik Lind, 2006 Char-Broil Grilling Team Chef.

2 4-ounce boneless, skinless
   chicken breasts
1 cup BBQ sauce of your choice
2 whole heads romaine lettuce
½ cup extra-virgin olive oil
½ cup minced shallot
½ cup minced fresh garlic
Salt and pepper
Bamboo skewers soaked in white
   wine for 1 hour
1 prepared log herbed polenta
1 cup balsamic vinegar
1 jar of your favorite
   Caesar dressing

Cut the chicken breasts lengthwise into four equal slices. Place chicken in a plastic bag with the BBQ sauce; seal; and marinate for 1 to 2 hours or overnight. Cut the romaine heads in half lengthwise. Drizzle the olive oil over both sides. Spread the shallot, garlic, salt, and pepper over the cut side of the heads. Set lettuce aside.

Preheat grill to high. Place chicken on skewers, and grill until the meat reaches 165°F. Slice the polenta into ¼-inch slices, and spray with nonstick cooking spray. Grill polenta 5 to 8 minutes on each side to ensure even grill marks. To make the balsamic reduction, place vinegar in a pan over medium heat, and cook until it reduces into syrup. Cool, and reserve. Grill the romaine heads on both sides for 2 to 3 minutes until just wilted. Remove and slice lengthwise; then roughly chop. Toss lettuce very lightly with Caesar dressing. Place a small amount on each plate. Cut the polenta circles in half, and arrange them across the salad. Place the chicken skewers in an "X" over the salad, and drizzle with the balsamic reduction.

BBQ THAI CHICKEN SALAD

6 SERVINGS • PREP: 15 MIN. • MARINATE: 4 HR.–OVERNIGHT • GRILL: 25–30 MIN.

1 broiler-fryer chicken, about 3½ pounds
1 tablespoon curry powder
1 14-ounce can unsweetened coconut milk, regular or low fat
1 tablespoon lime juice
1 tablespoon fish sauce
3 garlic cloves, minced
¼ cup chopped cilantro leaves
2 tablespoons brown sugar
12 red lettuce leaves, rinsed
1 medium head lettuce, shredded
1 large red bell pepper, sliced
½ cup torn mint leaves
⅓ cup finely chopped peanuts

SWEET & SOUR CILANTRO DRESSING

⅔ cup rice vinegar
¼ cup sugar
¼ cup minced cilantro
¼ teaspoon salt
½ teaspoon chili paste
⅓ cup safflower or canola oil

Rinse the chicken, and pat it dry. Split the chicken in half with a large, sharp knife. In a large bowl, whisk the curry powder into the coconut milk. Blend in the lime juice, fish sauce, garlic, cilantro, and brown sugar. Add the chicken, turning to coat it in the marinade. Cover, and refrigerate 4 hours to overnight.

Preheat the grill to medium. Place the chicken on the grill, skin side down. Turn after about 10 minutes, and continue cooking until the juices run clear or a fork can be inserted into the chicken with ease, about 30 minutes. Cool the chicken slightly; cut it into strips.

Prepare the dressing. Combine all of the ingredients; stir until the sugar dissolves. Arrange the red lettuce leaves on six plates. Combine the shreds of lettuce, bell pepper, and mint; distribute onto lettuce leaves. Scatter the chicken on top. Sprinkle the salad with peanuts; serve with dressing.

GREEK SALAD OLIVE-GRILLED CHICKEN

6 SERVINGS • PREP: 10 MIN. • MARINATE: 4–24 HR.
GRILL: 30 MIN. (UNTIL THICK BREAST TEMP. IS 165°F)

6 split chicken breasts, bone-in
¼ cup olive oil
1 4½-ounce jar prepared black
    olive tapenade
¼ cup lemon juice
¼ cup chopped fresh oregano

GREEK SALAD

1 cup grape tomatoes, halved
12 pitted kalamata olives
6 ounces feta cheese, cubed
½ small red onion, diced
¼ cup extra-virgin olive oil
3 tablespoons lemon juice
1 tablespoon chopped
    fresh oregano
8 cups mixed greens, preferably
    spinach, arugula, and romaine

Place the first four ingredients in a resealable plastic bag; add chicken; seal bag; and shake gently to coat chicken with marinade. Refrigerate 4 to 24 hours.

Preheat grill to medium high. Remove chicken from bag, and discard marinade. Arrange chicken on grill. Close lid, and open vents. Cook chicken, turning occasionally to cook all pieces evenly, for about 30 minutes or until a meat thermometer inserted in thickest part of breast registers 165°F.

For the salad: Toss together the first seven ingredients in a bowl. Gently stir in greens. To serve, divide Greek Salad among plates, and top with chicken.

GRILLED SALMON SALAD VINAIGRETTE

4 SERVINGS • PREP: 30 MIN. • GRILL: 10–15 MIN.

SALAD DRESSING

⅓ cup extra-virgin olive oil

¼ cup tarragon vinegar

1 tablespoon Dijon mustard

1 clove garlic, pressed

SALAD

4 salmon steaks or fillets (4 to 6 ounces each), fresh, thawed, or frozen

1 large apple, cored and chopped

1 ripe avocado, peeled and chopped

1 tablespoon lemon juice

1 package (10 ounces) prepared salad greens

1 navel orange, peeled and chopped

¼ medium red onion, sliced very thin

⅓ cup slivered almonds

⅓ cup raisins

2 teaspoons olive, canola, peanut, or grape-seed oil

Salt and pepper

Rinse any ice from frozen fish under cold water; pat dry with paper towel. Preheat the grill to medium high. Brush both sides of salmon with oil. Place salmon on grill, and cook about 3 to 4 minutes until good sear marks appear. Turn salmon, and season with salt and pepper. Reduce heat to medium, and close grill lid. Cook an additional 6 to 8 minutes for frozen salmon or 3 to 4 minutes for fresh or thawed fish. Cook just until fish is opaque throughout.

Divide salad among four plates; place salmon portion on top. Drizzle with vinaigrette dressing, and serve.

For the salad: Mix dressing ingredients in a small bowl; set aside. Place chopped apple and avocado in a large salad bowl. Drizzle with lemon juice. Add salad greens, orange, onion, almonds, and raisins; mix.

GREEK BEEF SALAD

2 SERVINGS • PREP: 20 MIN. • MARINATE: 6 HR.–OVERNIGHT • GRILL: 15 MIN.

1 pound top round steak,
    approximately 1 inch thick
6 cups romaine lettuce
1 medium cucumber, thinly sliced
½ small red onion, cut into
    thin wedges
2 tablespoons crumbled
    feta cheese
8 Greek or black olives
2 pita breads, toasted, cut
    into wedges

MARINADE

⅔ cup fresh lemon juice
⅓ cup olive oil
½ teaspoon dried oregano
½ teaspoon salt and pepper

Whisk marinade ingredients in a small bowl. Place steak and one-half of marinade in plastic bag; turn to coat. Seal bag securely, and marinate in refrigerator 6 hours or overnight, turning occasionally. Refrigerate remaining half of marinade.

Remove steak; discard marinade. Place steak on medium-high grill, 12 to 15 minutes for medium rare, turning occasionally. Remove and let stand 10 minutes. Carve into thin slices. Combine sliced steak, lettuce, cucumber, and onion in a large bowl. Toss with reserved marinade mixture. Sprinkle with cheese and olives. Serve with pita wedges.

SIRLOIN, PASTA & ARTICHOKE SALAD WITH BALSAMIC VINAIGRETTE

4 SERVINGS • PREP: 20 MIN. • MARINATE: 2 HR. MINIMUM • GRILL: 15 MIN.

1 pound boneless top sirloin steak, cut 1 inch thick

¼ cup tricolored fusilli or rotini pasta, cooked and drained

1 14-ounce can quartered artichoke hearts, drained

1 large red bell pepper, cut into thin strips

1 cup small, pitted, ripe olives

½ tablespoon fresh basil, chopped

1 cup prepared balsamic vinaigrette dressing

Place steak and ½ cup of dressing into a plastic bag; seal; and turn to coat. Marinate for 2 hours or overnight. Thirty minutes before cooking, remove steak from refrigerator. Remove from bag; discard marinade.

Cook steak on medium-high grill, 13 to 17 minutes, turning occasionally. Remove; let stand 10 minutes. Cut steak lengthwise in half; then slice crosswise thinly. Combine steak, pasta, artichoke hearts, bell pepper, olives, and basil in a large bowl. Add vinaigrette; toss. Serve immediately.

STEAK & ROASTED VEGETABLE SALAD

4 SERVINGS • PREP: 20 MIN. • GRILL: 15 MIN.

1 pound boneless beef top loin or
   tenderloin, cut 1 inch thick
8 cups torn salad greens
¾ cup prepared Italian dressing

GRILLED VEGETABLES

2 portabella mushroom caps
1 large red, yellow, or green
   bell pepper, cut into 1-inch-
   wide strips
1 medium Japanese eggplant,
   sliced lengthwise in ¼-
   inch slices
1 medium red onion, cut into ½-
   inch slices
1 zucchini, sliced lengthwise in
   ¼-inch slices
½ tablespoon balsamic vinegar
½ large clove garlic, minced
1 teaspoon dried rosemary

Coat vegetables with vinegar, garlic, rosemary, salt, and pepper. Grill vegetables; then cool slightly.

Place steaks on grill for 8 to 11 minutes for medium-rare to medium doneness, turning occasionally. Remove; let stand 10 minutes.

Carve steaks and roughly chop vegetables; season with salt. Arrange beef and vegetables on greens. Serve with dressing.

JAPANESE STEAK SALAD WITH SESAME

4 SERVINGS • PREP: 20 MIN. • MARINATE: 2 HR. • GRILL: 20 MIN.

1 pound boneless top sirloin, cut
   1 inch thick
3 cups each sliced Napa cabbage
   and romaine lettuce
½ cup each thinly sliced carrot,
   cucumber and radish
1 cup hot cooked rice
24 pea pods, blanched

MARINADE AND DRESSING

3 tablespoons each dry sherry,
   reduced-sodium soy sauce,
   and rice wine vinegar
2 tablespoons hoisin sauce
½ teaspoon grated fresh ginger
2 tablespoons green
   onion, chopped
1 tablespoon each sugar and dark
   sesame oil

Prepare marinade by combining sherry, soy sauce, vinegar, hoisin sauce, and ginger in a small bowl. Place steak and ⅓ cup marinade in plastic bag. Close bag securely, and marinate in refrigerator 2 hours, turning once.

For dressing, add ¼ cup water, green onion, sugar, and sesame oil to remaining marinade; mix well. Remove steak; discard marinade. Place steak on medium-high grill, 13 to 17 minutes for medium-rare to medium doneness, turning occasionally. Let stand 5 minutes. Carve steak.

Combine cabbage, lettuce, carrot, and radishes; divide among 4 plates. Arrange cucumber, rice, pea pods, and steak on salads. Top with dressing.

8

A grill is just a source of heat. Just like a stove, it is very user-friendly.
–Bobby Flay

Desserts

PUMPKIN STICKY TOFFEE PUDDING CAKE

PREP: 10 MIN. • COOK: 50 MIN.

CAKE

1 can pumpkin puree (this is *not* pumpkin pie filling)

2 eggs

½ cup vegetable oil

1 teaspoon vanilla

1 teaspoon maple syrup

1 cup granulated sugar

1 cup all-purpose flour

½ teaspoon salt

¾ teaspoon baking soda

½ teaspoon baking powder

1 teaspoon cinnamon

½ teaspoon ground ginger

½ teaspoon ground nutmeg

⅛ teaspoon ground cloves

STREUSEL TOPPING

¼ cup granulated sugar

¼ cup brown sugar

⅓ cup chopped walnuts or pecans

¼ cup all-purpose flour

¼ teaspoon salt

2 tablespoons butter, melted

STICKY TOFFEE SAUCE

½ cup unsalted butter

⅔ cup heavy cream

1 cup brown sugar

Pinch of salt

Preheat your Char-Broil Big Easy Oil-less Turkey Fryer for 15 minutes. Combine pumpkin puree, eggs, vegetable oil, vanilla and maple syrup. Add the sugar and mix well. Combine the flour, salt, baking soda, baking powder and spices. Whisk to combine and add to the wet mixture. Combine all of the ingredients for the streusel topping and set aside.

Pour pumpkin batter into a greased 9" round cake pan and sprinkle evenly with the Streusel Topping. Lower the cake plate into the stackable oven accessory and secure the lid. Carefully lower the stackable oven down into the cooking chamber of The Big Easy. Do not put the mesh lid on The Big Easy.

Meanwhile, make the sauce by combining all of the ingredients in a small saucepan. Cook on medium and let come to a boil. Stir frequently and let cook for 3 to 4 minutes to thicken. After 50 minutes, insert a toothpick into the cake and check for doneness. This can be tricky for a pudding cake, because it is normal for the toothpick to come out only mostly clean. As long as your toothpick doesn't come out with wet cake batter, you're good to go. If it needs more time to cook, check back every 5 minutes. Serve cake warm, drizzled with warm sticky toffee sauce. You can also top with vanilla ice cream.

CB'S GRILLED PEARS WITH HONEY & THYME

2 SERVINGS • PREP: 10 MIN. • GRILL: 5–10 MIN.

Canola oil spray
1 ripe pear, cored and sliced into eighths

1 tablespoon honey
1 teaspoon chopped fresh thyme

Preheat the grill to medium. Spray the pear slices with canola oil, and grill, turning as needed, until they are slightly soft and grill marks appear. Arrange four slices in a fan shape on each plate. Drizzle with honey, and sprinkle with thyme. Serve as is or with a dollop of ice cream or whipped cream if desired.

Vegetables are a must on a diet. I suggest carrot cake, zucchini bread and pumpkin pie.

–Jim Davis

GRILLED PEACHES WITH RASPBERRY PUREE

4 SERVINGS • PREP: 10 MIN. • GRILL: 5–10 MIN.

4 medium peaches, sliced in half and pitted
3 teaspoons honey
2 tablespoons brown sugar

1 cup raspberries
¼ cup orange juice
¼ cup butter

Preheat grill to medium. Combine butter, 1 teaspoon of honey, and brown sugar in a medium saucepan. Bring to a low boil. Place the peaches in the sauce; let simmer 4 to 5 minutes.

Remove the peaches from the sauce; place on grill, cut side down. Turn peaches over when grill marks appear, about 2 to 3 minutes. Continue grilling 2 to 3 minutes more.

Remove peaches from the grill. In a blender, puree orange juice, raspberries, and remaining 2 teaspoons of honey to a sauce-like consistency. Place the peaches on a plate, and drizzle them with the raspberry mixture.

GRILLED PINEAPPLE WITH RUM & COCONUT

6 SERVINGS • PREP: 5 MIN. • MARINATE: 3–5 MIN. • GRILL: 10 MIN.

1 ripe pineapple, peeled and cut crosswise into 6 slices
2 to 3 tablespoons dark rum
1 teaspoon granulated sugar
1 cup whipped cream
¼ cup shredded coconut, toasted

Pour the rum and sugar into a bowl with the pineapple. Mix to coat the slices evenly, cover with plastic wrap, and let rest for 3 to 5 minutes. Preheat the grill to medium high.

Lightly sear the pineapple directly over the heat for about 10 minutes, using tongs to turn once. Make sure the fruit does not become overly charred.

Remove pineapple from grill, and top with whipped cream and coconut. You can also add a heaping scoop of your favorite ice cream if desired.

GRILLED POUND CAKE WITH CHERRY-NUT ICE CREAM

8 SERVINGS • PREP: 2½ HR. (INCLUDING FREEZING TIME) • GRILL: 1 MIN.

¾ cup dried cherries
1 cup boiling water
5 tablespoons brandy
1½ pints vanilla ice cream,
    softened slightly
4 tablespoons coarsely chopped
    semisweet chocolate
⅓ cup coarsely chopped nuts
    (pecans, walnuts, or almonds)
1 loaf pound cake
¼ cup unsalted butter

Place the cherries in a medium bowl. Pour 1 cup of boiling water over them. Let them stand until softened, about 10 minutes. Drain and pat them dry. Mix the cherries and 1 tablespoon of brandy in a small bowl. Place the ice cream in a large bowl. Mix in the cherries, chocolate, and nuts. Cover the ice cream mixture; freeze until firm, about 2 hours.

Preheat the grill to medium. Cut the pound cake into ½-inch slices. Brush both sides of each slice with melted butter. Grill the slices until lightly toasted, about 30 seconds per side.

Place two cake slices on each of eight dessert plates. Place a scoop of ice cream on top. Drizzle 1½ teaspoons of brandy over each serving.

CB'S NUTELLA & MARSHMALLOW QUESADILLAS

4 SERVINGS • PREP: 5 MIN. • GRILL: 5–7 MIN.

4 soft flour tortillas
8 tablespoons Nutella or thick
   chocolate sauce
8 tablespoons marshmallow creme

2 tablespoons butter, melted
   (½ tablespoon per tortilla)
2 teaspoons cinnamon
2 teaspoons sugar

Preheat grill to low. Warm, but do not brown, the tortillas; then lay them flat on a work surface. Spread 2 tablespoons of Nutella and 2 tablespoons of marshmallow creme on top of each one; fold them in half; and return them to the grill. Cover with an inverted aluminum pan for quick heating.

When the Nutella and marshmallow are sufficiently heated and oozing slightly out of the tortillas, remove the quesadillas from the grill, and quickly brush them with melted butter. Finish with a sprinkling of cinnamon and sugar. Serve warm.

BANANA BLISS

4 SERVINGS • PREP: 5 MIN.
GRILL: 7–10 MIN.

2 ripe bananas, unpeeled
2 cups miniature marshmallows
2 cups semisweet chocolate chips
Brown sugar

Leaving the peel on, slit the bananas lengthwise, but not all the way through the peel. Put half of the marshmallows and chocolate chips in the slit of each banana. Lightly sprinkle brown sugar on top of each banana. Wrap each banana tightly in foil, making sure to seal ends. Place on a medium-hot grill, seam side up, for about 7 minutes. Carefully remove bananas from grill; place in serving dish; unwrap; and serve hot.

CB'S CRANBERRY-APPLE SKILLET CRISP

8–10 SERVINGS • PREP: 30 MIN. • CHILL: 1 HR. • GRILL: 30 MIN.

FILLING

1 pound cranberries, fresh
   or frozen
1¼ cups granulated sugar
3 tablespoons grated orange peel
¼ cup water
5 pounds apples (combination of
   Granny Smith, Honey Crisp,
   or other firm baking apple),
   peeled, cored, and cut into
   ½-inch pieces
1 cup raisins
3 tablespoons instant tapioca
1 teaspoon vanilla extract
1 teaspoon nutmeg
1 teaspoon pumpkin pie spice

TOPPING

¾ cup all-purpose flour
½ cup packed light-brown sugar
½ cup granulated sugar
1 teaspoon ground cinnamon
12 tablespoons (1½ sticks)
   unsalted butter, cut into ½-
   inch pieces and chilled
¾ cup old-fashioned oats

Simmer the cranberries, ¾ cup of the sugar, grated orange peel, and water in an ovenproof pot over medium-high heat. When the mixture has a jam-like consistency, remove to a bowl.

Add the apple slices, remaining sugar, and raisins to the pot to cook. When the apples have softened, about 5 to 10 minutes, combine them in the bowl with the cranberries. Blend in the remaining filling ingredients.

For the topping: In a food processor, blend the flour, sugars, cinnamon, and butter. Remove to a medium-size bowl. Pour oats into the food processor, and pulse until they are the texture of coarse crumbs. Combine with the flour mixture and, using your fingers, pinch the topping to make peanut-size clumps. Chill for 1 hour.

Preheat grill to medium-high. Pour filling into a greased cast-iron skillet; scatter topping over it.

Bake over indirect heat, hood closed, for about 30 minutes. (Rotate the pan after 15 minutes for even baking.) The crisp is done when the juices are bubbling and the topping is brown. Serve hot with whipped cream or vanilla ice cream.

PEANUT BUTTER & MARSHMALLOW FINGER SANDWICHES

12 SERVINGS • PREP: 15 MIN. • GRILL: 3–5 MIN.

½ cup heavy cream

2 ounces semisweet chocolate, chopped

1 pound cake

½ cup peanut butter

⅓ cup marshmallow creme

2 tablespoons unsalted butter, melted

In a microwave-safe bowl, heat cream and chocolate on high for 30 seconds; stir; heat for about another 30 seconds, making sure that cream does not boil. Let the mixture stand until the chocolate is melted, about 5 minutes, stirring occasionally.

Preheat the grill to medium high. Using a knife, trim off the top of the cake so that it is even on all sides. Cut the cake in half horizontally. Spread the peanut butter on one half and the marshmallow on the other. Put the two halves together, and brush the top and bottom with butter.

Grill, turning once, until both sides are warm and golden, about 3 to 5 minutes. Transfer to a platter, and cut the cake into thin finger sandwiches. Serve with the chocolate dipping sauce.

GRILLED BROWNIE SUNDAE WITH BLUEBERRY SAUCE

9 SERVINGS • PREP: 15 MIN. • GRILL: 30 MIN.

BLUEBERRY SAUCE

¼ cup sugar

2 tablespoons lemon juice

2 cups blueberries, fresh or frozen

BROWNIES

½ cup sugar

2 tablespoons butter

2 tablespoons water

1½ cups semisweet
    chocolate chips

2 eggs, slightly beaten

½ teaspoon vanilla

⅔ cup flour

¼ teaspoon baking soda

½ teaspoon salt

SUNDAE & TOPPINGS

Vanilla ice cream or frozen yogurt

Whipped cream (optional)

Chopped nuts (optional)

In a small saucepan, bring the Blueberry Sauce ingredients to a boil. Stir for 1 minute, and remove from heat. Set aside. Bring sugar, butter, and water to a boil in a medium saucepan over low heat; remove from heat, and add chocolate chips, stirring until melted. Blend in eggs and vanilla. In a separate bowl, combine flour, baking soda, and salt; then add to the chocolate mixture.

Preheat grill to medium. Spoon batter into an oiled 9 × 9-inch metal pan. Bake over indirect heat with the lid down for 30 minutes or until a toothpick inserted into the center of the brownies comes out clean. Cool before slicing.

Scoop ice cream onto each brownie, sprinkle with nuts if desired, and drizzle sauce over the top.

GRILLED S'MORES

8 SERVINGS • PREP: 5 MIN. • GRILL: 3 MIN.

8 graham crackers, each one split in half to make 16 pieces

8 chocolate squares
16 large marshmallows

Preheat the grill to high. If using wooden skewers, soak them in water before using them on the grill. Place the graham cracker halves on a warming tray. Set a square of chocolate on top of half of the crackers. Thread the marshmallows onto the end of each skewer. Hold the marshmallows just above the grill grate directly over high heat, turning slowly until lightly browned, about 2 to 3 minutes. Meanwhile, warm the graham crackers and chocolate over indirect heat. Place two roasted marshmallows on top of the melted chocolate, and gently press down with the top half of graham cracker. Serve immediately.

GRILLED BANANA SPLITS

6 SERVINGS • PREP: 10 MIN. • GRILL: 5–8 MIN.

2 tablespoons butter, melted
6 large ripe bananas
18 large scoops of your favorite ice cream

Chocolate sauce, as desired
Whipped cream, as desired
Chopped toasted nuts, as desired
6 maraschino cherries

Preheat the grill to medium. Melt the butter in a saucepan. Slice the bananas, still in their peels, lengthwise. Place the bananas cut side down onto the grates; grill for 3 to 4 minutes. Flip the bananas to the other side (peel side down). Brush the cut surfaces with melted butter, and grill for 2 to 3 additional minutes until the bananas are soft and light brown.

Remove the bananas from the grill, and let them cool. Remove the bananas from peels, and cut them into 1-inch chunks. Divide the cut bananas evenly among six serving dishes, and top each with three scoops of ice cream. Top each with chocolate sauce, whipped cream, nuts, and a cherry.

HOT tip! Let your guests customize their own banana splits. Set up a banana-split bar with a variety of sauces and toppings.

BACON CHOCOLATE-CHIP COOKIES

24 SERVINGS • PREP: 20 MIN. • GRILL: 16–18 MIN.

1 cup all-purpose flour
1 cup bread flour
½ teaspoon salt
½ teaspoon baking soda
1½ cup turbinado sugar or light
   brown sugar
¾ cup unsalted butter, melted
1 egg
1 egg yolk
⅛ teaspoon cinnamon
1 tablespoon vanilla extract
2 cups semisweet chocolate
   chips or chunks
¼ pound bacon, fried crisp
   and crumbled

Preheat the grill to 325°F, and set it up for indirect cooking. Grease cookie sheets, or line them with parchment paper or baking mats. Sift the flour, salt, and baking soda; set aside.

Using a mixer, combine the sugar and butter; add eggs, cinnamon, and vanilla; and mix until creamy. Blend in the sifted ingredients; then fold in the chocolate chips and crumbled bacon, using a spatula or a wooden spoon.

Drop ¼-cup-size dough balls onto a cookie sheet, spaced about 3 inches apart, and bake for 9 minutes; then turn and bake for an additional 7 to 9 minutes. Let the cookies cool slightly on the sheet for a few minutes before moving them to a rack to finish cooling.

FROZEN STRAWBERRY PIE

6–8 SERVINGS • PREP: 20 MIN. • BAKE: 6–7 MIN. • FREEZE: 2 HR.–OVERNIGHT

CRUST

4 tablespoons sugar
14 chocolate graham
    crackers, crushed
1 tablespoon butter, melted

FILLING

12 ounces white-chocolate chips
6 egg whites
1 pint heavy cream, sweetened
1 teaspoon vanilla
1 pound fresh strawberries
1 cup strawberry glaze or jelly

Combine sugar with chocolate graham crackers; add butter; press into a springform pan; and bake at 375°F for 6 to 7 minutes. Set aside to cool.

Melt white-chocolate chips in a double boiler, and let cool slightly. Beat egg whites until stiff, and then set aside. Whip the heavy cream with vanilla; set aside.

Wash the strawberries; pat dry with paper towels; and chop, reserving a few for garnish. Place into a bowl with the strawberry jelly. Fold the egg whites into the whipped cream; then fold in the strawberry mixture, followed by the white chocolate. Pour the filling into the pie crust, and freeze.

Remove the pie from the freezer about 15 minutes before serving to soften slightly. Garnish with the reserved strawberries.

MISSISSIPPI RIVER PIE

8–12 SERVINGS • PREP: 30 MIN. • BAKE: 14–16 MIN. • FREEZE: 2¼ HR.

1½ cups crumbled chocolate sandwich cookies

2 tablespoons unsalted butter, melted

1½ quarts coffee ice cream

1 cup chunky-style peanut butter

8 ounces semisweet chocolate chips

2 cups heavy cream

1½ tablespoons confectioners' sugar

Preheat the oven to 350°F. Combine the crumbled cookies together with the melted butter in a medium bowl. Press the crumb mixture over the bottom of a 10-inch springform pan. Bake for about 14 to 16 minutes or until firm. Chill the crust in the freezer for about 15 minutes.

Place the ice cream in a large bowl, and allow it to soften slightly. Stir in the peanut butter; then press the mixture into the chilled crust. Quickly return the ice cream to the freezer for about 2 hours.

Just before serving, remove ice cream from the freezer. Next, make the chocolate sauce by slowly melting the chocolate chips and ½ cup of cream in a microwave or over a double boiler. Whip the remaining 1½ cups of cream until soft peaks form. Sprinkle the cream with sugar, and continue whipping until stiff peaks form. Release the pie from the springform pan, and cut it into wedges. To serve, pour warm chocolate sauce over each wedge, and top with whipped cream.

RICE PUDDING WITH DARK-CHOCOLATE SAUCE

4 SERVINGS • PREP: 15 MIN.

This dessert is courtesy of Adam Byrd, who says, "This is the most decadent thing I have made to date."

5 ounces uncooked white rice
2 pints milk
7 tablespoons butter
½ teaspoon vanilla extract
⅓ cup sugar
¼ teaspoon nutmeg

SAUCE

5 ounces dark-chocolate chips
2 tablespoons water
1 tablespoon butter

In a medium saucepan, combine the rice, milk, butter, vanilla, nutmeg, and sugar. Bring the mixture to a gentle simmer over medium-high heat. Reduce the heat to low; cover; and simmer until the mixture is thick and pudding-like, about 10 minutes. Be careful not to scorch the bottom.

In a separate saucepan, heat the chocolate, water, and butter over low heat, and stir until the mixture is smooth and shiny, about 5 minutes. Add 2 to 3 heaping spoonfuls of chocolate sauce to each serving of the rice pudding.

CB'S PIE-IRON PEACH PIE

2 SERVINGS • PREP: 5 MIN. • GRILL: 5 MIN.

Canola oil spray
1 can (8 ounces) sliced
  peaches, drained
2 teaspoons brown sugar, plus
  extra for topping
2 teaspoons butter
Lemon zest to taste
4 slices sandwich bread
Cinnamon

Preheat the grill to medium. Get the pie iron hot by placing it, closed, over the heat for 5 minutes on each side. Then open it, and lightly grease the inside with canola oil spray.

Mix together the peaches, brown sugar, butter, and lemon zest. For each pie, place a slice of bread on one side of the iron. Add about 2 to 3 tablespoons of the peach mixture to the center of the slice. Top with a second slice of bread. Close the pie iron, and return to the grill. Heat for about 5 minutes or until the bread toasts.

Remove, and sprinkle with brown sugar and cinnamon before serving.

A pie iron is an old-fashioned cooking device with a long, wooden handle that is used to make grilled sandwiches or pies over an open fire. They're pretty easy to find online or at a camping supply store.

CHOCOLATE-CHIP COOKIE-DOUGH DIP

---

4 SERVINGS • PREP: 10 MIN. • CHILL: 1 HR.–OVERNIGHT

½ cup (1 stick) butter

⅓ cup brown sugar

1 teaspoon vanilla extract

1 package (8 ounces) cream cheese

½ cup confectioners' sugar

¾ cup semi-sweet mini chocolate chips

Fresh fruit for dipping (such as strawberries, pineapple, peaches, melon, grapes, or bananas)

1 package vanilla wafers or graham crackers

Melt the butter with the brown sugar in a small saucepan over medium heat. Stir continuously until the brown sugar dissolves. Remove from heat, whisk in vanilla extract, and set aside to cool.

Using a hand mixer, beat the cream cheese and confectioners' sugar for 1 minute. Slowly add the cooled butter mixture, and beat 1 more minute. Stir in the chocolate chips, using a spatula or a wooden spoon. Transfer the dip to a serving bowl, and refrigerate at least 1 hour and as long as 24 hours. (Remove the dip from the refrigerator about 15 to 30 minutes before serving to allow it to soften.)

Garnish with additional chocolate chips if desired. Serve with fresh fruit and vanilla wafers or graham crackers.

NECTARINE PIZZA WITH GOAT CHEESE & THYME

4 SERVINGS • PREP: 10 MIN. • GRILL: 6–7 MIN.

Courtesy of Liz Vidyarthi at zested.wordpress.com

¼ cup water
3 tablespoons honey
Few sprigs thyme
2 teaspoons balsamic vinegar
Prepared pizza dough (one-fourth package per pie)
Olive oil, for brushing
¾ cup goat cheese, crumbled
2 to 3 nectarines, thinly sliced
Coarse salt, to taste

Preheat grill to high. Heat water until boiling; then add honey and thyme. When the liquid is reduced by half, stir in the balsamic vinegar; set aside.

Divide the dough into four equal parts. On a well-floured surface, roll out one-quarter of the dough into an 8-inch round "pie." Refrigerate until ready to grill. (If you will only be making one pie, refrigerate the rest of the dough for up to two days.)

Brush one side of the pie lightly with olive oil, and place it, oiled side down, directly on the grill. After about 1 minute, rotate the pie 180 degrees to cook it evenly. Dough will begin to puff or bubble and brown in about 2 to 3 minutes.

Slide the pie off the grill and onto a flat surface, such as a cutting board, and flip it over. Reduce the heat to low. Lightly brush the pie with olive oil. Sprinkle with the goat cheese; then top with the nectarines. Return it to the grill, and close grill lid. Let the dough become crisp and the cheese soften, about 3 minutes.

Remove from grill, and drizzle immediately with the honey-balsamic reduction and a pinch of coarse salt. You can garnish with more crumbled cheese if desired. Slice into 4 wedges and serve warm.

DULCE DE LECHE GRILLED CHEESE

4 SERVINGS • PREP: 15 MIN. • GRILL: 3 MIN.

1 teaspoon vanilla extract

8 ounces mascarpone cheese, room temperature

8 slices cinnamon-raisin bread

6 tablespoons butter, softened

4 tablespoons raspberry preserves

1 jar (14 to 16 ounces) of dulce de leche*

Fresh red raspberries for garnish, optional

Whipped cream for garnish, optional

*Dulce de leche is a thick, creamy spread made from caramelized milk and sugar. It is much-loved in Latin American countries.

In a bowl, stir vanilla into the mascarpone. Stirring will make the cheese lighter and easier to spread. Butter one side of each bread slice.

Preheat grill to medium. Place the bread slices, buttered side down, in a cast-iron or other heavy skillet over direct heat. Grill until golden brown and crisp, about 3 minutes. Place the bread, toasted side down, on a clean work surface. Spread 1 tablespoon of raspberry preserves, 2 tablespoons of mascarpone cheese, and 1 tablespoon dulce de leche over each slice. Top with another piece of bread, toasted side up, and drizzle with more dulce de leche. Garnish with fresh raspberries or whipped cream if desired.

WOOD-FIRED APPLE-PECAN PIE

8 SERVINGS • PREP: 20 MIN. • GRILL: 40–45 MIN.

CRUST

1½ cups flour
¾ teaspoon salt
1½ tablespoons sugar
½ cup shortening
½ tablespoon butter
5 tablespoons water

FILLING

4 Granny Smith apples
3 Gala apples
2 cups pecans
1 cup brown sugar
1 tablespoon cinnamon
¾ cup flour

CRUMB TOPPING

1 cup flour
1 cup sugar
3 teaspoons cinnamon
½ cup (1 stick) butter, softened

For the crust, mix the flour, salt, and sugar. Cut in the shortening and butter. Mix in the water 1 tablespoon at a time using a fork. Roll out the dough, and shape it into a pie plate. Set aside.

For the filling, peel, core, and slice the apples; then mix them with the other filling ingredients. Place the mixture in the crust, creating a mound in the middle.

For the crumb top, mix the flour, sugar, and cinnamon in a bowl. Cut in the butter until the mixture forms pea-size crumbs. Cover the apples with the crumb topping. Bake the pie in a smoker at 375°F for 40 to 45 minutes or until golden brown.

ADAM BYRD'S GRILLED BLACKBERRY COBBLER

6 SERVINGS • PREP: 15 MIN. • GRILL: 20–25 MIN.

2 tablespoons cornstarch

¼ cup cold water

1½ cups sugar

1 tablespoon lemon juice

4 cups blackberries, picked over, rinsed, and drained

1 cup flour

1 teaspoon baking powder

½ teaspoon salt

8 tablespoons cold butter, cut in small pieces

¼ cup boiling water

In a large bowl, stir together the cornstarch and ¼ cup cold water until the cornstarch is completely dissolved. Add 1 cup sugar, lemon juice, and blackberries; combine gently. Transfer the mixture to an 8-inch cast-iron skillet.

In a bowl, combine the flour, remaining sugar, baking powder, and salt. Blend in the butter until mixture resembles coarse meal. Add ¼ cup boiling water, and stir the mixture until it just forms dough.

Light the outer two burners of a three-burner grill to maximum heat. (I used the infrared burner and the right-hand burner on a Char-Broil Quantum.) Preheat until the temperature gauge on the lid reads 400°F. Light the side burner to medium-high heat; place skillet over this side. Bring the blackberry mixture to a boil, stirring constantly. Drop spoonfuls of dough carefully into the bubbling mixture. Transfer the cobbler to the center of the grill, and close the lid. Bake for 20 minutes or until the topping is golden. Serve warm.

WHOOPIE PIES

18 SERVINGS • PREP: 15 MIN. • BAKE: 15–20 MIN.

2 cups flour

1 cup sugar

5 tablespoons baking cocoa

1½ teaspoons baking soda

1 cup milk

1 egg, beaten

5 tablespoons
     margarine, softened

½ cup butter, softened

½ cup shortening

1 cup marshmallow crème

1 teaspoon vanilla extract

1 cup confectioners' sugar

Combine the flour, sugar, baking cocoa, and baking soda in a bowl; mix well. Add the milk, egg, and margarine, beating until blended. Drop 1 teaspoonful of the batter at a time onto an ungreased cookie sheet. Bake at 350°F for 10 to 15 minutes, or until the edges are crisp. Remove, and place on a wire rack to cool.

Beat the butter, shortening, and marshmallow crème in a mixer bowl until creamy. Add the vanilla, beating until blended. Add the confectioners' sugar. Beat for 2 minutes, scraping the bowl occasionally. Spread over half of the cookies, and top those with the remaining cookies.

9

You don't have to cook fancy or complicated masterpieces—just good food from fresh ingredients.
–Julia Child

Marinades, Sauces & Rubs

SMOKED BRISKET MARINADE

YIELD: 2 CUPS • MARINATE: OVERNIGHT
USE WITH: BRISKET

2 cups beef broth
¼ cup Worcestershire sauce
1 tablespoon onion powder

1 tablespoon garlic powder
1 teaspoon cayenne pepper
½ teaspoon black pepper

Avoid reduced-sodium beef broth.
The salt helps tenderize the brisket as well as season it.

In a large pan, mix all ingredients until well combined. Add the brisket. Using a marinade injector, inject the brisket with the marinade all the way down the brisket. Do this in about 1-inch increments. Let rest overnight in the fridge. Discard the marinade after use. Because it has been in contact with raw meat, it is not safe to use again.

HOT tip! Seal brisket and marinade in a container while it rests in fridge. This will prevent cross contamination with other foods.

PLUM MARINADE

YIELD: APPROX. ¾ CUP • PREP: 5 MIN. • MARINATE:
4–6 HR. • USE WITH: STEAK

½ cup plum preserves
3 tablespoons minced green onion
2 tablespoons white vinegar
2 tablespoons hoisin sauce

2 teaspoons minced fresh ginger
1 teaspoon dry mustard
½ teaspoon ground red pepper
Green onion, minced (optional)

In a bowl, whisk together all of the ingredients until completely emulsified. Marinate meat in a sealable plastic bag or covered container in the refrigerator.

THREE-WAY MARINADE

YIELD: 1 CUP • PREP: 5 MIN. • MARINATE: 4–12 HR.
USE WITH: FLANK STEAK, LONDON BROIL

CLASSIC MARINADE

1 cup prepared Italian-
    style vinaigrette
1 teaspoon minced garlic
¼ teaspoon coarsely ground
    black pepper

MEXICAN VARIATION

To classic marinade, add
1 tablespoon fresh lime juice
1 teaspoon ground cumin
1 teaspoon chipotle chili powder
½ teaspoon salt

ASIAN VARIATION

To classic marinade, add
2 tablespoons reduced-sodium
    soy sauce
2 tablespoons minced fresh ginger
1 tablespoon packed brown sugar
1 tablespoon sesame seeds, toasted
1½ teaspoons dark sesame oil

In a bowl, whisk together all ingredients until completely emulsified. Marinate meat in a sealable plastic bag or covered container in the refrigerator.

CAPTAIN JESSIE'S JAMAICAN JERK MARINADE

YIELD: 1 CUP • PREP: 10 MIN. • MARINATE: 4 HR.–OVERNIGHT
USE WITH: BEEF AND PORK

1 white onion, chopped
½ cup chopped scallions
2 teaspoons fresh thyme or 1 teaspoon dried thyme
1 whole Scotch Bonnet or habanero pepper,
    seeded and chopped
1 teaspoon coarse salt
2 teaspoons light brown sugar
1 teaspoon allspice

½ teaspoon ground nutmeg
½ teaspoon ground cinnamon
1 teaspoon black pepper
1 tablespoon soy sauce
1 tablespoon Worcestershire sauce
1 tablespoon vegetable oil
1 tablespoon apple cider vinegar

Spices from the Caribbean give this marinade a kick to heat up your mouth!

In a food processor or blender, add the onions, scallions, thyme, and peppers. Stir in the other ingredients, and pulse until mixture becomes a light slurry. Marinate meat in a sealable plastic bag or covered container in the refrigerator.

*Note: When working with fresh peppers,
use food-safe gloves; do not touch your eyes,
mouth, or nose until you have washed your
hands with soap and water.*

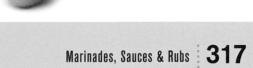

KOREAN KALBI MARINADE

YIELD: APPROX. 1 CUP • PREP: 5 MIN.
MARINATE: OVERNIGHT • USE WITH: SHORT RIBS

1 tablespoon soy sauce
¼ cup sugar
2 tablespoons honey
¼ cup Chinese rice wine
2 teaspoons Korean toasted-
    sesame oil
2 green onions, minced

4 teaspoons (1 to 2 cloves)
    chopped garlic
2 tablespoons toasted
    sesame seeds
2 tablespoons water
1 teaspoon grated ginger root

**The recipe is a classic one used for most
Korean kalbi (grilled short ribs).**

Mix ingredients in a nonreactive bowl. Use some as an overnight marinade for meat—placed in a sealable plastic bag or covered container in the refrigerator—and reserve some for glazing during the final 5 to 7 minutes of cooking.

MAÎTRE D' BUTTER

YIELD: 2 CUPS • PREP: 10 MIN.
REFRIGERATE: 1 HR.–OVERNIGHT
USE WITH: STEAK, FISH, VEGETABLES

1 pound (4 sticks) unsalted butter, softened
3 tablespoons lemon juice (about 1 lemon)
¼ cup chopped Italian (flat-leaf) parsley, or other herbs or spices
    as desired

In a large bowl, mash the butter. Add lemon juice and parsley and, using a wooden spoon, blend.

Spread a 1-foot-square piece of plastic wrap across a work surface, and scoop the butter mixture on top. Gently wrap the plastic film around the butter, forming a cylinder. Tie off the ends of the wrap with string or a twist tie. Chill or freeze until needed.

Maître d' Butter is simply softened butter with seasonings that is rolled and chilled. You can serve it in slices on top of grilled steaks, fish, or vegetables. Experiment by combining your favorite herbs and spices.

SPICY GRILLED-VEGGIE MARINADE

YIELD: 1½ CUPS • PREP: 5 MIN. • MARINATE: 1 HR.
USE WITH: VEGETABLES

⅔ cup white wine vinegar
½ cup soy sauce
2 tablespoons minced fresh ginger
2 tablespoons olive oil

2 tablespoons sesame oil
2 large cloves garlic, minced
2 teaspoons Tabasco sauce

In a bowl, whisk together all ingredients until completely emulsified. Marinate in a sealable plastic bag or covered container in the refrigerator.

CB'S WET SALT RUB FOR FISH

PREP: 5 MIN. • USE WITH: FISH

1 part coarse salt
1 part finely minced fresh
   lemon thyme

½ part anchovy paste
2½ parts dry white vermouth

Whisk together all ingredients until blended.

SAVANNAH SMOKER'S MOHUNKEN RUB

YIELD: 3+ CUPS • PREP: 5 MIN. • USE WITH: PORK

½ cup brown sugar
1 cup white sugar
1 cup paprika
¼ cup garlic powder
¼ cup coarse salt
2 tablespoons chili powder
2 teaspoons cayenne pepper

4 teaspoons black pepper
2 teaspoons dried oregano or
   Italian seasoning
2 teaspoons cumin
1 tablespoon mustard powder
Yellow mustard to taste

Blend all ingredients in a small bowl.

PROVENÇAL CITRUS-TARRAGON SAUCE

YIELD: 1½ CUPS • PREP: 5 MIN. • USE WITH: HALIBUT, SALMON, CRAB, SCALLOPS

¼ cup apple cider vinegar
2 tablespoons Dijon mustard
⅓ cup olive oil
2 tablespoons honey
⅓ cup fresh tarragon leaves

1 can (11 ounces) mandarin orange slices, drained,
    or 2 fresh mandarin oranges, peeled, sectioned,
    and seeded
½ teaspoon coarse salt

Combine the vinegar and mustard in a blender or food processor, and pulse until smooth; slowly add olive oil until fully incorporated. Add the honey, tarragon, and oranges; blend or pulse again until almost smooth. Salt to taste.

GREEN-CHILI PESTO

YIELD: APPROX. 2 CUPS • PREP: 15 MIN. • USE WITH: MEAT AND FISH

6 large, long green chilies or 4 medium poblano chilies,
    roasted, peeled, and seeded
¾ cup pine nuts
2 cups lightly packed fresh basil leaves and stems
6 garlic cloves, chopped

1 cup extra-virgin olive oil
¾ cup grated Parmesan cheese
½ cup grated Romano cheese
½ teaspoon salt
½ teaspoon ground black pepper

Chop the chilies, and set aside.

In a skillet over medium heat, toast the pine nuts; then let them cool to room temperature.

In a food processor, combine chilies, pine nuts, basil, and garlic. Process, scraping down sides of the bowl once or twice, until smooth. Drizzle in olive oil. Transfer the mixture to a bowl, and blend in the cheese, salt, and pepper. Use immediately, or cover and refrigerate for up to 3 days; freeze (without cheese) for up to 3 months.

CHIPOTLE MARINADE

YIELD: ½ CUP • PREP: 5–10 MIN. • MARINATE: 2 HR.–OVERNIGHT
USE WITH: STEAK OR SEAFOOD

⅓ cup fresh lime juice
¼ cup chopped fresh cilantro
1 tablespoon packed brown sugar

2 teaspoons minced chipotle chilies in adobo sauce
2 tablespoons adobo sauce (from chilies)
2 cloves garlic, minced

This Southwestern marinade is great for flank steak or pork tenderloin.–CB

Combine ingredients well; then pour marinade over meat or seafood. Marinate in a sealable plastic bag or covered dish in the refrigerator.

ADOBO MARINADE

YIELD: 1 CUP • PREP: 5–10 MIN. • MARINATE: 2 HR.– OVERNIGHT • USE WITH: PORK OR FISH

½ cup fresh orange juice
2 tablespoons lime juice
2 tablespoons wine vinegar
3 canned chipotle chilis
3 garlic cloves

2 teaspoons oregano
½ teaspoon black pepper
½ teaspoon salt
½ teaspoon ground cumin

Adobo means seasoning or marinade in Spanish. This dark-red marinade is often used in Filipino and Puerto Rican cooking.–CB

In the bowl of a food processor, place all ingredients; puree. Makes enough marinade for six to eight pork chops. Place meat in self-sealing plastic bag; add marinade.

ASIAN MARINADE

YIELD: ½ CUP • PREP: 5–10 MIN. MARINATE: 1 HR.–OVERNIGHT • USE WITH: PORK CHOPS, STEAK, CHICKEN THIGHS, SHRIMP

¼ cup green onions, chopped
¼ cup hoisin sauce
1 tablespoon fresh ginger, minced

Combine ingredients well; then pour marinade over meat, poultry, or seafood. Marinate in a sealable plastic bag or covered dish in the refrigerator.

GEORGE JV'S SECRET BEEF JERKY MARINADE

YIELD: 1 CUP • PREP: 5–10 MIN. • MARINATE: 6 HR.–OVERNIGHT
USE WITH: BEEF RIBS, BRISKET, STEAK

½ cup soy sauce
1 clove garlic, mashed
2 tablespoons brown sugar
2 tablespoons ketchup

½ cup Worcestershire sauce
1¼ teaspoons salt
½ teaspoon onion powder
½ teaspoon pepper

George JV is a "Sizzle On the Grill" reader and frequent recipe contributor.–CB

Marinate in plastic bag or covered container in the refrigerator for at least 6 hours or overnight.

QUICK CHIMICHURRI MARINADE

YIELD: 1½ CUPS • PREP: 5–10 MIN. • MARINATE: 2 HR.–OVERNIGHT
USE WITH: LONDON BROIL, FLANK STEAK, FILET MIGNON

¾ cup prepared, non-creamy Caesar dressing
½ cup chopped fresh parsley

¾ teaspoon crushed red pepper
Salt and pepper

Chimichurri originated in Argentina where it is a popular accompaniment
to all types of grilled meats, especially steak.–CB

Combine ingredients well; then pour marinade over meat. Marinate in a sealable
plastic bag or covered dish in the refrigerator.

CB'S BASIC BEER SAUCE

YIELD: 3 CUPS • PREP: 15 MIN.
USE WITH: SMOKED BEEF BRISKET, PORK BUTT, RIBS

1 12-ounce can or bottle of ale or dark beer
½ cup apple cider
½ cup water
¼ cup peanut oil

2 medium shallots, chopped
3 garlic cloves, chopped
1 tablespoon Worcestershire sauce
1 teaspoon hot sauce

Beer seems to be plentiful around many backyard barbecues. Try using a richer beer to make this
excellent "mop" for your low- and slow-cooking barbecue or grilled meats.–CB

Combine the ingredients in a saucepan. Heat the mixture, and brush it on the meat during the final minutes
of grilling.

MOROCCAN SAUCE

YIELD: APPROX. 1 CUP • PREP: 5 MIN.
COOK: 12–13 MIN. • USE WITH: COD, HALIBUT,
SALMON, CRAB, SCALLOPS

1½ tablespoons minced garlic
½ cup olive oil
½ cup unsalted butter
2 tablespoons harissa
1½ tablespoons fresh lemon juice or
   1 to 2 tablespoons sherry

Coarse salt, to taste
Cracked black pepper, to taste
2 tablespoons chopped Italian
   (flat-leaf) parsley
2 tablespoons chopped salted
   almonds (optional)

**Discover the flavors of North Africa in this zesty sauce
made using fiery-hot harissa, a traditional seasoning for couscous.
If harissa is not available, substitute 1 tablespoon of
pimenton (smoked Spanish paprika).**

Place the garlic, olive oil, and butter in a small saucepan over low
heat. Cook until the garlic begins to soften, about 10 minutes. Add the
harissa and lemon juice, blending with a whisk; continue cooking 2 to
3 minutes more. Season to taste with salt and pepper. Garnish with
parsley and, if desired, almonds.

MEMPHIS BBQ SAUCE

YIELD: 3 CUPS • PREP: 15 MIN. • COOK: 25 MIN.
USE WITH: PORK RIBS, BEEF RIBS,
BRISKET, PORK BUTT

¼ cup apple cider vinegar
½ cup prepared mustard
2 cups ketchup
3 tablespoons
   Worcestershire sauce
1 tablespoon finely ground
   black pepper
¼ cup brown sugar

2 teaspoons celery salt
2 tablespoons chili powder
1 tablespoon onion powder
2 teaspoons garlic powder
¼ to ½ teaspoon cayenne pepper
   (optional)
2 teaspoons liquid smoke (optional)
2 tablespoons canola oil

Combine all ingredients, except the oil, in a saucepan. Bring them
to a boil, stirring to dissolve the sugar. Reduce the heat, and simmer
for 25 minutes, stirring occasionally. Using a whisk, blend in the oil
until incorporated.

HORSERADISH SAUCE

YIELD: 1 ½ CUPS • PREP: 15 MIN.
USE WITH: SMOKED PRIME RIB

1 3-ounce package cream cheese

1 cup sour cream

1 teaspoon grated onion

2 tablespoons horseradish

¼ teaspoon sugar

¼ teaspoon salt

¼ teaspoon pepper

This is a perfect accompaniment to a smoked rib roast.–CB

Combine all ingredients in a blender.

SWEET ALE MUSTARD

YIELD: 2 CUPS • PREP: 20 MIN. • MARINATE: 1 HR.–
OVERNIGHT • USE WITH: BRATS, SAUSAGE, BURGERS

½ heaping cup mustard seeds

¼ cup dry mustard

½ cup malt vinegar

1 cup medium-bodied ale

3 tablespoons honey

2 teaspoons salt

¼ teaspoon cayenne pepper

¼ teaspoon paprika

Combine the mustard seeds and mustard with the vinegar, and cover. Allow the mixture to sit at room temperature for at least 1 hour or longer to mellow the strong flavors.

Combine the mustard mixture with the remaining ingredients in a food processor; blend to a coarse puree. Refrigerate mixture for at least 24 hours; then taste, and adjust the seasoning to your preference.

CB'S LAVENDER RUB FOR LAMB

PREP: 5 MIN. • USE WITH: LAMB

3 parts lavender flowers

1 part fresh lemon sage,
   finely chopped

1 part fresh rosemary, chopped

½ part coarse salt

½ part cumin, ground

Blend ingredients in a spice mill or with a mortar and pestle until the mixture becomes a coarse paste.

CB'S SOUTHWEST-STYLE RUB

YIELD: 1 CUP • PREP: 10 MIN. • MARINATE: 20 MIN.
USE WITH: PORK, BEEF

DRY INGREDIENTS

¼ cup chili powder

¼ cup packed brown sugar

⅛ cup ground cumin

⅛ cup kosher salt

⅛ cup black pepper

1 teaspoon ground cinnamon

WET INGREDIENTS

1 tablespoon Worcestershire sauce

⅛ cup apple cider vinegar

1 tablespoon minced fresh garlic
(or 1 tablespoon garlic powder)

1 teaspoon hot sauce

I developed this rub to please guests who enjoy something a little spicy on their ribs or other slow-cooked meat. I think it works well with just about any meat, but particularly with pork when rubbed on about 20 minutes or so before you start the slow-cooking process.–CB

Mix the dry ingredients; add the wet ingredients; mix again. Store mixture in the refrigerator for up to 3 days. Apply the rub to meat; let meat rest for about 20 minutes before slow cooking. Note: Use plastic gloves or plastic sandwich bags over your hands to prevent irritation from the spices.

CB'S HERBED POULTRY RUB

PREP: 5 MIN. • USE WITH: CHICKEN, TURKEY

Equal parts fresh parsley, sage, rosemary, and thyme, finely chopped

½ part coarse salt

Blend ingredients in a spice mill or with a mortar and pestle until the mixture becomes a coarse paste.

CHILI-CINNAMON RUB FOR CHICKEN

YIELD: APPROX. ¼ CUP • PREP: 5 MIN.
USE WITH: CHICKEN

2 teaspoons ancho chili powder
2 teaspoons cinnamon, ground
2 teaspoons cumin, ground

4 teaspoons fresh thyme
2 teaspoons salt
2 teaspoons brown sugar

Blend the spices, salt, and sugar in a small bowl.

HOT tip! Ancho chili powder works well in this recipe, but you can use chipotle or other, milder chili powders.

SAVORY RUB FOR SMOKY PULLED PORK

YIELD: APPROX. 4½ TBSP. • USE WITH: PORK

4 teaspoons salt
2 teaspoons seasoning salt
2 teaspoons brown sugar
2 teaspoons garlic powder
2 teaspoons onion powder

½ teaspoon paprika
¼ teaspoon cumin
¼ teaspoon black pepper
¼ teaspoon cayenne pepper
¼ teaspoon dry mustard

In a bowl, mix ingredients together and rub onto meat before smoking.

CREAMY GORGONZOLA SAUCE

YIELD: 2+ CUPS • PREP: 5 MIN. • CHILL: 30 MIN.–1 HR.
USE WITH: STEAKS, VEGETABLES

1 cup reduced-fat cream
   cheese, softened
1 cup plain non-fat yogurt

½ cup Gorgonzola
   cheese, crumbled
¼ cup onion, minced
1 teaspoon pepper

Combine all ingredients in a small bowl; mix well. Chill for 30 minutes to 1 hour before serving.

SMOKED TURKEY RUB

¼ cup vegetable oil

2 tablespoons onion powder

1 tablespoon paprika

2 teaspoons garlic powder

2 teaspoons kosher salt

2 teaspoons white pepper

1 teaspoon powdered ginger

½ teaspoon powdered sage

A wet rub holds better to the outside of your bird and also aids in moisture retention.

Mix all dry ingredients together. Dust the inner cavity of the turkey with one tablespoon of the dry ingredients. Mix the remaining dry ingredients with the vegetable oil to make a wet rub or paste. Gently separate the skin from the meat of the bird. Message the wet rub into the meat underneath the skin. Be careful: Do not completely remove the skin from the bird. Use all remaining wet rub to coat the outside of the bird.

HOT tip!
When finished, use toothpicks to hold the skin in place.

SMOKED BRISKET RUB

SERVES 1 BRISKET

8 tablespoons of butter

1 tablespoon of chili powder

3 tablespoons of salt

½ teaspoon of smoked paprika

½ teaspoon black pepper

½ teaspoon of garlic powder

½ teaspoon of cayenne

½ teaspoon of cumin

½ teaspoon dried parsley

Mix all ingredients together in a medium-sized bowl. Use paper towels to dry the brisket. This will prevent the rub from clumping together in wetter areas. Spread the rub generously over the brisket before smoking. Be sure to coat all sides.

HOT tip! Gently press the rub into the surface of the brisket to help the spices stick throughout a long cook time.

PERFECT RUB FOR SMOKED PORK LOIN

YIELD: APPROX. 3 CUPS • USE WITH: PORK

½ cup brown sugar

1 cup white sugar

1 cup paprika

¼ cup garlic powder

¼ cup coarse salt

2 tablespoons chili powder

2 teaspoons cayenne pepper

4 teaspoons black pepper

2 teaspoons dried oregano or
    Italian seasoning

2 teaspoons cumin

1 tablespoon mustard powder

Yellow mustard to taste

In a small bowl, blend all ingredients. Rub liberally on pork loin before smoking.

EASY SMOKED TURKEY BRINE

YIELD: 2 GALLONS • USE WITH: TURKEY

2 gallons water

1 cup sugar

1 cup salt

4 bay leaves

2 lemons, cut in slices

4 sprigs fresh thyme

2 tablespoons sage

2 tablespoons onion powder

2 tablespoons garlic powder

¾ tablespoon cumin

¾ tablespoon smoked paprika

In a large saucepan, combine water, sugar, salt, bay leaves, lemon slices, thyme, sage, onion powder, garlic powder, cumin, and smoked paprika over medium heat until the sugar dissolves. Remove from heat. Add ice or place in refrigerator until completely cooled.

Select a container large enough to hold all of the brine and turkey. Add the turkey, making sure to stretch the skin of the turkey away from the legs. This will allow the brine to get as close as possible to the surface of the meat. Let it sit overnight. Remove the turkey. Rinse to wash off any excess salt or spice on and under the skin. Smoke and enjoy.

HOT tip! Place a bag of ice or plate over the turkey to keep it fully submerged while brining.

SMOKED CHICKEN BRINE

YIELD: 2 GALLONS • USE WITH: CHICKEN

2 gallons water

1 whole chicken

10 garlic cloves

2 tablespoons peppercorns

2 cups salt

½ cup vinegar

1½ cups sugar

2 tablespoons rosemary

2 tablespoons thyme

In a large saucepan, combine water, garlic cloves, peppercorns, salt, vinegar, rosemary, and thyme. Mix over low heat until combined and sugar is dissolved. Let cool completely by using ice or placing in refrigerator. Place chicken in brine so that it is completely covered and place in the fridge for four to six hours. Remove chicken from brine and rinse before smoking.

HOT tip! Be sure to rinse excess brine before use and discard used brine; it has now been in contact with raw meat and is not safe to be used again.

SIMPLE BRINE FOR SMOKED FISH

YIELD: 5 CUPS • USE WITH: SMOKED FISH

4–5 pound fillets, skin on
4 cups water
1 cup soy sauce

¾ cup brown sugar
¼ cup sea salt
¾ tablespoon granulated garlic

Mix ingredients together in a large bowl. Pour mixture over fillets, making sure they are covered. Marinate for about 6 to 10 hours (or overnight) in the refrigerator. Remove fillets from brine and pat dry with paper towels. Preheat the digital smoker.

While the smoker is preheating, arrange the fish on racks and let the fillets dry for about an hour or until a glaze forms on the surface of the fish. Smoke the fish until the internal temperature is 165°F.

HOT tip! Be sure to let the brine cool completely before adding the fish. Additionally, use a container large enough to hold all of the brine and fish comfortably. Resealable zip-top bags or covered baking dishes are great options.

APPLE CIDER BRINE FOR SMOKED PORK LOIN

YIELD: 2+ GALLONS • PREP: 5 MIN. • BRINE: 24 HR.

2 gallons water
2 cups dark brown sugar
2 cups coarse salt
¼ cup ground ginger
¼ cup garlic powder
½ cup apple cider vinegar
¼ cup ground cumin
4 large sprigs fresh rosemary

¼ cup black pepper, coarsely ground
2 tablespoons Worcestershire sauce
2 tablespoons Tabasco sauce
2 medium-sized lemons, chopped, squeezed & smashed

Fill a large pot with the water. Then add the remainder of the ingredients, and stir. Brine meat overnight or 24 hours.

TIPS

- Use a pot large enough to hold brine and smoked pork loin comfortably.
- Rinse brine off before smoking to remove excess spice.
- This brine also works great with bone-in pork chops.

Resources

This list of manufacturers and associations is meant to be a general guide to additional industry and product-related sources. It is not intended as a listing of all of the products and manufacturers presented in this book.

COMPANIES AND ASSOCIATIONS

The Alaska Seafood Marketing Institute (ASMI)
www.alaskaseafood.org
Alaska's official seafood marketing agency offers a consumer recipe database on its website.

Butterball
www.butterball.com
The company provides recipes, tips, and ideas, and product information on its website.

Cattlemen's Beef Board and National Cattlemen's Beef Association
www.beefitswhatsfordinner.com
The beef industry offers tips, food safety information, and recipes for preparing beef through its website.

Char-Broil
www.charbroil.com
This is the official website for the Char-Broil company.

Christopher Ranch
www.christopherranch.com
Christopher Ranch provides product information and recipes on its website.

Lean on Lamb
www.leanonlamb.com
The Tri-Lamb group offers nutritional information, preparation and cooking tips, and recipes on its website.

Litehouse Foods
www.litehousefoods.com
The company's website features recipes and product information.

Louisiana Seafood Promotion & Marketing Board
http://louisianaseafood.com
The organization's website features news, information, and recipes.

Mann's Fresh Vegetables
www.veggiesmadeeasy.com
The company's website features product information and recipes.

Marie's
www.maries.com
The company's website features product information and recipes.

My Beef Checkoff
www.beefboard.org
The Cattlemen's Beef Board–sponsored website provides consumer and industry information and recipes.

National Pork Board
www.porkbeinspired.com
The National Pork Board's–sponsored website features information, nutrition, and recipes.

National Turkey Federation
www.eatturkey.com
The National Turkey Federation–sponsored website offers recipes, information, and merchandise.

Ocean Mist Farms
www.oceanmist.com
Ocean Mist Farms provides recipes, videos, and nutrition information on its website.

Perdue
www.perdue.com
Perdue provides recipes, information, and tips on its website.

Pillsbury

www.pillsbury.com

The company's website features recipes, holiday cooking guides, and product information.

Potatoes Goodness Unearthed

www.healthypotato.com

Recipes and information about healthy eating.

Sizzle on the Grill

www.charbroil.com/cook

Char-Broil sponsors this newsletter and website, which features grilling tips and recipes.

Tabasco

www.tabasco.com

The company's website features product information, recipes, and merchandise.

The Other White Meat

www.theotherwhitemeat.com

The National Pork Board's–sponsored website features information, nutrition, and recipes.

Tyson Foods

www.tyson.com

Provides recipes and product information.

United States Department of Agriculture (USDA) Food Safety and Inspection Service

www.fsis.usda.gov

The website offers consumer safety information on buying, storing, preparing, and cooking meat and poultry.

USDA Meat & Poultry Hotline

888-MPHotline

This hotline answers questions about safe storage, handling, and preparation of meat and poultry products.

USA Rice Federation

www.usarice.com

The organization's website features information, news, and recipes.

Virginia Seafood

www.virginiaseafood.org

News, information, and recipes.

FOOD BLOGS AND RECIPE DATABASES

Barry "CB" Martin

www.guysinaprons.com

Website featuring recipes, tips, and techniques.

Cookthink

www.cookthink.com

This website features a recipe database and kitchen tips.

Danica's Daily

http://danicasdaily.com

This blog focuses on recipes for a healthy lifestyle.

Girls on a Grill

www.girlsonagrill.com

These guest chefs are sisters who share their recipes featuring fresh ingredients cooked over an open fire.

Jess Thomson

www.jessthomson.wordpress.com

Jess Thomson is a Seattle-based, Bert Greene Award–nominated food writer, recipe developer, and food photographer.

Marcia's Kitchen

www.happyinthekitchen.com

Marcia Frankenberg lives in Minneapolis, where her main inspiration for cooking is hearing her daughter say, "Feed me, Mama!"

Not Eating Out in New York

www.noteatingoutinny.com

Cathy Erway is the author of *The Art of Eating In: How I Learned to Stop Spending and Love the Stove*, which is based on her two-year mission to forego restaurant food, and her blog, which is filled with original recipes for the busy-but-thrifty.

Liz Vidyarthi

https://lizvcommunication.com

Liz Vidyarthi, a freelance food photographer, chronicles her experiences eating in New York and traveling in East Africa.

Index